EARLY HAWAIIANS

EARLY HAWAIIANS

*An Initial Study of Skeletal Remains
from Mokapu, Oahu*

Charles E. Snow

The University Press of Kentucky

Frontispiece. Female figurine with a shaped head (flat forehead and back head), *ehu* hair, a rocker jaw contour, bent-knee posture, and a well-developed, muscular body. Probably from the premissionary period. Courtesy of Bernice P. Bishop Museum, Honolulu.

ISBN: 0–8131–1277–X

Library of Congress Catalog Card Number: 72–81317

Copyright © 1974 by The University Press of Kentucky

A statewide cooperative scholarly publishing agency serving Berea College, Centre College of Kentucky, Eastern Kentucky University, Kentucky Historical Society, Kentucky State University, Morehead State University, Murray State University, University of Kentucky, University of Louisville, and Western Kentucky University.

Editorial and Sales Offices: Lexington, Kentucky 40506

THIS STUDY *is dedicated to the memory of Sir Peter H. Buck (Te Rangi Hiroa) whose friendly words, "Haere Mai, Haere Mai, Haere Mai," first welcomed me to Bernice P. Bishop Museum; and to Alexander Spoehr, director of Bishop Museum during the time of this study, whose helpful and friendly encouragement made it possible to bring this report to publication.*

Contents

Tables

Preface

As the widow of the author and his "girl Friday" throughout this study, I am pleased to speak for him. The years 1951 and 1974 were auspicious years for us, the Alpha and Omega of this book; 1951 marked the beginning of the study of the physical characteristics of early Hawaiians and a happy experience of friendship with the Islands and her hospitable people; 1974 marks the publication of my husband's findings. The book is designed principally for students and scholars of physical anthropology but much of the descriptive text is presented, hopefully, in a manner understandable to the interested lay person.

Several organizations have been most generous in providing the funds necessary to support this project. Lilly Endowment, Inc., of Indianapolis granted money for publication expenses in 1957 and again in 1971. The Wenner-Gren Foundation for Anthropological Research made grants that initiated the study in 1951–1952 and in the summer of 1955. A grant from the National Science Foundation supported the final year of field work, 1956–1957. In addition, the University of Kentucky Research Fund Committee was generous in supplementing these grants.

The fulfillment of the study required not only financial support but the interest and labor of many people and organizations. The cooperation and active interest of Bernice P. Bishop Museum and especially the people who were staff members during the field work years made the study possible in the first place and greatly enriched this book and our personal lives. The late Sir Peter Buck, director of the museum in 1952, first welcomed Dr. Snow. Alexander Spoehr, director from 1953 to 1961, actively supported the project during that period and has rendered valuable assistance since that time.

This book has been enriched by appendixes by several individuals. Robert N. Bowen, who has described the archaeology of the site, was a graduate assistant in the department of anthropology at the University of Hawaii in 1956–1957, the period of the last excavation, which he directed. From 1961 to 1969 he was associated with the Pacific Science In-

formation Center at Bishop Museum, and taught at the University of Hawaii and the Kamehameha Schools in Honolulu. At present he is assistant director and curator of anthropology at Cranbrook Institute of Science, Bloomfield Hills, Michigan.

The detailed report on the pathology of several bone specimens was prepared by Lent C. Johnson with the assistance of Ellis R. Kerley at the Armed Forces Institute of Pathology, Washington, D.C. Dr. Johnson received his medical education at the University of Chicago and is senior pathologist at the institute, in charge of musculo-skeletal pathology. Dr. Kerley, whose research experience at the institute included skeletal variations, received his doctorate in physical anthropology at the University of Michigan. He is now head of the department of anthropology, University of Maryland.

Leonard J. L. Lai, who writes on the dental conditions of the early Hawaiians, practiced dentistry in Honolulu during the time of our study. At present he practices in Canoga Park, California.

Mary Kawena Pukui, associate in Hawaiian culture at Bishop Museum, was the source of much information and understanding of Hawaiian folkways. Mrs. Pukui, whose first language was Hawaiian, for twenty years collected Hawaiian words, culminating in the publication of the Hawaiian-English Dictionary in collaboration with Dr. Samuel H. Elbert. In June 1960 the University of Hawaii awarded her an honorary degree, thus recognizing her knowledge of and contributions to Hawaiiana. Her study of posture and body-molding practices is included here as an appendix.

Carey D. Miller, professor (now emeritus) of foods and nutrition, University of Hawaii, and former nutritionist, Hawaii Agricultural Experiment Station, provided the valuable information on the probable nutrition of the ancient Hawaiians.

Many others—anthropologists, doctors, dentists, and associates with special skills and knowledge—assisted the author in interpretation and presentation of the material.

The names of the many people who assisted in the essential tasks of recording and compiling data, computing statistics, and preparing the illustrations and manuscript are recorded in my memory. I'm confident they are aware of Dr. Snow's appreciation of their contribution and interest.

Finally, I personally appreciate the invaluable assistance of a long-time friend, William M. Bass, professor of anthropology at the University of

Tennessee, in the final preparation of this manuscript. He has given generously of his time and skill in the final review of the material for publication.

For my husband and myself, I am grateful to each person who has contributed knowledge, facilities, work, time, funds, and good will. *Aloha* and *mahalo nui* (thank you).

Katherine B. Snow

Introduction

HISTORY OF THE STUDY

The discovery of the Sandwich Islands (present-day Hawaii) by Captain James Cook in 1778 brought about the first recorded contact of Europeans with the descendants of the original inhabitants of these northernmost islands of Polynesia. Descriptions of the physical traits of these early Hawaiians exist in the records and diaries of the early explorers but, as Sir Peter Buck has said, "Until recent years our knowledge of the racial characteristics of the Polynesians was extremely scanty" (1938, p. 64). The recovery of skeletal material from the sand dunes of Mokapu afforded the opportunity for scientific investigation of the physical characteristics of the Hawaiians who lived and died before European contact, thereby adding a chapter to our knowledge of their racial heritage. The material is believed to represent a breeding isolate and as such stands as one of the unique collections in the Pacific island world.

Attempts to assign a relative date to these burials have been inconclusive. (See Appendix A, pp. 134–36.) However, the designation pre-European or "early" is justified for two reasons. First, trade objects commonly found with burials of the historic period are absent from Mokapu. Second, according to Buck, "Sand burials are found on all of the Hawaiian Islands, but the present population has no knowledge of their use as recognized cemeteries in the past" (1957, p. 570).

My personal involvement with the Mokapu burials began in 1947–1948 when I was serving with the American Graves Repatriation Program of the United States Army at Schofield Barracks, directing the identification of unknown war dead. On an errand to Bishop Museum my interest was sparked when I saw the skeletal remains recovered from Mokapu. Permission for me to study the material was granted by Sir Peter Buck, director of the museum at the time, and by Dr. Gordon T. Bowles, who had directed the field work at Mokapu before World War II and had started a study of the pelves. My study was initiated in September 1951, continued until April 1952, resumed during the summer of

1955, and completed after a year's work in 1956–1957.

The first bones from Mokapu were accessioned by Bishop Museum in November 1932. The first major excavation began in October 1938 and ended in January 1940. During the war years and until 1957, undocumented remains were brought to the museum by visitors to the peninsula as well as by residents. The second major excavation was conducted by Robert N. Bowen in 1957. An account of the discovery of the Mokapu burials and the subsequent recovery of the bones of over a thousand individuals is told by Bowen in Appendix A to this book.

All the skeletal material from Mokapu is stored at Bishop Museum. Each bone bears not only an identifying number but also a letter, H, C, N, or W. The letters H, C, and N designate specific locations within the Mokapu burial area (see map, p. 128). The letter W was assigned to miscellaneous material recovered in a manner that precluded documentation of a definite location. The skeletons of over 100 individuals recovered by Bowen in the spring of 1957 were not available for study until my field work was nearing completion. Time did not permit thorough study or measurement of this material but it was carefully examined and the age and sex of each skeleton determined. These data appear in the census as the C–2 series. The original C area material is designated C–1. (Tables of measurement and observation do not include the C–2 materials.) Nothing of archaeological significance was evident to warrant a separation of the bones into series other than on the basis of location, nor were any physical traits found which would suggest any significant differences among them. Therefore the series presented in the section on census are treated elsewhere as one series, namely, Mokapu.[1]

OBJECTIVES OF THE STUDY

Since no adequate and comprehensive description of early Hawaiian skeletal material now exists, it was my task to find out as much as possible about these pre-European Hawaiians. Who were these people, from the standpoint of their physical attributes? How many were men, how many women? How many children were there? How big were they?

1. The original data, notes, and photographs for this study are available at the University of Tennessee, Department of Anthropology, Dr. William M. Bass, chairman. All photographs, unless otherwise indicated, are by Dr. Snow.

FIG. 1. Dr. Snow and his assistant, Mrs. Clay, with skeletal remains from Mokapu. These 257 adult skulls are shown atop Bishop Museum's Paki Hall. Courtesy of *Honolulu Star Bulletin.*

What did they look like? With what diseases were they afflicted? How long did each live? How do they compare with us, with people in other parts of the world, and with people of previous times? What can be learned of their activities and habits from the bones? What kind of injuries did they sustain? Did they have unique physical characteristics?

An adequate and objective description of the people of Mokapu from their skeletal remains is the ultimate purpose of this study. It is hoped that the description of the morphology and an attempt to assess the roles of function, culture, and physical environment in the shaping of certain features will throw more light on the problem of the ecology of the Polynesian people. The compilation of these data forms the demographic record of this population.

METHODS

The first step necessary in examining the Mokapu collection was to measure in detail the major bones of each adult individual and to make morphological observations and classifications of those features that do not yield easily to measurement. Age and sex were determined by several methods. Finally, the remains of each individual were assembled so that data determined from the various parts could be used in assessing the individual as a whole.

Assembling Individual Burials: As the bones were brought into Bishop Museum they were properly numbered, as indicated above. But until the last period of recovery in 1957, they were not stored as individual burials but were separated into groups by kind of bone—skulls, jaws, humeri, and so forth —and boxed separately. Articulated pelves gave evidence of the study begun by Gordon T. Bowles. The pelvic bones (the innominates and the sacra) had been cleaned and prepared with dental wax for articulation. Moreover, John de Young, a student of Dr. Bowles, studied some of the skulls for his master's thesis (De Young, 1941). These special studies may explain why the bones of some individual burials had been separated out.

Beginning in the summer of 1955 and continuing in 1956–1957, I reassembled the parts into as complete individual skeletons as possible. Each bone was cleaned and then immersed in a solution of vinyl acetate for storage. A card prepared for each burial lists the following information: number of the burial; sex and age assessment; bones present; bones measured; pathology or anomalies, when present; distinguishing characteristics, such as the presence of the rocker jaw; notes on the condition of the bones when excavated, with other pertinent remarks; and, finally, which bones were photo-

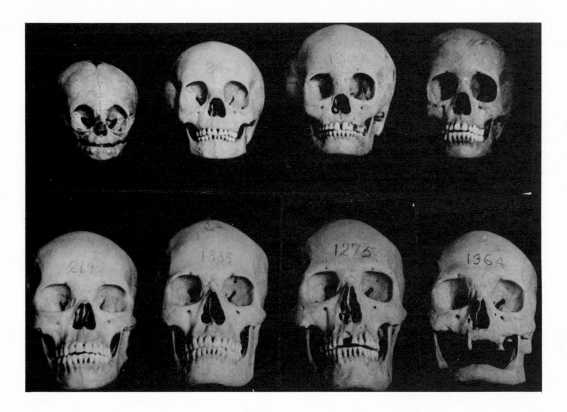

Fig. 2. Age changes from infancy to old age. A series of skulls of various ages. Left to right, top row: 4 months, 4 to 5 years, 7 to 8 years, 11 to 12 years. Bottom row: 19 to 20 years, 23 years, 37 years, 45 years.

graphed or X-rayed. From this card file the census was compiled.

It should be pointed out that many of the burials were not complete skeletons. Occasionally only a skull or sometimes a single bone was found. These parts were considered as representing individual burials and were numbered accordingly. Every effort was made to avoid counting any individual more than once. Since the bones of each person are unique as to articulating joint surfaces, bone texture, muscle markings, and other characteristics, it was possible to sort out the bones into individuals in nearly all cases. This matching of isolated bones is in itself a fascinating challenge of detection in human anatomy.

Why certain bodies had been dismembered before, during, or after burial is not clear, but some explanations have been advanced and these will be discussed later. In some instances, burials that had probably been complete were disturbed by bulldozers and some bones lost. And often the amateurs who worked on the excavations lacked the neces-

sary experience and skill to recover all the bones of an entire skeleton.

Age Determination: In assessing the age of each individual in such a wide range, from fetuses to old adults, several keys were used. In all cases, the criteria rested upon the known age factors observed in normal growth of modern Americans. (See Fig. 2.)

Laboratory studies for determining age have long utilized such phenomena as the eruption of both the deciduous and the permanent teeth; wear on the dentition (useful only when some measure of the rate of tooth wear and type of diet are known); the size and development of all bones, particularly the skull, spine, limb, shoulder, and pelvic girdle; and finally, in adults, the completion of the growth pattern after the rapid growth and development of adolescence and the subsequent degenerative processes. The age changes of the surfaces of the pubic symphysis, the closure of the cranial sutures, the onset of arthritis with lipping and exostoses of the joints, and finally the changes in bone texture (thinning and absorption processes) of such bones as the scapulae and innominates—all were utilized. One, some, or all of these age changes were used to estimate the age of each individual remains, whether represented by a single bone or by the complete skeleton.

The ages of the smallest infants were assessed by the stage of tooth calcification and the eruption of the deciduous teeth. The relative size of the major limb bones, the growth stages of fontanel ossification, and the degree of union of the chin symphysis were used to classify the ages up to about 2 years. Children from 2 to 6 years of age were classed according to the size and development of the major long bones and the degree of wear of the deciduous dentition.

At about 6 years of age, the permanent dentition begins to appear. Thus, an individual 6 to 12 years old was aged according to the eruption of the permanent teeth, as well as the wear upon the deciduous teeth and the initial wear on the permanent molars and incisors. Also during this period the epiphyses of the long bones appear as new centers of bone formation. Again, the general size and development of the major long bones were used as guides to the average age.

Teen-agers are easy to identify. Twenty-eight permanent teeth—that is, all but the third molar, which in American whites erupts irregularly from age 17 on—have erupted and show their first abrasion. The epiphyses begin to unite with the shafts of the bones, and final growth of all the long bones except the clavicle, the sternum, the vertebral bodies, and the hip bones is complete at approximately 20 years of age.

Adults, of course, show completed growth of all bones and usually complete eruption of the permanent dentition, including the third molar. The union of the sternal epiphysis on the clavicle was useful to determine the age of individuals 26 years or older. The best criterion of all was the age phase of the surface of the pubic symphysis. Similar but more limited bone change takes place in the sternum and sacrum, as recently revealed by McKern and Stewart (1957). Lastly, the union and obliteration of the sutures of the cranial vault were used to indicate wide age limits.

Changes involving arthritic degeneration of joint tissue as well as exostoses, seen particularly in the spine, are phenomena of older adults. Degenerative

changes in the scapulae and the innominates were useful in detecting persons of older age.

One, some, or all of these keys to age were used to define the adult group. No skull with an open basal suture, which closes at about 20 years of age, and no limb bones without attached epiphyses, indicating terminal growth phases, were included in the adult series.

Sex Assessment: On the basis of extensive experience in studying and observing morphological differences, I assigned the sex to most of the individuals. In the cases of infants, children, and youths, these appear as "possible male" or "possible female" because of the absence of clear-cut differences until after the hormone-molded growth of puberty (Boucher, 1957, pp. 598–99). Whenever possible, the bones of every part were examined carefully. For infants and children, the size of the teeth, the contours and nature of the superior orbital edge, the structure of the chin, and width and nature of the sciatic notch, as well as the relative gross size and development of all bones were the criteria. For youths, the same criteria were used, plus eruption of the permanent dentition. After puberty, the usual skeletal sexual differences were apparent in the bony frame for the near-adult and adult groups.

Accordingly, whenever present, the pelvis, that most functionally important structure, served as ultimate reference and criterion for sex determination of adults (Fig. 3). The following observations or measurements of the hip-girdle structure were made: the general contour; the size and opening of the pelvic brim; the width and shape of the subpubic angle; the width and depth of the greater sciatic notch; the shape of the obturator foramen; the width between the ischial tuberosities; the ischiopubic index, which is a diagnostic ratio according to Washburn (1948); the comparative lengths of the pubic and ischiatic bones; and finally, the maximum and minimum diameter and depth measurements of the left acetabulum. From these it was possible to assign the sex of each individual satisfactorily, even if only one hip bone was present.

Certain features of the skull were carefully examined for telltale indications of sex. The typical Mokapu male skull could be identified by the following: on the frontal bone, a large glabella flanked by well-rounded brow ridges; a deep nasion depression; large, well-marked nuchal and temporal areas

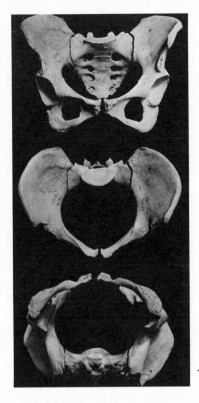 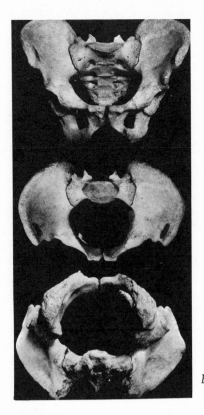

FIG. 3. Sex differences of the pelvis. Front oblique, top, and bottom views of *A*, female pelvis (W-41) and *B*, male pelvis (H-190).

of musculature, especially a sharp, well marked supramastoid crest; large, rough, deeply grooved mastoid processes; a capacious palate with large teeth; and a large, deeper-chinned mandible. Conversely, the female skull was typified by a fineness of features and a smaller, smoother skull. In particular, the facial features have a gracility of all bones—the brows, nose, mouth, jowls, and chin. The last also has a characteristic sharp point.

When only a few bones or sometimes a single bone remained, the gross size was used to assign sex. The size of the articular ends of the long bones was particularly useful, especially in the case of the femoral and humeral heads (Thieme and Schull, 1957).

In the normal distribution of typical sex characters, only a few of the overlapping extremes of male and female caused concern. Thus, I soon became cognizant of the usual size-association of most of the material, particularly because of considerable previous experience with skeletal series.

During the early part of the study, the sex of each individual adult was assessed from the skull alone, since the rest of the skeletal parts had not been assembled at that time. After assembling, it was neces-

sary to change the sex-assessment of only eleven individuals—seven males to females (1.8 percent) and four females to males (.9 percent).

Measurements: Each adult skeleton from skull to ankle was described as fully as possible by the accepted and standard anthropometric techniques and with the use of precise instruments. I followed procedures of the Martin school of anthropology (Martin, 1928) which are used throughout the world by virtue of international agreement among scientists. When I observed that some features could not be adequately described by the usual procedures, I devised new procedures. These original devices are defined in the text.

Detailed measurements and classifications were made of the major skeletal parts of each adult. These were compiled by sex, and statistical measures of the inherent variability were computed; the data are presented in the tables beginning on p. 79. Limb-bone dimensions provided the necessary data for making stature estimations; interbone comparisons (indices or percentage ratios) provided a means of understanding the shape of the body and its proportions. On the complete skull alone, some 43 measurements were used in 24 indices in addition to detailed measurements of the upper jaw and of eleven selected teeth of both jaws. In all, 101 measurements describe the cranium.

The bones of the arms and legs, the lumbar vertebrae, the pelvis, and the ankle bones were measured (a total of 95 measurements and indices on the postcranial skeleton) and were described in the effort to bring their owners "back to life" and to portray their separate characteristics in such a way as to be comprehensible to both scientific and lay readers. Measurements of all the postcranial bones were systematically taken on a standard osteometric board made of aluminum and plastic.[2] All maximum measurements were obtained by placing one end of the bone, usually the distal end, against the upright, and by moving the shaft of the bone through a small arc. Physiological bone lengths were obtained on the humeri and femora by placing the bone diagonally on the board with both condyles against the stationary upright and measuring the length at the head. In the case of the tibiae, a bolt placed through the wall of the upright and extending three centimeters from its inside surface was used. The most distal and center eminence of the inferior (distal) facet was carefully placed upon the rounded head of the bolt and the physiological length obtained by placing the plastic block against the anterior rim of the lateral condyle of the head. This technique permits the measurement of shin bones on which the internal malleolus is missing—all too frequently the case in archaeological specimens.

The maximum diameters of the heads of the upper arm and leg bones were obtained with a sliding caliper. All shaft diameters were likewise measured with the same caliper. In addition, a midshaft circumference of all long bones was obtained by using fresh waxed dental tape one-eighth of an inch wide. This flat tape was carefully placed at the midshaft and applied with the fingers to all of the contour surfaces of the bone. The place where the ends overlapped was pinched off with a pair of straight-edged forceps. The tape was then measured on the scale of the osteometric board. This girth measurement, when compared with the maximum length of the bone, yielded the "index of robustness," a useful measure of bone ruggedness or gracility.

A measure of the condylodiaphysial angle of the humerus (slope at the elbow joint) was obtained with a modified Bodel apparatus (Snow, 1940, p. 8). The angle between the shaft and the plane of the humeral condyles was measured to the nearest half-degree with a standard transparent protractor.

The postcranial bones were divided into two series for study: total series and paired series. The total series—or all the bones, single and paired, of the same sex and by left and right side—are treated together statistically. The paired series is composed of cases where bones of both sides of the same individual were present. This last group, necessarily smaller than the total series, is of more significance, since the differences between the bones of the two limbs due to function are revealed and can be analyzed and interpreted.

All efforts were made to obtain as many measurements of each part as possible. In dealing with skeletal material of fragmentary nature, measurements were made and close approximations included in the series. Frequently in such fragile bones as scapulae and delicate parts of long bones, the upper or lower tips of the bone—often the exact point for measurement—were missing. In such cases, by close comparison using one bone to "complete" the other, it was possible to obtain a valid approximation of the dimension. I believe that, in the main, the individuality of the bone of either side was still preserved. These approximated measurements were recorded, enclosed within parentheses, and included in the series.

All measurements, with the exception of those of the teeth, were made with standard anthropometric instruments of the Martin design and recorded to the nearest millimeter. The teeth were measured to the nearest tenth of a millimeter with a vernier scale.

The instruments used for skull measurements were a craniophore with protractor and calibrated rod attachments, and a sliding caliper with coordinate attachment.[3] Modifications in the form of the latter included the lengthening of the arms so as to span the length of the palate and provide clearance for such measurements as nasion–basion diameter. A very useful coordinate attachment with its own calibrated rod has been designed to fit between the caliper arms. This is so compact that it permits width measurements to 5 millimeters and at the same time can caliper elevation or depression to 5 centimeters (50 mm.) each way. Measurements termed "sub-

2. Manufactured by K. O. Lange Instrument Co., Lexington, Kentucky.

3. Both instruments were made by Karl A. Schneider, Department of Physics, University of Kentucky, and have been described elsewhere (Snow, 1946).

tense" by Neumann (1946) were all obtained by using these coordinate calipers.

In addition, spreading calipers with dial calibration,[4] a linen tape, a sliding caliper with vernier attachment for teeth,[5] and a goniometer with protractor and hinge plate[6] were used in cranial measurements.

The instruments for postcranial measurements were an osteometer of special aluminum and plastic design, a modified Bodel apparatus to measure the condylar angles of the humeri at the elbow joint (Snow, 1940, pp. 7–35), a sliding caliper with coordinate attachment, flat dental tape (1/8 in.), and small forceps, templates (three sizes) to gauge the diameters of the sciatic notches of the hip bones, and a sheet of aluminum (6 cm. × 10 cm. × 1 mm.) to aid in measuring the calcanei and tali of the foot bones.

CENSUS

Skeletal demography holds much of interest to the scientific understanding of man. This Mokapu series, representative as it is of a breeding isolate, is an extensive one. The Mokapuans interred their dead in family plots in the sand dunes within their *ilis* (small land sections) at Mokapu. The skeletal remains provide a great deal of information regarding their vital statistics and living conditions.

After the bones were assembled into individual burials and a card was made for each burial, a census was taken. This census enabled us to determine the number of individuals involved: 1,171, not all of them complete skeletons (some with but one bone), but nonetheless separate individuals. From the census information it was also possible to ascertain each individual's approximate age at the time of death. Of the total group, 28.43 percent were under 20.6 years of age (subadults) and 71.57 percent were 20.6 years or older (adults). (See Table 1.)

The average adult age at death for the 631 Mokapuans whose remains permitted a precise age estimate was 30.45 years, both sexes included. For the 336 females, the average was 28.99 years; for the 295 males, 31.91 years. These data are presented in Table 4. Age estimation was based on the phase of the face of the pubic symphysis, the sternal union, the sternal epiphyseal union of the clavicle, and the amount of tooth wear and/or cranial

4. Lange Instrument Co., Lexington, Kentucky.
5. Kurval Tool Co., Buffalo, New York.
6. Made by Dr. Gordon T. Bowles.

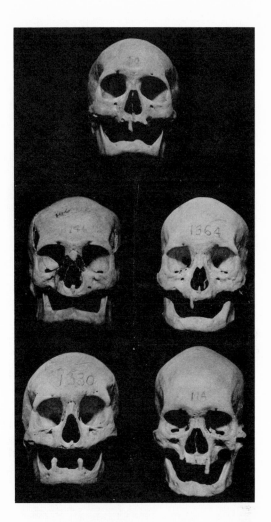

FIG. 4. Elderly Hawaiians; skulls of one woman (top) and four men. Note loss of teeth and absorption of alveolar ridges.

suture closure. Thus the sample size in Table 4 is smaller than the total sample in Table 2.

The section of Table 2 headed "Total Series" reveals a slightly larger female population recovered (52.45 percent) than male (47.55 percent). Sampling is probably responsible for some of this discrepancy; and until the entire dune area is excavated, the true distribution between the sexes cannot be ascertained. Some factors may explain it, however, if the sampling is a true one. High-ranking males may have been buried secretly elsewhere and accidents while fishing and fighting, as well as war casualties, both peculiar to males, might account for the difference in number of the sexes.[7]

7. Mary Kawena Pukui, personal correspondence.

FIG. 5. Well-preserved skulls of children and subadults.

It will be noted that 64 percent of the women in this series are found in the 20- to 30-year age group, and only 43 percent of the men; the men exceeded the women in the older age groups. The average age of death reflects this longevity of men in comparison with women and is similar to that found in another early skeletal series, Indian Knoll. The figures for modern American whites provide a decided contrast: women live longer than men and the average age for both sexes is more than double that of these early folk. (See Table 4.)

Virtually a third of the entire Mokapu series consists of subadults—that is, individuals below 20.6 years of age (Fig. 5; see also Tables 1 and 3). It should be noted also that infanticide may have claimed an unknown number of infants, presumably newborn, who may not have been accorded the usual pattern of burial.[8]

The high incidence of early childhood deaths astounded the early medical missionaries to Hawaii. Similar, if not perhaps poorer, conditions prevailed during the early nineteenth century compared with the prehistoric life in the islands as revealed by the Mokapu series. Contact-period Hawaiians were borrowing ideas and augmenting their native diets with the newly introduced food of the white men, but also the far-reaching effects of "civilized diseases" were making themselves felt. All in all, the remarks quoted below reveal in part the demography of the historic Hawaiians before they were decimated, intermixed, and absorbed. In 1778 the estimated native population was listed at 300,000; by 1836 this had dropped to less than one-half—107,000—in a mere 68 years.

Halford (1954, p. 173) quotes Seth Lathrop Andrews, one of the medical missionaries of the eighth company to Hawaii in 1838, who wrote:

I have recently made an effort to ascertain what proportion of the native children survive. The result shows that more than one half die under two years of age, most of these at from six to twelve months. Of those who survive the first two years, but a very small portion die in childhood.

That so large a proportion of deaths in infancy is not attributable to an unhealthy climate is manifest from the fact that of those who survive that tender age, but a small number die early. . . .

8. We note in the modern populations of Egypt, Turkey, Greece, and Italy that the high infant mortality rate has been taken for granted since history began. Ancient skeletal series from these countries confirm this fact.

To those acquainted with the habits of the Sandwich Islanders, the cause of so many early deaths is plain. It is to be found in the insufficient clothing or, as often the case, in an entire destitution of covering, improper food and want of cleanliness. It is the practice of the natives to feed their children at a very early age and often from birth, with poi, fish, sea eggs, seaweed, and whatever else they themselves eat. The consequence is indigestion, dropsy, diarrhoea, and other complaints. Disease having supervened, no alteration is made in the diet but a mistakened kindness indulges the sufferer in everything his appetite craves until death closes the scene. With such treatment, the wonder is not that so many perish, but that any survive.

Examination of Table 3 reveals that 46.2 percent of the subadults in the Mokapu series were 3.5 years old or younger, and an additional 11.4 percent were from 3.6 to 5.5 years of age. Over half of the children did not reach our present-day school age. Myron E. Wegman of the Pan-American Sanitary Bureau (World Health Organization, Washington, D.C.) observes:

Whether general death rates are high or low, the school age period is [at present] generally that of the lowest mortality rate in the lifetime. You can see . . . for example, that the chances of finding a skeleton in the age group 1 to 4 years would be perhaps ten times that for the 10 to 14 year group, ranging from a maximum of about 16 times in Barbados Island to about 6 times in Malaya.[9]

It is interesting to compare in more detail this census of early Hawaiians with other peoples, both prehistoric and modern. Harrison (1958, p. 294) has presented a chart showing the average length of life from ancient to modern times. The sharp upswing toward present-day longevity from the 33- to the 35-year level that was common for centuries, started in 1789, about the time Captain Cook's voyages to Hawaii ushered in the modern, historic period there.

When age groups from Mokapu are compared with those of another extensive skeletal series (see Table 4; also Fig. 6), the similarity of both incidence and curve is striking. This is especially surprising when one considers that the Indian Knoll series from Kentucky has been dated at 5,000 to 7,000 years old.

The outstanding fact to be learned from the comparison of these data is that in early times, among peoples of both different racial origins and different

9. Letter to Dr. Warner F. Bowers, October 15, 1956.

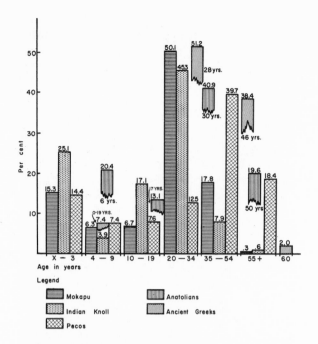

FIG. 6. A histogram comparing age group distribution of Mokapu population with other prehistoric populations. Graph by Dorothy T. Rainwater.

cultural levels (from the early American Indian hunting and gathering economy to the sophisticated agrarian Roman system), life expectancy was short and seems to have centered at about 30 years of age. Today it stands revealed that in the so-called unprogressive countries around the world, much the same limitations of human life prevail. The public health problems that cause high infant and child mortality, combined with all the diseases prevalent among the vast majority of the world's peoples, seemingly set a definite and early limit to the length of human life. Only in our modern scientific age and in those countries in which nutriture, adequate medical care, and the myriad new drugs are common components of the culture—Western Europe, Scandinavia in particular, and the United States—has it been possible to extend human life to such a remarkable old age, and that only in the last 50 years.

Krogman (1958) indicates very clearly that short life for most adults has been the rule from the beginning. He even includes (p. 246) a census for a series of both Neanderthal and Cro-Magnon fossil populations to indicate the low life expectancy during the Pleistocene. Thus we can understand that the people from Mokapu are typical of the "unprogressive" populations found today, quite in contrast to the life-expectancy figures on the American

white population, where the average age at death is 70.4 years for both sexes: males, 67.3 years; females, 73.6 years.

SYNOPSIS

The Mokapu skeletons form a large, statistically representative sample of an early Hawaiian population on windward Oahu. The skeletons excavated to date number some 1,171 individuals, 72 percent identified as adults and 28 percent as subadults. The absence of any European trade objects indicates that this group of people lived on Oahu before contact with the white man—that is, before the arrival of Captain James Cook and his crew in 1778. Fluorine tests (chemical analyses) have suggested a possible date of from 200 to 800 years ago.

The life span of these pre-European Hawaiians—approximately 32 years for men and 29 years for women—is comparable to that of ancient Greeks and Romans and of many people in the world today, such as the living Egyptians, American Indians, and Chinese. The same is true of the ratio of subadults to adults, and similarly the greatest mortality occurs between birth and 3 years (see Table 3).

These Hawaiians were a remarkably homogeneous group, as would be expected in view of their geographic isolation. This fact has been established by many measures of variability. They were in many ways quite similar in body build to typical American whites. Men stood 5 feet 7 inches tall and women 5 feet 3 inches, on the average, virtually identical to living Hawaiians measured in 1920 by Sullivan (1927). (See Table 26.) To be sure, there was a range of variation as there is today in the typical American population, and there were some unusual deviants in size and appearance.

These were large-headed people and some distinctive features were present in the skulls (Fig. 7). Many Mokapuans had a curved lower border to the mandible called a "rocker jaw." They had prominent chins that were arched at the midline, large parietal eminences, and flat-sided faces with large cheek bones. The men had larger-than-usual brow ridges and glabellas, and had deep nasal-root depressions. The results of the custom of head-shaping—the binding of the moldable heads of infants—were evident in many individuals of all ages. The effects of this were a flat fore- and back head and a short, broad, high vault. Their noses had narrow roots and medium high concavo-convex bridges. Sometimes the nasal sills were quite rounded, and some individuals had blunt double sills. Two individuals had no nasal bones, and five individuals had only one bone and part of the other.

Their palates are unique for straight-sided shapes and large teeth; many had shovel-shaped incisors. Frequently the central incisors had an inward midline twist. There was a conspicuous absence of the third molars and little wear on the teeth. Extra cusps (a hereditary trait) were frequent both on the inner front portions of the upper molar teeth (Carabelli's cusp) and on the facial and front sides of the lower molar teeth (protostylids). Supernumerary teeth were found in only one case—that of a youth. Some protrusion of the mouth parts (alveolar prognathism) was common.

Limb bone descriptions are based principally on the paired series; that is, the corresponding arm and leg bones of the same individuals. Comparisons of the different bones give accurate concepts of body proportions and build. Muscular bodies with very narrow hips were characteristic of these island people. The limb and hip bones showed an extraordinary muscular development, in women as well as men. Indeed, all of their bones bespeak the vigorous and strenuous outdoor existence of these people, and confirm what we have already learned of it through other sources. Septal apertures of the humeri of the women are among the highest number recorded throughout the world. This perforation, which permits hyperextension of the forearm, may be a functional characteristic.

Many functional adaptations were noted which affected these early Hawaiians in walking, running, swimming, and standing, and in other postures. The tilt of the tibial plateau reveals that they habitually kept their knees bent, both when in motion and when standing. Interestingly enough, their carved figurines are represented in this position (see Frontispiece). All who could (a few adults with clubfeet or foot injuries and stiff joints excepted) squatted with their feet flat on the ground, as do all young children, and thus marked their bones with extra facets (squatting facets) on the hip, knee, and ankle joints.

A curious anomaly, apparently unique here, was a V-shaped groove on the top surface of the sacrum. This, together with the separated neural arch of the lower lumbar vertebrae (spondylolisthesis), V-shaped and wrap-around articular facets of the bones of the lower back, and numerous accessory sacroiliac articulations, form an interesting group

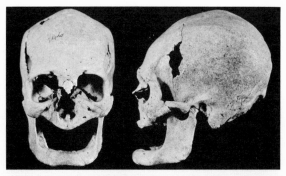

A

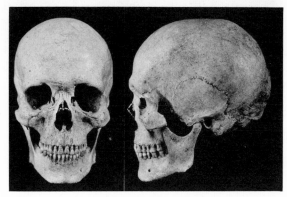

B

FIG. 7. Male skulls showing contrasts of age changes and shape. *A*, an old toothless man (146) with a shaped head; *B*, a young man (H-88) with an unshaped skull who was very short in stature but had the largest skull in the series. Note the expanded ascending ramus of the jaw.

of associated traits that are probably functionally connected with age.

Few bones were found to have been broken during the individual's lifetime, even though these were a people who fought close in with spears, daggers, and clubs. Of those bones that had been fractured, nearly all were perfectly set and healed. It is notable that no healed fractures are recorded for the entire subadult group. There is one interesting case of an adult with an arm amputation above the left elbow. Almost all adults had some form of chronic arthritis or osteophytosis. Osteoarthritis, either in the small of the back or in the major limb joints, occurred most commonly, and two cases of rheumatoid arthritis were found.

Bowers, in his discussion of the bone pathology (1966), reports tuberculosis, osteomyelitis, neuroarthropathy, and possibly yaws. Dental conditions are generally better than our own American population, says Lai (Appendix C), but caries, gum recession (pyorrhea, alveoclasia), and a little crowding of the Type II class of occlusion are characteristic. Miller (Appendix E) concludes that the known foods available to these people were adequate for the promotion and maintenance of good health except when food shortages and famine occurred.

These conclusions are the results of some 202 measurements and indices plus observation of several hundred classified morphological features on the skull and postcranial skeleton. All of these traits, most of them hereditary in origin but some clearly involving functional responses, together mark these early Hawaiians and set them apart from all other peoples in the world. These observations, together with the pictures and sketches of early historic people and Sullivan's study (1927) on Hawaiians living in 1920, afford an interesting picture in depth of the Hawaiian people.

Cranium

MEASUREMENTS AND INDICES

The human skull has been of particular interest to all people, ancient and modern. In recent studies this portion of the skeleton, and especially the dentition with its useful genetic structure, has received extensive description. The skull is a means of identifying individuals, bears the marks of certain racial traits, and also reveals acquired or cultural characteristics. It is by far the most complicated of skeletal structures, housing man's most distinctive organ—the brain.

The largest Hawaiian series hitherto available (British Museum, London), measured by Konrad A. Wagner, is compared with Mokapu in Table 5. Wagner (1937, p. 8) refers to his series of fifty-six males and forty-six females as "Sandwich Islanders . . . from Havaii, Oahu and Owhyee," early names for the Hawaiian Islands. The similarities between the two series are remarkable.

The low average differences between the two series would indicate an extremely high degree of homogeneity in these early Hawaiian crania. The average difference for the thirty-one measures that could be compared is only 2.2 millimeters for males, 1.5 millimeters for females; 16 indices average .63 units for males, .74 units for females. The similarity of these skulls probably represents the genetic response to a common physical and cultural environment.

Additional measurements and indices have been computed using the values of the means listed in Wagner's data. It should be noted, however, that Wagner tried to eliminate those skulls which showed a definite degree of deformation. This was not done with the Mokapu series, since those skulls that had been shaped were included as part of the ordinary population.

In general we can say that the Mokapu skulls appear to be a little larger than those examined by Wagner in almost all dimensions of the vault and face. The amazing number of indices that agree within 1 or 2 tenths of a unit is even more remarkable than the similarity of the measurements themselves.

Judging from the Wagner series, if the known groups of Hawaiian skulls available in this country—those at the United States National Museum in Washington, D.C., the American Museum of Natural History in New York City, and the Peabody Museum at Harvard University—follow suit, they will indicate a remarkable similarity which I interpret as indicative of homogeneity.

When the Mokapu crania are compared with skull dimensions listed by Martin (1928, pp. 747–78) for all parts of the world, we are in a position to evaluate the former. The Mokapu crania are large in overall size as measured by capacity, horizontal circumference, and other arcs in the transverse and sagittal planes, as well as the diameters themselves. The vault is moderately long and wide but very high (all three dimensions are affected by head-shaping, with length decreased and width and height increased). We find, too, that the height of the skull base from the basion to the poria is likewise very high (Fig. 8).

As for facial features (Martin, 1928, pp. 894–910), the forehead is rather narrow but the dimensions of the face in breadth and across the jowl region, and the facial height, both total and upper, are large. The nose is long but moderate in breadth (ibid., pp. 939–40). The orbits are wide (breadth) and medium in height (ibid., pp. 959–62). The measurements of the nasal bridge tend to run moderately high with the root noticeably lower. The palate is large. The projection of the face, as measured by the total facial angle (84°), approaches the straight-faced profile found in most Europeans. On the other hand, the alveolar projection tends to be outstanding, with a very low angle (about 64°) for both sexes (ibid., p. 913). The height of the chin at the symphysis is remarkably low for both sexes. This shallow mandibular character undoubtedly accounts for the medium proportions of the otherwise big facial size (Fig. 9).

It appears now (too late) that a standardized method of measuring and describing the rocker jaw can be suggested. At the time of measuring and studying the Mokapu collection at Bishop Museum, I followed the standard procedures in measuring the mandible. The rocker jaws, with their unstable rounded lower borders, presented some very real problems of orientation and deep concern for me regarding technique. Martin (1928, p. 981) indicates that the usual mandible has three points of contact on a smooth surface; it touches at the gonial points

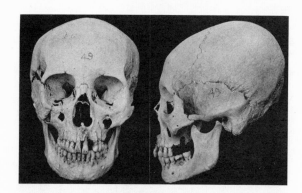

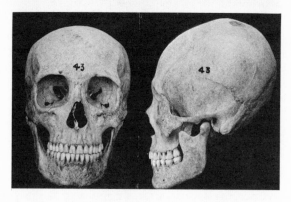

FIG. 8. Front and side views of two female skulls (H-49 and H-43) with shaped contours.

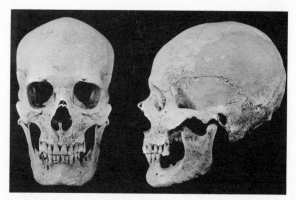

A

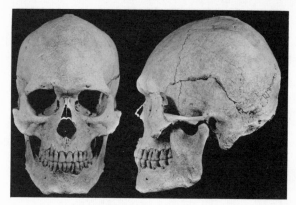

B

FIG. 9. Male skulls. *A,* (1261) with a high nose and long, flat-sided face; *B,* (1366) with shaped and rugged contours.

and at the chin. It is simple to place the "standard" lower jaw at rest and measure it. With the Mokapu sample, wide variations were experienced in measuring the angle and the length and height due simply to the unusual contours of these curious jaws.

In measuring the gonial angle and the diameters of height and length, I selected a compromised middle point along the lower border, which represented more or less the position at rest. (See Hrdlička, 1940, p. 288.) Since then it has been discerned that this sometimes resulted in the oblique anterior sloping of the occlusal plane, a poor orientation, which should have been used as a plane of reference. By keeping the level of the tooth row horizontal to the supporting surfaces, a standard position could have been maintained for measuring and otherwise describing the rocker mandibles. Experimentation has indicated that a variation in the height of the mandible up to two centimeters may result from the compromised position up to the horizontal occlusal plane (see Table 5). It also seems clear that the variations of length and of the

angle likewise resulted from the lack of a standard position. In other words, if the occlusal plane horizontal had been adopted during the period of measurement, it would have eliminated the variables due to position. The trend, since over half of the adult mandibles were rocker-jawed, would then be toward a slightly shorter mandible with less angle (that is, more upright) and one with a greater height to the top of the condyles.

When the cranial proportions and indices are considered (these values reflect the shapes of the parts concerned), we have a superior means of comparison. The Mokapu skulls, both sexes alike, can be described in these terms: they are brachycranic, hypsy and acrocranic (deformation involved), with projecting and deep skull bases; the faces are meso-prosopic and mesene (upper face); the orbits are mesoconch; the nasal structure mesorrhine; and the palates brachyuranic. These are large-sized crania.

Using the universal Lee-Pearson formula for skull

capacity (Martin, 1928, p. 647), which utilizes the basion-bregma height, we find that the males average 1,540 cc. and females, 1,329 cc. Both of these values are slightly higher than the world average. This overall large size is again reflected in the high cranial module: 157 for males; 151 for females.

In Hawaii today, there are many opportunities to observe the head and facial features of the native populations and to compare them with the Mokapu group, as well as with recorded observations and descriptions left by the early European explorers and navigators and the sketches made by artists (e.g., Webber and Choris) aboard their ships. In addition, there are the contemporary Hawaiians who were measured, studied, and photographed by Sullivan (1927) in 1920–1921.

Charlot (1958, p. 47) provides a description and illustrations from the original 1816 Choris sketches of Kamehameha (Fig. 10) which depict a Negroid cast of the face. These physical features, present in modern-day Hawaiians and in their ancient carved statues of wood and stone, are so classified because of the full lips, the slight bulge of the mouth parts, and particularly the flare of the nostrils. In these respects, there is a similarity between certain Hawaiians and some American Negroes. On the other hand, the early observers also emphasized the regularity of the Hawaiian face and commented on its Europeanlike features, except for the nose.

When we consider the bony nose structure of the Mokapu people, we note that it is quite long, moderately high, but characterized sometimes by dull nasal sills and by prenasal fossae. In side-profile we observe that the face protrudes slightly and that the chin is prominent, terminating the curved sweep of the lower face line to the chin point.

A comparison between the Mokapu male skulls and other Polynesian crania presented by Marshall and Snow (1956, p. 419) indicates some interesting relationships, if the samples available, despite their small size, are representative. The Mokapu figures are larger in all measurements except those of interorbital and biorbital diameters, wherein a difference of about 1 millimeter exists.

Hawaiian skulls, as represented by the Mokapuans, resemble more the larger skulls from the Society, Chatham, and New Zealand (Moa-hunter and Maori) series than those from the Marquesas and Tonga. We note too that the Mokapu series contains shaped (deformed) skulls as perhaps does that from Tonga (Life, January 24, 1955, p. 64). It appears

FIG. 10. Portrait of Kamehameha I (1816) by Louis Choris. Courtesy of Bernice P. Bishop Museum, Honolulu.

obvious that the Tonga crania with the highest cranial index measured by Marshall show the expected deviations associated with skull deformation. The Mokapu skulls have the longest noses (heights) and, like those from Tonga, have shorter, wider, and higher vaults. It is important to watch for the cultural mark of head-shaping practices in all Polynesian samples (Figs. 11 and 12).

The usual statistical measures have been applied to the Mokapu series and they may be easily compared with those of Wagner (Table 5). Standard errors of the mean and standard deviations were computed. The standard deviation (SD) and the coefficient of variation (V) are devices used to gauge the extent to which the average measurement or index deviates from the mean, and we can easily determine this. Even though the Mokapu group is about three times as large as the Wagner series, the SDs and Vs have similar values, despite the much greater probability of including in the Mokapu group more variation simply because it is a larger sample—that is, more cases of differing sizes are involved. Overall uniformity of the physical type and all its sizes is indicated.

In comparing these statistical values further, it

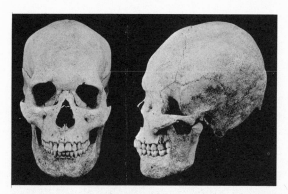

A

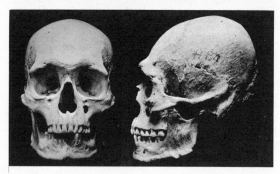
B

FIG. 11. Male skulls, *A* (120) and *B* (H-80), with rugged contours and some head shaping. Note in *B* the wide-chinned, nonrocker jaw.

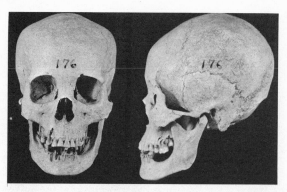
A

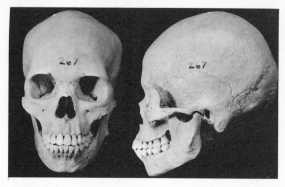
B

FIG. 12. Front and side views of two female skulls. *A* (176) has a big flat face and head shaping; *B* (267) (not shaped) has facial projection, large teeth, and a receding chin profile.

appears in most cases that they are larger in both groups in those diameters and indices most likely to be affected by the head-shaping custom. Larger SDs are indicated for the length and breadth of the skull vault, for the orbital height, the external dimensions of the palate, and the facial length (basion-prosthion) than for the other measurements and their indices. The other tests used for homogeneity likewise point out these same items (that is, diameters and their proportions) as the larger deviants.

These variations of skull dimensions and indices present within the population can be tested again by using the mean sigma ratio as a standard of reference. In analyzing European populations, Howells (1936 and 1941) and Stewart (1943), and, in analyzing American Indian populations, Snow (1948a) found this test to be of value; that is, a comparison of the SDs of an unknown series (to be so tested) with one of proven and accepted homogeneity.

When these mean sigma ratios were computed for the Mokapu male series, an average figure of 106.2 for thirty-four items (measurements and indices)

was obtained. This is six units higher than the ideal 100 level; yet many of the items scored below 100. Indeed, those with the highest values—that is, those farthest from the ideal—were the very same dimensions which yielded the largest differences in the Wagner Hawaiian analyses. These appear to center about those parts affected by the deformations of head shaping.

Using the *F* test for variance (Yule and Kendall, 1953, p. 495), we obtain another useful viewpoint in measuring the uniformity of the Mokapu male skulls. It should be noted here that the female skull series, even with its greater number, has smaller SDs and Vs, hence is regarded as more consistent and homogeneous. This is true of other prehistoric populations (Angel, 1944, p. 334; Snow, 1948a, p. 443).

F tests were computed between Mokapu and a very large, homogeneous European series compiled by Howells (1941, p. 145). The overall average value, using the SDs of thirty-three measurements

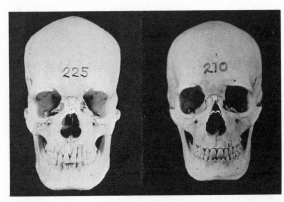

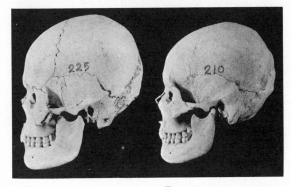

FIG. 13. Male (*A* and *C*, H-225) and female (*B* and *D*, H-210) skulls showing typical contours. Note the flat-sided faces, straight facial profiles, and rocker jaws with arched chins.

and indices, is 1.215. Both of the limits for significance (lack of variance) at the 5 percent level of 1.25–1.00, and even at the 1 percent level of 1.38–1.00, suggest that this Mokapu group of male skulls is truly a homogeneous one—that is, in all but those same critical dimensions and indices most clearly affected by the pressure changes of head shaping. In other words, the inclusion of individual skulls with obvious head-shaping deformations brought about the greatest variations (deviations).

Thus if these tests for homogeneity have validity for the Mokapu research, they appear to confirm my surmise: namely, that these early Hawaiians at Mokapu do indeed represent an inbred, isolated population characterized by a remarkable uniformity of physical form in their skulls.

MORPHOLOGY

In analyzing the morphological expression of the Mokapu skulls, we come to deal not merely with size and shape but with the sum total phenotype of each individual. These developmental wholes require a qualitative as well as a quantitative measure. Hence, they are classified by kind, size, development, and so forth, and presented in Table 6 by frequency and percentage distributions.

To define this phenotype, the following explanation of just how heredity and environment cooperate (Dobzhansky, 1959, pp. 90–91) may be helpful:

The action of heredity consists basically in transforming a susceptible component of the environment, *food*, into a living body. Before all else, genes reproduce themselves. The sum total of genes which an individual receives from his parents is his *genotype*; the genotype interacts with the environment and makes the body grow and develop; the *state* or appearance of the body at a given moment is its *phenotype*. In a sense, our bodies, and hence our phenotypes, are *by-products* of the process of self-reproduction of the genes. . . . In short, the genes determine processes, not states.

The Mokapu "states"—the skulls—are the subject of this interpretation. The genetic systems (or gene constellations) of these early Hawaiians undoubtedly were truly isolated, owing to the location of their island world.

I am aware of limitations in the use of the classification "physical type" as ably set down by Hunt (1959, p. 81). This category-grouping of like external appearances has been widely used in this country to indicate a total morphological impression (Hrdlička, 1922, 1927; Neumann, 1952; Hooton, 1930; Angel, 1944; Krogman, 1940; Briggs, 1955; Brues, 1958, 1959; Coon, 1939; and Snow, 1945, 1948a). In Polynesia, Shapiro (1943) and Sullivan (1924) have likewise tried to group and analyze these physical type differences.

The skull is a valid piece of anatomy, a phenotype bone-assemblage, which can be classified as can any other life form, whether plant or animal. Simpson (1947, p. xvii) has aptly stated, "The paleontologist is given only phenotypes (bones), and attempts to relate these to genotypes have so far had little success." This statement applies to all skeletal remains of past life, including those of Mokapu.

Grouping by phenotype has been useful to me in attempting to depict the compiled and significant data of this large series. Much of the distinctive morphology may be portrayed in the facial view, other aspects in an oblique or full-side profile.

The morphological types are in essence the sum

total of all the features found in Table 6. Taken together, Hawaiians or mixed Hawaiians make up 82.5 percent of the series (Fig. 13). The small "minority groups" remaining, some 17.5 percent, are distributed nearly equally between white, Mongoloid, Negroid and Australoid (combined), and others. The Mokapu wheel (Fig. 14) illustrates this grouping.

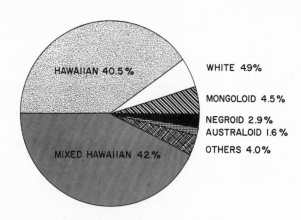

FIG. 14. Gross composition of the Mokapu skulls, sexes combined and based on the total morphology. Drawing by Robert Herndon.

These physical-type designations do not imply genetic relationships. Rather they are names given to groups of individuals with physical features in common. However, this common, consistently appearing type—the phenotype—must represent the genotype as it was expressed in this particular physical environment on Oahu (Fig. 15).

In Table 6, the detailed classification of the morphology of the skulls of both men and women is compared with the average male skull of northwestern European origin. The categories marked S are those which show the greatest sex difference. Those with H (for Hawaiian) reflect what appear to be features of genetic (racial) import. Sometimes both sex differences and racial features appear to be involved within the same set of classified morphology. An important factor in the categories is age, A, indicated by tooth wear and decay, the closure of cranial sutures, and the incidence of diseases involving the alveolus and other portions of the cranial bones. Cultural trait, C, appears with those features affected by head shaping.

A generalized description of the most outstanding features follows. The number of individuals of each

sex varies according to the preservation of the part in question on each skull. Percentage distribution provides a fair basis for making comparisons.

These Mokapu skulls tend to be large and heavy, marked by the usual sex differences. The bone tissue is hard, ivorylike, and massive in many instances. In the more rugged individuals, the zygomatic arch is thick and wide. An exceptionally flat temporal region is present on most skulls. Areas covered by muscles—temporal, nuchal, and facial—tend to be large and well marked. Large divided brow-ridges along with an unusual prominence of glabella set these Hawaiians apart, even in some indisputable females. (See De Young, 1953, p. 79.) Deep-set nasal roots at nasion, very low nasion-metopic angles, and long frontal diameters add to this distinction. Sloping but often high foreheads, frequently flattened from shaping, with distinct temporal lines and marked postorbital constrictions in many cases, and small to average-sized bosses are common. Howells (1959, p. 209) has used the term "strongly built" skull to refer to his "type" for *Homo sapiens* —a Melanesian skull from Fiji. He describes the population as one which "probably represents a blend of the main races of modern man." This statement might well apply to many of the skull structures found at Mokapu. (See Figs. 16 and 17.)

Viewed from above (horizontal shape) these skulls are oval for the most part. Outstanding parietal bosses form flat sides; prominent brow-ridges in front, and flattened occipital curves at the back make pentagonal and rhomboid shapes.

From behind (vertical transverse) these skulls present high, flat-sided pentagonal outlines with sagittal crests and pointed parietal bosses, but softer, more rounded sides occur in many females. Suture patterns tend to be simple to average, with pterion-in-K lines. Wormian bones (separate islands) occur in about 70 percent of all adult skulls.

From the side these skulls have another distinctive profile: a shallow, prominent, pointed chin (Fig. 18); some alveolar bulge of the mouth parts, but nonprojecting, upright faces; small nasal spines; and distinctive concavo-convex, moderately projecting nasal profiles.

Frequently the lower borders of the orbits lie anterior to the upper edge and often they are associated with large-sized, projecting cheek bones (Fig. 19). Strong jut of the lower border of the maxillomalar joint along with a full suborbital region (antra) of the forward plane of the cheek

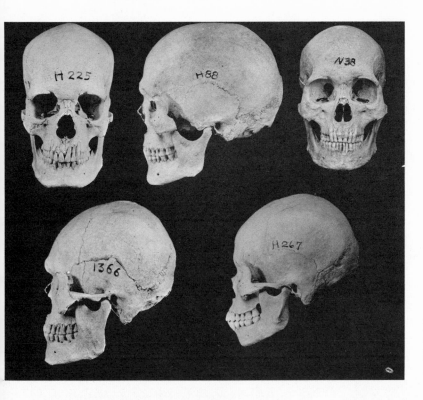

FIG. 15. Physical types in skulls. Clockwise from upper left: Hawaiian, European, Mongoloid, Negroid, Australoid.

FIG. 16. Male skulls, *A* (1282) and *B* (N-48), in front and side views. Compare the shaped skull *A* with the undeformed contours of *B*.

A

B

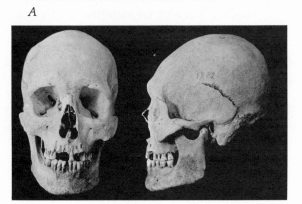
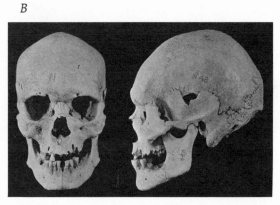

FIG. 17. Female skulls contrasting *A*, "normal" unshaped, prognathous youth (H-200), with shaped adults *B* (H-49), *C* (H-62), and *D* (H-83).

A   *B*

C   *D*

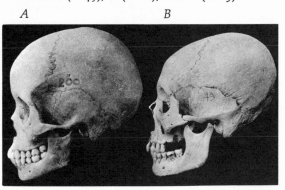
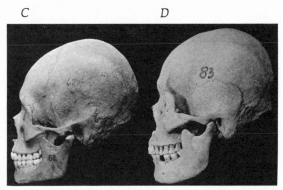

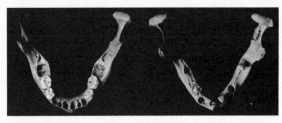

A   B

FIG. 18. Top view of mandibles of *A*, a 6-year-old child (N-55), and *B*, an old woman (H-30) showing sharp chin crests. Note the dental caries in large molar teeth in *A* and loss of teeth and other age changes in *B*.

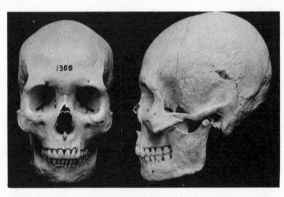

A

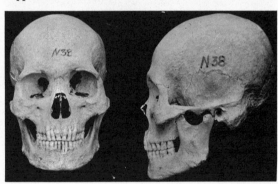

B

FIG. 19. Front and side views of the skulls of *A*, a female (1305), and *B*, a male (N-38). Note the large, heavy, Mongoloid faces, large cheek bones, and converted types of bite (edge to edge in *B*).

bones produces a flat, blunt face. A few Hawaiians have conspicuous suborbital (canine) fossae. They have a deep-set nasion and large, heavy glabella flanked by medium-to-large, usually divided brow-ridges; a high but often quite sloping forehead, sometimes rounded by frontal bosses; a moderate vertex curve, sharply bent in cases with deformation; and the occipital region of small to average projection (depending on the degree of shaping). Lambda usually is located high upon the profile. Inca bones occur in 6.4 percent (ten) females and in 17 percent (twenty-five) males.

Neck muscles form ridged tori (small to large for both sexes). There are frequent neck pegs (external protuberances). Bone extensions, ridges which run from the nuchal lines down to the mastoid notch, are common on the occipital base. Both mastoid size and supramastoid crests run large and are well marked by sharp crests. Some men have very large, prominent, and deeply notched mastoids, and many females show unusual medium-to-large crests along with other equally well-marked muscle areas. The cerebellar area (occipital base) often bulges downward, sometimes with lateral bosses directly behind and obliquely median to the mastoids. In most cases the contours of the base are flat.

Viewed from below, the typical skull shows some interesting if not unique features (Fig. 20*B*). The large, hyperbolic palate with straight sides and large teeth comes to view. Shovel-shaped incisors are common in both the maxillae (44 percent) and the mandible (43 percent). Almost all adults and sub-adults have the midline inward twist (mesiolingual torsion) of the upper central front teeth (Fig. 20*B*). The palate is usually smooth with only small ridges near the midline.

The plane of the face is blunt since the cheek bones extend directly sideways from the edges of the palate. Often at the union of the malar and maxilla there is a right-angled corner and even a forward angulation or jut (Fig. 19). Usually the bottom edge of the cheek bone is thick and rough for the insertion of the powerful masseter muscles which pull at the jaw angles to close the mouth and clench it in a forward, oblique grip (Fig. 20*B*).

The inferior surface of the palate and pterygoid base below is often scored with pinhole-sized perforations. This condition is usually associated with other cortex bone porosities of the vault, the cause of which is unknown (McKern and Stewart, 1957, pp. 14–15).

Well-formed, often large, articular eminences (the portion where the mandibular condyles ride as the mouth is opened) curve backward or actually upward into deep, well-defined sockets (temporal-mandibular fossae) (Fig. 20B).

In an unusual number of cases the skull base shows peculiar bone formations. These are masses of spongy bone and are part of the basilar portion of the occipital bone; they extend against the petrous portions of the temporals anterior to the jugular foramina and occipital condyles. These condyles stand high and are well-defined and curved (Fig. 21).

The mastoid processes are large with unusually deep notches which extend onto and may be continuous with the occipital tori. Other occipital rugosites, including the external crest and the lateral bosses which bulge downward, model the nuchal region (Figs. 20B and 22).

The face gives the "character" to the skull; hence its importance in skeletal description. The characteristic contours of the typical Mokapu male face have been described by Marshall and Snow (1956, pp. 415–16). The following is revised and modified from the original.

The Polynesian face, as reflected in the skulls from Mokapu, has a narrow forehead, but orbits, noses and faces of average proportions. The lower margins of the face have typically rounded contours, with the Rocker Jaw frequently present. Perhaps the most interesting feature of the face (next to the Rocker Jaw) is the flat-sided nature of the cheekbones. The Hawaiian malars are typically large in size with considerable anterior prominence (jut). On the lateral aspects, from the frontal processes down to the middle, the malar bones show a flatness which brings the surfaces parallel with the sides of the cranial vault. This bony "plane" must have provided the structure for a rather flat-sided facial contour, discernible on so many present-day Hawaiian faces.

Nasal fossae with interesting rounded sills to the lower margins of the nasal apertures, are common. Some have double sills, internal and external, which form prenasal fossae. Nasal spines are of a small to average size. Another common characteristic is the narrow-rooted nature of the nose bones. Both upper and lower jaws are large in size, show little anterior projection and contain large teeth with some caries and commonly with abscesses. The dentition as a whole is characterized by little wear, close overbite, and the recession of the bony borders of the alveoli; some 34 percent of the men and 51 percent of the women have excellent to perfect teeth. In Hawaii, the shape of the palate frequently is flat-sided. From the canines back to the second and third molars, the upper alveolus is straight-sided. The Rocker

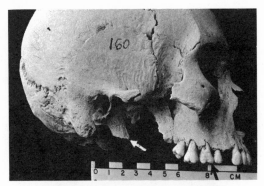

A

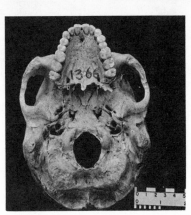

B

FIG. 20. Skull base anomalies. In A (H-160), the arrow points to a remarkable development of the temporal part of the stylohyoid. Note the first molar tooth (black arrow) with a ring on the crown indicating an interruption of growth. B, base view of male skull (1366). Note the palate shape, the massive bone and muscle areas of the zygoma, and the modeling of the mastoid-occipital regions. The occipital crest continues to the mastoid processes.

Jaw, with its characteristic rounded lower border, frequently has an arch under the chin. Usually there is a median and sharply pointed eminence here and the chin height is low, i.e., shallow, in most cases. The jowl region shows little gonial eversion and is wide and full. [See Figs. 23 and 24.]

The typical female Mokapuan (Fig. 25) is simply a smaller, smoother version of the rugged males described above. Her facial features, in particular, are finer, with a gracility present in all parts, including the chin and lower jaw. The same rounded contours are found in the lower borders of the faces with rocker jaws and their characteristic smooth curves. Prominent, sharply pointed chins are also typical of most of the Mokapu women.

Undoubtedly many of these classified skull fea-

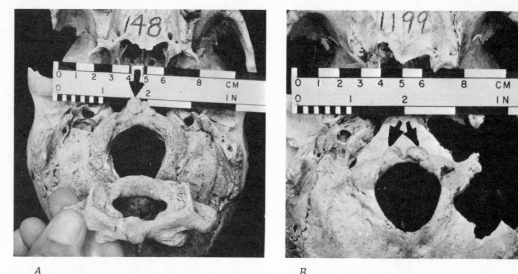

A   B

FIG. 21. Views of *A*, male (148), and *B*, female (1199) skulls with basilar tubercles on occipital base (arrows).

FIG. 23. *A*, male skull (1275) with shaped contours and rocker jaw, compared with *B*, unshaped skull (N-47) with a nonrocker jaw.

A

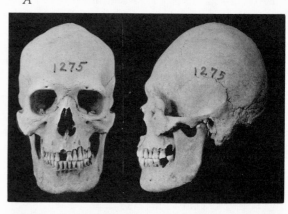

FIG. 22. Front and side views of *A*, female skull (H-255), and *B*, rugged male skull (248). Both demonstrate shaped contours.

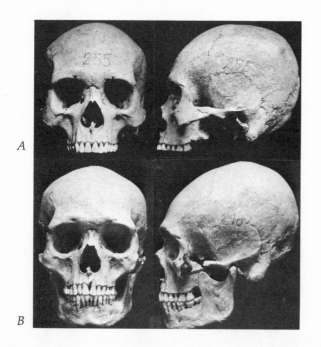

A

B

B

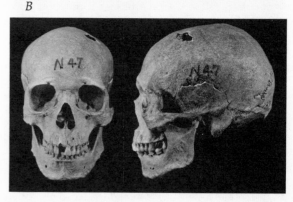

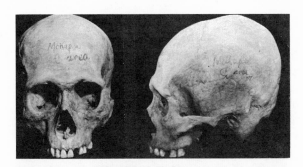

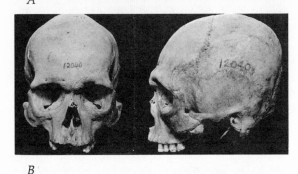

FIG. 24. Front and side views of two shaped male skulls. *A*, from C-2 area, Mokapu, and *B* (12040) from Hawaii. Note the bony plugs (exostoses) which fill the ear holes.

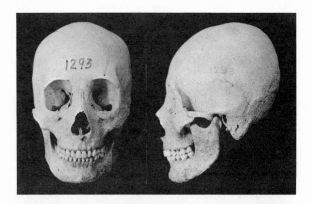

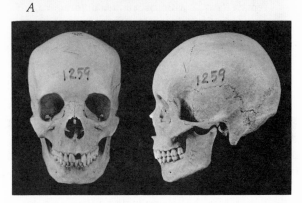

FIG. 25. Female skulls shown in front and side views for comparison of *A*, shaped (1293), and *B*, nonshaped (1259) contours.

tures are of more significance from a genetic point of view than are some of the measurements and their dependent indices. It is obvious that the size of any individual in the series was dependent upon growth factors and other environmental conditions. Thus, absolute sizes may simply reflect either optimal or minimal nutriture factors.

There were many additional morphological features which, because of their rarity, do not appear in Table 6, but are here described to complete the morphological observations.

Most of the skulls from Mokapu show left cranial, facial, and nasal asymmetries. That is, the left side of the vault of the skull and of the face were larger and extended on the left side. Most noses showed definite left deflections.

Separate bony protuberances or tubercles (Marshall, 1955, p. 148) associated with the occipital condyles were found in thirty-six instances, twenty-five of which were female and eleven male (Fig 21). In the female skulls, these tubercles in seven cases were anterior to and toward the middle of the basilar portions, usually bilateral with the left side better developed and larger, thirteen were unilateral and

situated near the left condyle, while five others were near the right side. For the male skulls, two were bilateral between the condyles, six were unilateral to the left and three to the right side. Double occipital condyles were found unilaterally on four female skulls, three on the left and one on the right. Noticeable depressions were observed along the sagittal suture near obelion in fourteen females and five males. These may be age changes or may be associated with healed osteoporosis. (See Fig. 55; see also Bowers, 1966, p. 214.) Extensions of bone from the temporal portion of the skull (styloid sheaths) were found in seven individuals, four female and three male. They were usually of equal size on both sides. In one case this protective styloid sheath measured 33 millimeters in length (see Fig. 20A).

There were several dental anomalies. Rotation of premolar and molar teeth was present. There were seven females with 20- to 90-degree rotation of the upper premolars and six with a slight rotation of the lower ones. Only two males showed this twist of

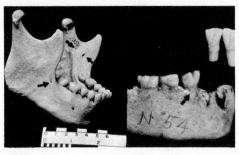

FIG. 26. Anomalies. *A,* an adult mandible, female (1354) with two unusual foramina (arrows). Scale in centimeters and inches. *B,* a child's jaw (N-54) with a divided right deciduous canine tooth (arrow). The inset shows "twinned" lower permanent incisors (HX series), slightly enlarged.

the upper premolars. Rotation of the upper right molars occurred in two females and one male. Another anomaly was three-rooted lower first molars in two males, one on the left side, the other on the right. A persistent trace of the premaxillary suture was detected on two skulls, one male and one female.

Dental pearls were observed in seven individuals, four female and three male. These, of course, occur primarily on the molar teeth above the level of the alveolus. There was no attempt to observe this feature either by extraction of the teeth or by X-ray.

Supernumerary teeth were found in gross examination in only one instance, in the lower jaw of a youth. Congenital absence of teeth other than third molars was low. There was an absence of lower right central incisors in two females, of upper second premolars in one female, and of the upper right lateral incisor in one male. Large lower premolars with three cusps were observed in three females and two males.

Bridges of bone over the mylohyoid grooves were observed in eighteen cases. In the females, six were on the left, three on the right; in one case there was a double bridge over the left groove. The eight males have an even frequency—four on the left and four on the right.

The enlargement of the tip of the inferior orbital fissure into a large oval expansion was bilaterally present in seven individuals, six being females.

Additional foramina in the mandible, involving perhaps both nerves and blood vessels, were found in two adult males. There were three extra foramina in the lower jaw; two were at the opposite ends of the same canal, which was located inside and below the left mandibular notch; the other was on the right ramus opening from above downward near the anterior border (Fig. 26). This same structure was present in two subadults, one a 6-year-old. Another unusual opening was found in the right malar bone which opened vertically from above near the upper end.

In one-third of these anomalous features, the clear-cut preponderance of females suggests that these traits may be sex-associated.

Several other anomalies were noted among the subadults; two open metopic sutures, one in a 6-year-old and one in a 13-year-old; two examples of Inca bones; and one child with a double left mental foramen.

DENTITION

The teeth and jaws, a specialized portion of the masticatory structures of the cranium, deserve and require a separate discussion. Measurements were made of the dental arches of 180 individuals and of tooth crown dimensions for 25 males and 25 females, and the indices for both were computed (Tables 7–17). The teeth of all the skulls were studied and the morphological observations are presented in Table 6.

Many measurements were made using standard dental techniques to describe the characteristically shaped dental arch and palate of these people from Mokapu. With the skull resting upside down, the dental arch length was measured from the posterior or mesial surfaces of the second molars forward to the most anterior plane formed by the medial anterior corners of the upper central incisors at the midline. The width of the dental arch was obtained by measuring at right angles to the median sagittal plane, again on the second molars, at the point where the maximum measurement on the rounded buccal surface of the crown was obtained. In order to describe more precisely the interesting and different contours of the Hawaiian palate, a series of maximum breadths was measured across at the levels of the canines, first premolars, first molars, and, of course, the second molars (see Fig. 27).

In an effort to measure palatal heights accurately, the Kentucky-designed coordinate caliper was employed, placing the sharp tips of the caliper arms on the major anterior fissures of the first molars; then the coordinate attachment was adjusted vertically against the midline of the palate. Both the breadth of the first molar fissures (occlusal diameter) and the height of the palate above this occlusal level were recorded to the nearest millimeter.

These dimensions and the proportions formed by comparing one with the other are listed in Table 7. The statistical measures of the variation present and their standard errors are included. It appears that every dimension for the arch and the height of the palate, as well as the indices, shows significant sex differences. Furthermore, the indices portray very well the typically flat-sided dental arch of these Hawaiians—that is, there is little increase of the index as we move from the front to the back of the arch (from the canines to the level of the second molars).

The usual external palatal measurements employed in anthropological studies were taken upon the bone of the alveolus (see Table 5). The palatal length was measured from the anterior alveolar landmark, prosthion, back to the line of the posterior tuberosities of the maxillae. The outside palatal width was measured at the point of maximum reading. This point usually occurred near the level of the second molars, but in very wide palates the maximum width occurred near the third molar (Fig. 28C, D).

In order to compare these dental arch dimensions with data on American whites compiled by Moorrees (1959), an estimated standard of difference was added which adjusted the values. These values are recorded in parentheses in Table 8. If these estimated differences have validity, the Hawaiian dental arches, of both men and women, are absolutely larger than Moorrees's (1959) young American population.

The difference in palatal dimensions is perhaps to be expected when the physical composition of the two groups is considered. The Hawaiians from Mokapu were a people whose vigorous mode of living influenced the development of the masticatory structures as well as other parts of the body. Contemporary Americans, as we know, are reared amid comparatively soft living conditions and certainly nourished on soft foods that lead to less-well-developed jaws and dentition. The two groups also have different racial ancestry with implied genetic differences that influence the shape of face and jaw.

Another comparison was possible with the Aleut data from Moorrees (1957). These data are presented in Table 9, with the addition of the North

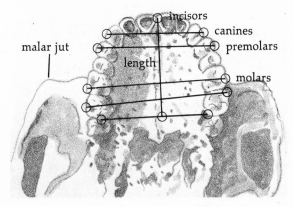

FIG. 27. Dental arch dimensions drawn to points of maximum size. In actual practice the caliper arms were parallel to the midline. Note the malar jut. Drawing by Robert Herndon.

American white data where the mode of measurement was identical. Table 8 represents measurements according to usual dental technique, while arch length and breadth in Table 9 are according to anthropological methods. Two interesting indices are available here: Berger's, wherein the first molar breadth is compared with the breadth of the face (bizygomatic); and Izard's, a similar comparison using the second molar breadth and that of the face. In both cases Mokapu has a larger value, hence relatively wider palates, in spite of the fact that the Mokapu faces tend to be flat-sided while the Aleuts have more laterally projecting faces.

In addition to measuring the maxillary dental arch, I also studied individual teeth of both jaws. The crown diameters, length and breadth, were obtained by means of a specially designed vernier caliper. All measurements were recorded to the nearest tenth of a millimeter, and a maximum dimension was obtained. The length of the tooth, the mesiodistal diameter, was measured between the interproximal facets. The crown breadth was measured at right angles to the length, that is, from outside to inside (faciolingually). Thus the back teeth were measured buccallingually, the front teeth, labiallingually. Each tooth—upper teeth on the left side and lower teeth on the right side—was thus measured according to dental techniques (Black, 1902, p. 14). These crown diameters appear in Tables 10–16.

Although the Mokapu tooth-dimension series, Tables 10 and 11, is small because it is selected from those males and females with all the necessary teeth, the measures of variation indicate that the individu-

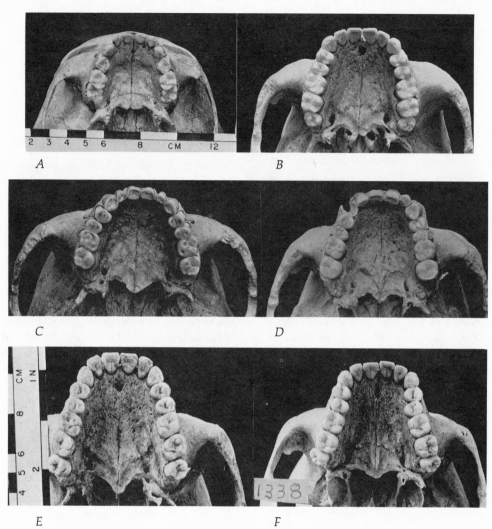

Fig. 28. Palate shapes. *A*, a child (1344) of 5 years, hyperbolic; *B*, a young adult female (1305), elliptical; *C*, an adult male (N-38), parabolic; *D* (122), *E* (190), and *F* (1338) are all adult males with typical flat-sided hyperbolic arches. In *C* and *D* note converging set of teeth.

als studied were quite homogeneous, and were similar in this respect to the other series available for comparison. Scanning all of the tables, two general statements can be made about all of the series reported. First, the upper teeth, with some exceptions, are larger than the corresponding teeth in the lower jaw. Second, there are sex differences, the teeth of males being larger than those of females. Table 12 indicates that in the Mokapu series these sex differences are significant for the dimensions of most of the teeth and for the indices (shapes) of three of the five upper teeth. The males tend to have higher indices, hence relatively wider teeth—that is, larger faciolingual diameters.

Moorrees (1959) has provided excellent additional data with which the Mokapu sample can be compared. Tables 13 and 14 show the place of these early Hawaiians with respect to other peoples of different racial ancestry and living at different times in human history. Indices for three groups were selected as representative for comparison with Mokapu and are presented in Table 15. Crown areas (length × breadth), Table 16, were likewise selected.

In general, the Mokapu men and women have characteristically moderate-sized to large maxillary teeth, canines, premolars, and molars in particular. The male teeth are larger in both length (mesiodistal) and breadth (faciolingual) when compared with other groups than are the Mokapu females. The mandibular teeth, on the other hand, are moderate in size, ranking second to fifth, with two exceptions: the first premolars are the second largest teeth and the incisors are among the smaller.

Martin (1928, p. 986) lists tooth-size ranges for various human groups (data compiled from De Terra, Black, Taylor, Muhlreiter, and Kajava). When Mokapu mesiodistal and faciolingual diameters are compared with these groups, they again rank from moderate to large.

No overall statement can be made as to the size of Hawaiian teeth when compared with other series. Tooth-by-tooth, measure-by-measure comparison is required for complete accuracy. However, it is true that by all available comparative data, the Mokapuans' teeth were large, especially their premolars and molars.

It was interesting to find several individuals with very large deciduous molars. In two instances of lower right second molars, faciolingual diameters of 10 millimeters were found. One of these same baby teeth had a mesiodistal diameter of 10.2 millimeters.

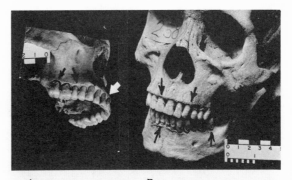

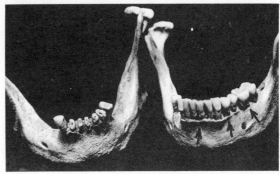

FIG. 29. Bone recession in jaws. Arrows indicate the general recession of bone of the alveolar borders, a common adult affliction: *A* (142), *B* (258), *C* (H-28), *D* (H-40). *C* and *D* show additional damage to the dentition caused by large abscesses and intensive wear of front teeth.

Although there were not enough regularly erupted third molars to merit a routine measurement, there was one lower right third molar with crown diameters of 12 millimeters square and another one of 12 millimeters (mesiodistal) by 13 millimeters (faciolingual), which is unusually large. On the other hand, some third molars were so reduced in size as to be peglike.

General examination of the dentition gives the impression that these ancient Hawaiians had good teeth. The general dental condition of 86 percent of the women (134) and 81 percent of the men (144) was rated as excellent. Dental decay was found in 14 percent of the females and 19 percent of the males. However, Lai in his study (Appendix C) reports, "Contrary to the common belief that the natives of Hawaii had teeth free of decay, this examination of their dentition showed that decay was definitely present." So careful and detailed

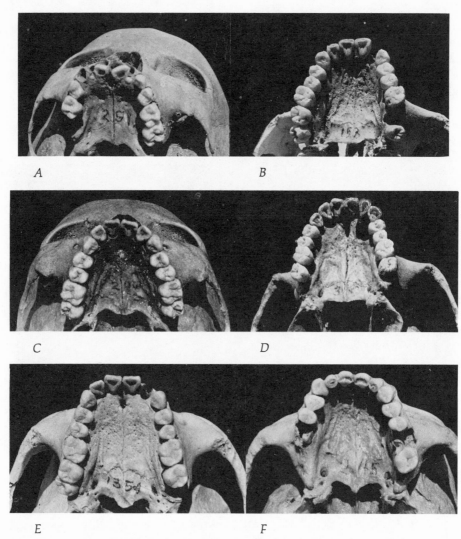

Fig. 30. Shovel-shaped incisors (upper jaw) in skulls ranging from that of a child, *A*, to that of a middle-aged adult, *F*. In *F* the lateral incisors show a tube or barrel condition wherein the margins of the teeth meet in a circle.

dental study reveals that the initial impression of perfect teeth is not borne out completely.

Some dietary factors may be responsible. Both Miller (Appendix E) and Lai (Appendix C) indicate the probable nature of the diet of the prehistoric people at Mokapu. It is believed that in historic times certain foods were *kapu* (forbidden) to women and that foods rich in vitamin C were scarce. Dr. Samuel B. Rabkin, an oral pathologist, commented, after examining the teeth at Bishop Museum, "It seems, judging from the tartar (calculus) on the teeth, that the prehistoric diet must have been a starchy one."[1]

Tooth wear was at a minimum. Eighty-nine percent of the females and 83 percent of the males had an estimated 3 millimeters or less of wear, while 71 percent of the women and 49 percent of the men showed 1 millimeter or less.

Rabkin was impressed with the condition of the alveolar borders. He said, "The alveolar borders, for some reason (as yet unknown) are subject to some changes quite different from those found in the long bones and other parts of the skeletons. The cells of bone tissue can go either of two ways: proliferation or necrosis. The breakdown in the alveolar tissue (necrosis) is remarkable among these early Hawaiians." (See Fig. 29.)

A condition rare in human jaws was observed. Two adult female mandibles had gaps between the canine and incisor teeth (Fig. 58E), the position of tusks in certain animal jaws. One adult female had this same gap present in the maxillae and there was one infant with canine gaps in the deciduous dentition of both jaws.

For comparison of some of this dental data, we are fortunate to have the detailed observations of the teeth of modern Hawaiians studied by Sullivan (1927, pp. 294–95). These data are presented in Table 17. I have equated Sullivan's "enamel rim on upper incisors" with shovel-shaped incisors, combining his "medium" and "marked" categories to indicate their presence. (See Fig. 30.) In spite of the probable discrepancies of techniques and dissimilar observations (Sullivan used children and youths with permanent dentition while I excluded this group), Table 17 reveals some remarkable continuities of dental traits. Therefore, these would appear to be significant genetic characters.

1. Personal correspondence and personal conferences at Bishop Museum, Honolulu, June 1957.

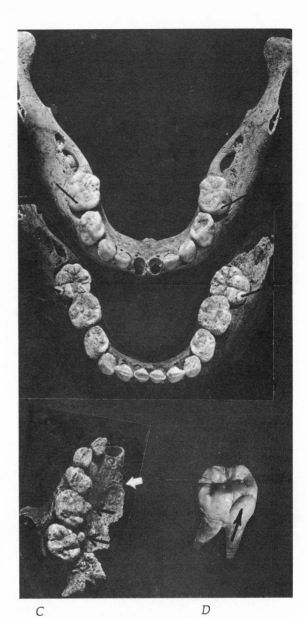

C   D

FIG. 31. Extra molar cusps. Two mandibles show protostylid cusps (anterior buccal): *A*, on the second deciduous molars, and *B*, on the first permanent molars with six instead of the usual five cusps (indicated by lines). *C*, an upper right jaw showing Carabelli's cusps on both the deciduous second molar and the first permanent molar; white arrow indicates a premaxillary suture. *D*, a lower right permanent molar with large protostylid (enlarged).

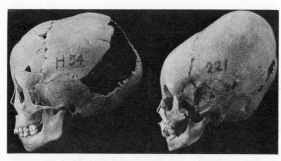

A   B

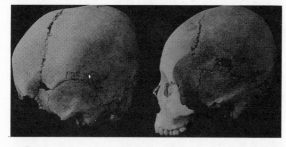

C   D

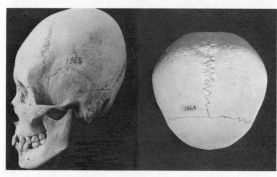

E   F

Fig. 32. Skulls of children of different ages showing the effects of acquired deformation. *A* (H-54), age 3 years, has the natural, unshaped form. The others all show the shortened, high crown shape produced by binding: *B* (271), age 1½ years; *C* (135a), age 4 to 5 years; *D* (229), age 12 years; *E* and *F* (1369), age 13 years.

A careful survey of the subadult crania revealed the following traits:

1) Shovel-shaped incisors: deciduous, four cases; permanent, fourteen cases; double-shovel (both lingual and labial surfaces indented) with pronounced rim development on both sides (Dahlberg, 1951, p. 142) on upper and lower incisors, two cases (Fig. 30C).

2) Mesiolingual torsion of central incisors: upper jaw, four cases; lower jaw, four cases.

3) Carabelli's cusps: deciduous second molars, twenty cases; permanent first and second molars, seven cases. (See Fig. 31C.)

4) Protostylids: deciduous molars, twenty-seven cases; permanent molars, twelve cases. (See Fig. 31A, B, D.)

5) Other variations, one case each: (a) deciduous lower right canine and lateral incisor fused; (b) canine-incisor diastema in child's jaw (deciduous dentition); (c) retention of two upper deciduous second molars in 17- to 18-year-old with worn stumps of lower left deciduous second molar; (d) lower left lateral permanent incisor congenitally absent; (e) upper and lower second premolar teeth on both sides absent in 14-year-old female; (f) incisor teeth with crowns longer than their roots in 6- to 7-year-old.

Albert Dahlberg, a practicing dentist, teacher, and dental researcher of Chicago, Illinois, has permitted me to quote the following statement:

I might say that as of this date it is not possible to determine the gene frequencies for tooth traits such as we can do for blood types, etc. However, in our reports we do list trait frequencies. Certain features, such as the five or four major cusps of upper and lower molars, no doubt, represent the genotype. The many variations occurring in and about these cusps mask their primary features and present us with phenotypes that are frequently described as positive entities. Also, these negative qualities (absence of teeth, loss of cusps, etc.) are not dependable as to penetrance and expressivity. Hence, although genetically inspired they must be studied cautiously. Carabelli's cusp and the protostylid, as well as the shovel-shaped trait, are useful and significant.[2]

Pedersen (1949, p. 213) and Moorrees (1957, p. 6) list the following dental characters as useful racial (genetic) clues to Mongoloid ancestry: 1) high incidence of shovel-shaped incisors; 2) very low incidence of Carabelli's tubercle; 3) high incidence

2. Personal correspondence, November 1958.

of three-rooted lower molars; and 4) high incidence of absence of lower third molars. These early Hawaiians qualify for Mongoloid ancestry in the first and fourth categories and possibly the third (three-rooted lower molars were present), but not in the second (in nearly one in three persons, Carabelli's tubercle was present). This variation suggests again the sort of trait that isolation might stamp on many of the individuals in the common gene pool of Mokapu.

Riesenfeld (1956, p. 519) has reported on the occurrence of shovel-shaped incisors in the Pacific. He finds an interesting west-to-east cline in the frequency of shovel-shaped types and the rounding of lateral incisors on an assumed Mongoloid cline from Indonesia through Micronesia to Polynesia. Such a cline, and the fact that shovel-shaped incisors are even more frequent among American Indians than in people from the western Pacific, seems incompatible with Heyerdahl's claim of an American origin for the Polynesians. It may well be, with our present knowledge, that these dental features and their variations are among the most useful clues in tracing the racial ancestry of these far-flung Polynesians. Yet much of useful nature in the solution of this problem lies in the rest of the skull.

HEAD-SHAPING OR DEFORMATION

Early in my study of the skulls from Mokapu, I found several with obviously flattened frontal and occipital regions. Skulls with flattened contours of the back head are conspicuous, rising as they do to a high-pitched crown on the parietals directly above or just behind the ear-holes (Figs. 32 and 33). In many cases, the flattening was so extreme as to place the back rim of the fleshy ear virtually at the back of the head. Another group was characterized by a markedly flattened area high on the center of the forehead above the bosses and in front of the coronal suture. This flattened plane continued the slope from the crown of the parietals. About 45 percent of the adults had a medium to pronounced degree of flattening (see Table 6). In extreme cases, the flattened plane of the occiput paralleled that of the flat forehead—in essence, parallel frontal-occipital deformation.

This general deformed shape was even more conspicuous among the skulls of infants and young children (Fig. 34). On many of these, the entire occipital bone sloped obliquely backward and upward to lambda, rather than curving forward from

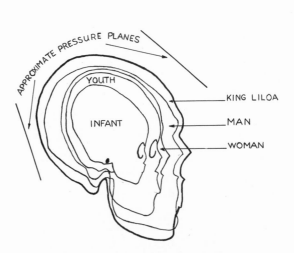

Fig. 33. Superimposed outlines of shaped skulls and approximate pressure planes which produced the characteristic head form.

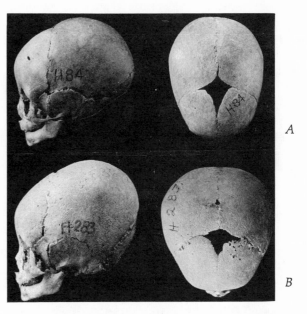

Fig. 34. *A*, side and top views of an unshaped infant skull (H-84) in contrast to *B*, the shaped contours of an older infant (H-283).

inion, so as to form a protruding back head with a convex boss, an oblique form of head deformation. This oblique plane might be called a "reversed occipital" (see Fig. 32B). In other cases, the forehead sloped toward the back at a 45° angle and the back head was nearly vertical instead of having a curved protrusion, with the resulting heightened or bulging crown, an extreme form of head shaping, that is, a vertical type (Fig. 32C, D).

It is an interesting coincidence that approximately the same percentage (44 percent) of shaped skulls was found among the youngsters as among the adults. Slightly more cases were found among the females. Hambley (1946, p. 187) reports that among the Arawe (Aruwi) in New Britain (the largest and southernmost island in the Bismarck Archipelago northeast of New Guinea), shapely, long heads were sexually the most desired and more time was spent on shaping the heads of girl babies than those of boy babies.

Although this head-shaping process is well known in Samoa and parts of western Polynesia and New Britain (Martin, 1928, p. 831, Fig. 358; Hambley, 1946, p. 187), I was surprised to find deformed skulls in this Hawaiian material. When the discovery was shared with Sir Peter Buck, who was himself part Polynesian and an authority on Hawaiian culture, his response was one of studied reserve.

Library sources revealed that Stokes had called attention to Hawaiian skull deformation in 1920 in a letter to Hrdlička (Stokes, 1920, pp. 489–91) and that Wagner had recognized it in the Hawaiian skulls he measured (1937, pp. 8, 67). An even earlier reference to cranial deformation (occipital) among Hawaiian skulls was made by Turner (1884). In reporting on skulls from Oahu and Waimea, Hawaii, he says (p. 63), "It is possible that the [occipital] flattening had been assisted by artificial pressure applied during infancy." He further indicates (p. 67) that this cultural mark is useful in separating skulls of Polynesians from those of other oceanic series, including Melanesians, Papuans, Australians, and Tasmanians. Ewing, in his study of hyperbrachycephaly (1950), includes Hawaii on his world map showing the distribution of round-headed peoples. Ploss in 1884 and Porter in 1889 (quoted by Ewing, 1950, p. 42) both indicate methods known to have prevailed in Hawaii.

Stokes (1920), then ethnologist at Bishop Mu-

seum, quoting from Andrews's *Anatomia*,[3] records the following:

In unenlightened countries, the people regarded as a matter of importance the changing of the natural forms of their children's heads into new shapes. Some pressed *opa* on the sides of the head to flatten it; other people manipulated the forehead. *The people of Hawaii regarded as the ideal head one which was flattened on the forehead and behind. . . . The molded head was said to have been the form admired by the chiefs.* In enlightened countries, the people allowed the heads of their children to remain in the beautiful form in which God made it. [Italics added.]

Stokes was able to furnish three contemporary accounts from women interviewed in Kona, Hawaii. All three agreed that the manipulations began as soon as the baby was born. One informant, aged 65 years, said that the infant was placed on its back with the head resting on a portion of coconut husk lined with *pulu*. In this position, the forehead was frequently pressed downward with the palm of the hand. It was stated that the treatment continued for a week or two until the bones were hardened. (Actually a year and a half to two years are required for the bones to conform to this external pressure.)

Another woman, about 45 years old, described a binding process by which two portions of the hard shell of the coconut were lined with *pulu*, then placed one at the forehead, the other at the back, and bound to the baby's head. They were removed whenever the child was bathed (once or twice a day), and the head was carefully massaged to keep up the circulation. The time required was about the same as in the preceding account.

The third, a grandmother over 60 years of age, stated that the baby was carefully laid with the back of the head resting on a piece of gourd lined with soft *kapa* and kept in that position. In this treatment, which continued for a week, the forehead was not touched or shaped by hand. This woman pointed out a middle-aged man (with decidedly Negroid hair) as one whose head had been reshaped by this means. The man's forehead was high (upright) and gave no indication of having been molded artificially, but the back of his head was almost flat in

3. Mission Press, Oahu, 1838; a text written in Hawaiian for the instruction of the pupils of Lahainaluna, Maui, School in Anatomy.

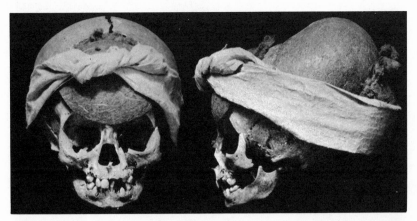

A

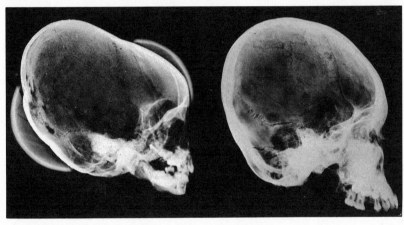

B   *C*

FIG. 35. Head shaping. *A*, front and side views of a year-old infant (H-271) with coconut shells padded with pulu and bound in place with a strip of *kapa*. *B*, the same skull by X-ray. *C*, an X-ray of the high-crowned, shortened skull of a female youth (1369).

a vertical line. His head seemed rounder and higher than those of his Hawaiian neighbors. Stokes says (1920, p. 489), "The custom fell into disuse some years ago, its initial breaking down being probably due to missionary teaching. . . . However, the mothers, generally conservative, were able to keep up the practice to a certain degree by keeping the infant lying on its back and thus attain their object without apparent conflict with the ideas of their new spiritual advisors."

This custom of shaping the infant head was still practiced at the turn of the century according to reliable information from several people, native born (*kama'aine*) or of Hawaiian descent. The following accounts were reported to me in 1951 by Amy V. H. Greenwell, a member of an old-time Hawaiian family of South Kona, Hawaii. Her aunt, Mrs. Caroline Greenwell Bryant of Kalukalu, South Kona, born in 1870, remembered that "bullet shaped heads were fairly common among the natives. Infants had their heads massaged into shape. Joe Pahana, born in the late 1880s or early 1890s, had such a head and was probably made that way with coconut shells. His forehead was very sloped. It was considered beautiful, and evidently done by all classes. His father, however, had a normal shaped head."

Mrs. Bryant's sister, Mrs. Christina Greenwell Natscheff, also of Kalukalu, born in 1876, remembers many "natives having heads flattened behind

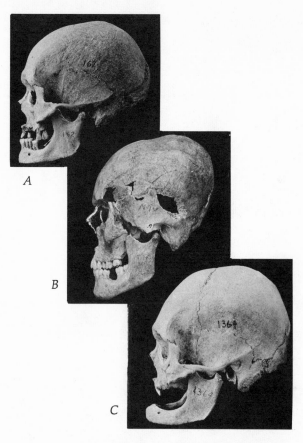

FIG. 36. Male skulls contrasting *A*, an unshaped "long head" (H-162), with *B*, a much shaped young man (N-13), and *C*, an old man (1364) with only one tooth.

and sharply sloping from the nose to the crest of the skull and bulging at the upper back portion of the vault."

Mary Kawena Pukui describes head-shaping practices in Appendix D, below. Another authentic account comes from an interview by Dr. Kenneth Emory with Mrs. K. Constable, a Hawaiian lady in her mid-eighties who prided herself on her *ali'i* descent. "My mother, Kaumaka O Kana, a full-blooded Hawaiian chiefess, had her head shaped in a calabash, and her sister also, but not the children who came after, because it was looked upon as a superstitious practice."

Figure 35 is an attempt to portray on a baby's skull the binding technique. Both gross and X-ray views show the two pieces of coconut shells padded with *pulu* (tree fern fluff), one piece on the forehead, the other on the back of the head, and bound in place by strips of *kapa* (bark cloth). Scott (1957, p. 208)

has explained the relationships of the head-shaping devices and the growth forces involved as follows: "These deformities are not produced by the pressure exerted by the apparatus itself but by a change in the direction of growth on the part of the growing brain or growth regulating cartilages." The results were indeed striking (Fig. 36).

A cultural factor that could have reinforced and continued the shaping process was the sleeping position. The old Hawaiians are known to have used a hard pillow covered with pandanus leaves under their heads, and they usually slept on mats rolled out upon the house floors. Thus both the bed and the pillow presented hard, flat surfaces on which the body and head rested, and the bones of the head responded to the pressure.

In one modern Oahu family the mother, of Samoan origin, still follows an old custom. The baby is placed on its back, with its head resting on a small bamboo pillow wrapped with cloth; flat stones are bound against the sides of the pillow. Confined thus in one position, face up, the baby's head becomes flat in back. One of this woman's children is shown in Figure 37A. Note the plane from the base of the neck to the high crown of the head, and the position of the ear far back on the head, close to a vertical line of the neck.[4] Figure 37B is of a man photographed by Louis Sullivan on which has been superimposed a male skull from Mokapu with similar contours.

It seems possible that this cultural practice was used to mark the heads of the chiefs or kings (*ali'i*) (Fig. 38A), since the conspicuous, high-crowned heads would set them apart for all to see and to respect. It was forbidden (*kapu*) for anyone to occupy a physical position higher than the chief's head, the recognized place of the mind. Buck (1957, pp. 238, 246) illustrates these typical shaped-head profiles in the plainwoven and feather-covered helmets worn by the Hawaiian chiefs. Obviously the heads of these *ali'i*, with their sloping foreheads and flat back heads had been shaped, and the helmets were made to fit the contours of their heads.

Nothing of an archaeological nature was found in any of the Mokapu graves which would indicate social distinction for those with shaped heads. Yet it is evident that the practice of head shaping did exist in both these early Hawaiians and their descendants for reasons that can only be surmised.

4. Personal communication from Edmond Hiram, April 1957.

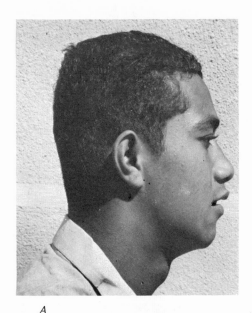
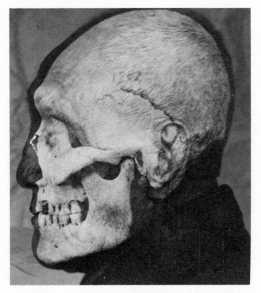

A   B

FIG. 37. Head shaping. *A*, profile of a Samoan boy with intentionally shaped head. *B*, superimposed photographs of modern and ancient Hawaiians. The skull of H-1282 is placed upon a profile photograph of Kauila by Louis Sullivan (photo courtesy of Bernice P. Bishop Museum). Note how perfectly the various parts of the head and face correspond, with the exception of the earholes.

THE ROCKER JAW

Many of the Mokapu skulls have a peculiarly shaped mandible with a rounded bottom. These jaws rest on only two points of support on the body or horizontal ramus of the mandible instead of the usual three or four points of the ordinary mandible described in the standard anatomy books. They are thus unstable and may be tilted chin to jowl, rocking back and forth. Figure 39 compares the rocker jaw to the nonrocker type. The extreme rocker jaw can only be fully appreciated when it is in action—that is, rocking. (See Fig. 40.)

Often associated with this rocker jaw is an arch below the chin (incisura submentalis; Martin, 1928, p. 98) which rises high in the center front and continues the curved lines of the lower borders of the body of the mandible. This structure is present in 48 percent of the adult male rocker jaws and 47 percent of the female.

Another feature of this mandible is the absence of the concavity (antegonial notch) in front of the gonial region marking the place where the facial artery ordinarily angles across the body of the mandible. Meredith (1957, p. 248) shows this notch as a constantly occurring feature in his study by X-ray of the shape of the normal chin and mandible of American white children.

Martin (1928, pp. 980–81) has given the following description of the rocker jaw:

The form of the lower border of the mandible and the manner in which the jaw rests upon a horizontal surface, depend in large measure upon the structure of the jaw angle, the "angular process of the mandible." As a rule this angle is strongly marked so that there is present a deep concavity, "the premuscular notch" (Klaatch) or the so-called preangular notch (Frizzi) which is more or less distinct from in front. Characteristically the mandible rests between the angles and a point in the vicinity of the first molar on the under surface. In the case of normal bilateral asymmetry the lower jaw lies equally on all the points named above so that 81 percent (84.6 percent according to Torok) of the mandibles rest not only on three but upon four points (Zoja). In case the angle is strongly curved, this characteristic concavity is missing and the entire lower border is convex. Such "Rocker Jaws" rest naturally on only two points when placed on a horizontal surface. These are seldom found in Europeans, but are especially characteristic of Maori and the Moriori (Polynesians) (Stahr).

The point of support of these rocker jaws falls farther forward in the neighborhood of the mental tubercles so that there is formed in the chin region an arch under the lower surface. This is particularly the case in those jaws wherein the lower border is cut out and there is present the so-called sub-mental notch (incisura sub-

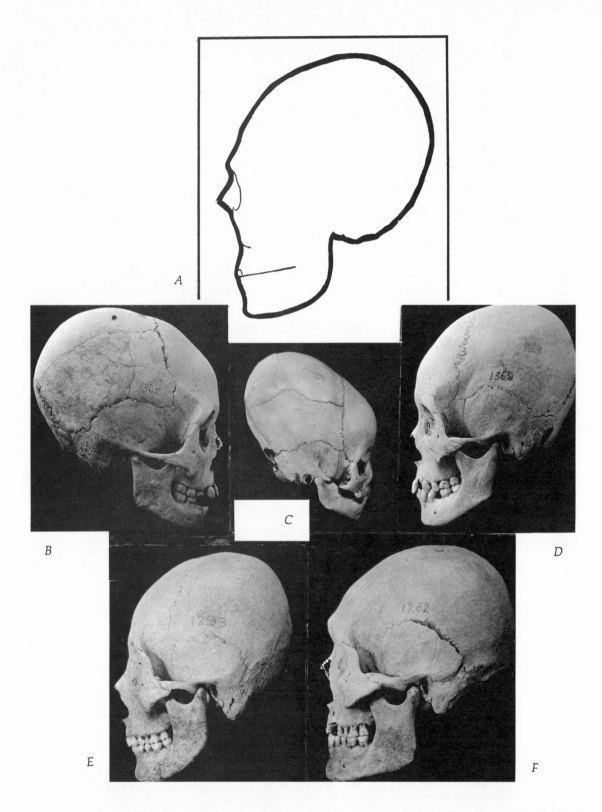

FIG. 38. Shaped skulls of different ages. *A*, outline from X-ray of King Liloa; *B*, a child (1367); *C*, an infant (Waipio 51); *D*, a teen-age girl (1369); *E*, a young woman (1293); and *F*, an adult male (1282).

mentalis). These chin arches are clearly present in the case of the mandible from Mauer (Heidelberg) and in other Neanderthaloid mandibles (Spy, Krapina, La Chapelle-aux-Saints). Also these have been observed in lower jaws of Australians and Melanesians and the ancestral gibbon.

Hooton, following Martin's excellent description along with his own observations, taught his classes at Harvard University that the rocker jaw was a diagnostic feature of Polynesian peoples. Therefore I found it readily recognizable.

At Mokapu, most of the adults (71 percent of the males, 88 percent of the females), and about a fourth of the children, showed this characteristic jaw structure in some degree. If the base of the mandible was sufficiently curved to be tilted back and forth, it was classified as a rocker jaw. A medium or large degree of the rocker form was found in 45 percent of the men and 54 percent of the women. It is significant that comparatively few subadults exhibited more than a slight degree of rocker jaw. No infant or child had the degree of roundness present in the average adult, and only two or three subadults possessed the typical rocker form. This shape definitely appears to be associated with full growth or maturity, and it occurs more commonly in mandibles of women than of men.

The typical curves of this form of lower jaw may be found in living Hawaiians today. Many photographs of front and side facial views taken by Sullivan in 1920–1921 (Bishop Museum Collection) show this contour. This same feature is found on both carved wooden and stone figurines. The carved wooden images of both sexes described by Buck (1957, pp. 471–93), and those from Necker Island fashioned from stone (ibid., Fig. 315, p. 501) all show the characteristic rocker jaw contour. The temple images with elaborate headdresses and hair (ibid., Fig. 308, p. 490) reveal the subchin arch as well. These representations would appear to be based on an intimate knowledge of the anatomy and contours of this facial feature. Regardless of their purposes and the materials used, these images apparently portray accurately the physiognomy of the typical Hawaiian of that time (see Frontispiece).

The rocker jaw occurs sporadically among individuals of other racial ancestry. I know, from personal communications from colleagues, of such jaws in the case of an Egyptian, a Hindu, a Melanesian, and American whites. In addition they have been found in an Australian (Martin, 1928, Fig. 456, p.

981) and in early American Indians (Snow, 1948a). Recently, rocker jaws have been reported in Oaxaca, Mexico (Genoves, 1958, pp. 472–73). The cast of the mandible of the Old Man of Cromagnon, as well as an occasional gorilla, shows this rocker tendency. The famous Mauer jaw (Heidelberg Man) has not only the curved mandible but the arch under the chin as well. Also the Old Man 101 from Choukoutien, North China, has a rocker jaw.

In an attempt to understand the high incidence of this trait in these Mokapu and Polynesian people, I explored many possible theories. In the first place, I have observed that in many nonrocker jaws, if the gonial region (angular process) were pulled up (elevated superiorly) so that the premuscular notch disappeared, there would be a continuous curved line from the chin to the gonial angle. Just how this change of line and rearrangement of structure could come about is not clear at present.

Although there is no dissection-room evidence, the curve of the rocker jaw may be due to anomalous slips of muscles, masseter, or pterygoid to the angle of the jaw. Both Washburn (1951, p. 302) and Scott (1957, pp. 198–99) have suggested that some sort of muscle-bone function is involved in shaping bone. This could apply to the rocker jaw.

Split-line techniques (Tappen, 1954, pp. 220–38) have demonstrated the structural lines of the mandible (Benninghoff's lines of trajectorial force). Many studies have been made of the stress systems set up in the movable and functional separate bones of the face (Krogman and Sassouni after Tappen, 1957; Seipel, 1948). Also DuBrul and Sicher (1954) emphasize that the chin and mandible respond as all bones do to mechanical stress. They state (p. 80) that "changes of the mandible are indivisible from those of the cranium." In addition, the type of occlusion and muscle movements, along with some peculiar postural habits, may be responsible for the rocker jaw. It may even be a trait-linked feature (Hughes, 1944, pp. 543–48).

Scott (1957, p. 228) has said "a large number of morphological features are latent and only find expression in the coordinated activity of genetic and environmental factors. In this the genetically determined plasticity of the skeleton, which enables it to respond to variations in functional activity, is important." The Sewall-Wright effect (genetic drift) associated with the almost completely isolated geographic location of the Hawaiian group, might well account for the high incidence of this feature at

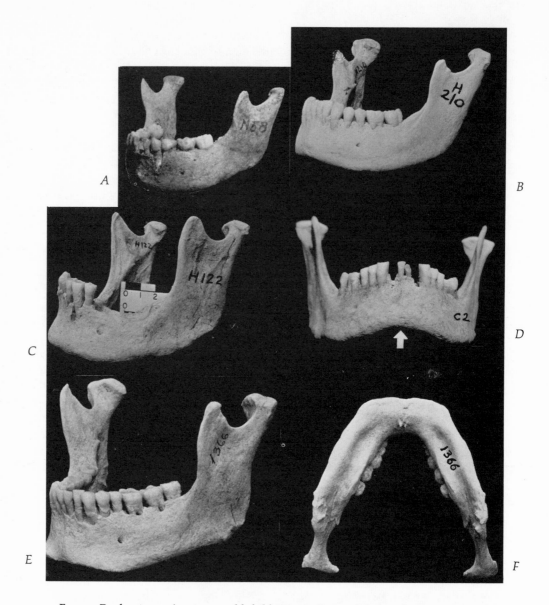

FIG. 39. Rocker jaws. *A*, a 6-year-old child (N-58); *B*, an adult female (H-210); *C*, an adult male (H-122). Scale in centimeters. Arrow in *D* points to chin arch. *E* and *F* show the contrasting wide-chinned, nonrocker jaw of a male (1366) with strong modeling and massive bone.

Mokapu, as well as its well known presence in other Polynesian series (Marshall and Snow, 1956, p. 414).

Another factor that may influence the structure of the jaw is the role of hormones in the body. Keith (1930, pp. 484–89) reports the rocker jaw as being associated with severe cases of hyperpituitarianism (gigantism), a hormonal disease. Only 26 percent of the subadult mandibles showed the rocker-jaw tendency, so obviously the full development occurs during puberty and early adult years, a period of increased hormone activity.

Thus growth factors, hormone interaction and influence during puberty, genetic potential, and certain muscle-bone functional relations may account for this unique facial structure common in the Mokapu crania.

A NOSE BONE ANOMALY

Six skulls are known which have no nose bones (ossa nasalis). Two of these skulls, a child 3 to 4 years old and a 25- to 30-year-old man, are from Mokapu (Fig. 41A, B). The other four are from the neighboring island to the north, Kauai. Three of these are in the United States National Museum collection, a child 5 to 6 years old (No. 217822), a 12- to 13-year-old female (No. 225481), and a female 14 to 20 years old (No. 225468). The fourth, an adult female, is in Bishop Museum. It is believed that the Kauai skulls came from old burial caves and, like those from Mokapu, they appear to be pre-European. Others from Mokapu, some five in number, show interesting nose bone variations. These range from a single bone (Fig. 41E, F) rather than two bones fused into one, to one of the pairs of bones being only one-quarter to one-half normal size (Fig. 42).

We have here an anomaly heretofore not described. Four of the seven instances from Mokapu are female and the two children are probably female. Thus this congenital absence or inhibition of development of the paired nose bones may be sex-linked among this inbred group.

The small size of the sample (2.7 percent) makes it impossible to assign definitely the significance of this feature. It may be a genetic expression. Dr. Montague Cobb of Howard University reports[5] the absence of nose bones in collections at both Western Reserve University at Cleveland, Ohio, and Wash-

5. Personal communication.

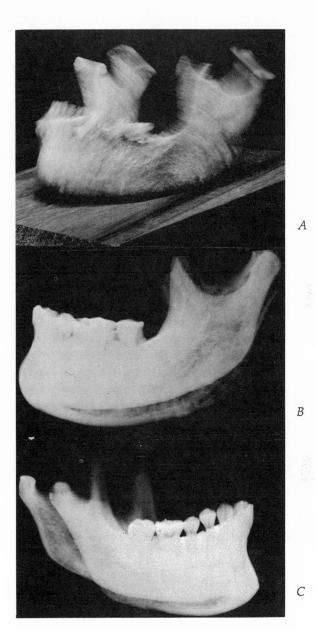

FIG. 40. A, a rocker jaw (N-27) in action. X-ray views of rocker jaws: B, a female (N-27), and C, a male (C-4).

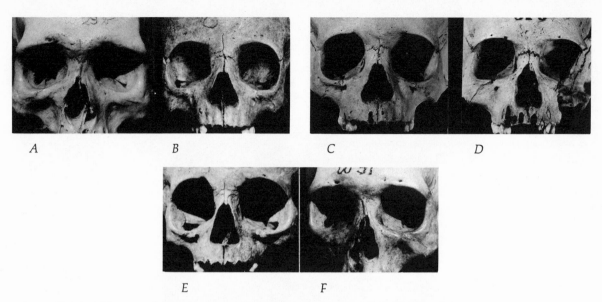

FIG. 41. Absence of the nose bones. *A*, an adult male (W-29b), and *B*, a child (H-65), have no visible nasal bones. *C*, a child and *D*, a teen-ager from Kauai, also have no nasal bones. *D* may possibly have had one part of the left nasal not articulating with the frontal suture. *E* (H-109) has a left portion only; *F* (W-31), another adult, appears to have a right nasal bone only. Photos *C* (USNM 217,822) and *D* (USNM 225,468) courtesy of the Smithsonian Institution.

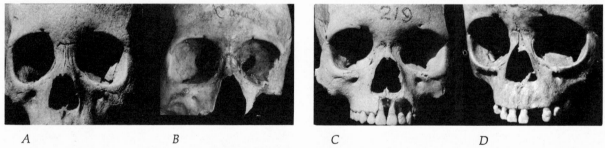

FIG. 42. Nose bone anomalies. *A* (H-77), a young girl whose nose bones taper to a very narrow root; *B*, (C-2 series), an adult woman with a single (right) nose bone; *C* (H-219), a youth with a single nose bone divided across the top; *D* (H-260), a child with an entire left nasal and only half of the right one.

ington University at St. Louis, Missouri. Further investigation of other collections is indicated.

SKULLS WITH RESTORED TISSUE

In an effort to visualize these Mokapu skulls as heads of living people, soft part tissue thicknesses as known today were added to the dimensions of both male and female skulls. Restoration measurements were compiled and compared with the measurements taken by Tozzer in 1916 and 1920 (Dunn and Tozzer, 1928), and by Louis Sullivan in 1920–1921 on living Hawaiians. The values used for restoration are from Stewart (1957), Wilder (1912), and Suzuki (1948). Although the sources of data are separated from Mokapu Hawaiians in both time and racial background, the result shows some interesting similarities and differences.

Table 18 lists some of the major dimensions of the skulls and faces of the Mokapu people, with restored tissue (European and Japanese data), and compares them with the dimensions of living Hawaiians. Most of the basic work in the past centering upon the restoration of facial features has been done to determine what famous persons may have looked like, or for legal identification. Using data supplied by Stewart and Wilder, I have added a compromise value to the Mokapu skull measurements to give the Restored Caucasoid (European and American) values, male and female. Very satisfactory measurements for the soft tissue of the face of Japanese are available from the work of Suzuki. These figures are presented to indicate a direct comparison between early and modern Hawaiians.

It appears that the early Hawaiians had larger heads and features than their descendants studied by Sullivan (Fig. 43). Specifically, the earlier Hawaiians had longer and relatively narrower cranial vaults which resulted in a lower cephalic index. However, modern (Sullivan) and early (Mokapu) Hawaiian skulls are also broad and high. The facial dimensions for Mokapu likewise are larger, with the exception of the total facial height. Here fairly close agreement is reached. Consideration should be given to the fact that an increase in facial length is often found in hybrid populations involving European ancestry.

The breadth of the forehead shows the greatest difference. Perhaps this may be explained by the fact that in the case of the living the landmarks on the frontal crests are often difficult to palpate and measure accurately. It seems odd that the early

A

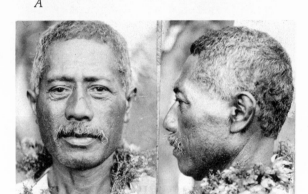

B

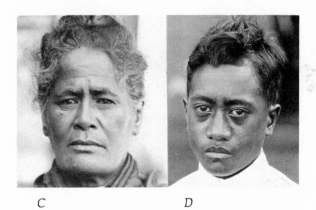

C   *D*

FIG. 43. Modern Hawaiians showing facial features similar to those found in Mokapu skulls. *A* and *B* are front and side views of typical Hawaiian men, *C* is a woman, and *D*, a boy. Note the head and facial contours including rocker jaw in *A* and *C*. Photographs from Louis Sullivan, courtesy of Bernice P. Bishop Museum, Honolulu.

Hawaiians with narrow foreheads would produce descendants with such wide foreheads.

Apparently most of these modern Hawaiians had more back-head flattening than Sullivan and Tozzer observed or at least reported. A case in point is the composite picture (Fig. 37B), in which one of the Mokapu skulls with head shaping is shown superimposed upon the left profile of one of Sullivan's Hawaiians. The conformity of contour is truly remarkable. Only the ear holes are not in alignment. The living man had a much greater flattening of his back-head than does the skull, which places the ear hole posteriorly.

Compared with data compiled by Krogman (1939, pp. 1–29), who makes allowances for the drying and subsequent shrinkage of both flesh and bone tissues, the Mokapu skull vaults are even larger than is shown in Table 18: 5 to 8 millimeters longer and 1 to 2 millimeters wider. The Krogman data provide for scalp thickness at both the front and the back of the head while the other European and American data do not include the posterior scalp thickness.

Hunt (1959, p. 77) in quoting Clark asserts that "limb lengths are slightly more heritable than are the dimensions of the head and face." This may apply to the modern descendants of these early Hawaiians. The stature estimates of Mokapu (Table 26) are much closer to the living Hawaiians than are the gross sizes of the head and face, if our restoration tissue estimates are correct.

It would be interesting and instructive to model the soft-part tissues, utilizing the Krogman data, on a Mokapu skull of representative proportions. With thickness markers placed on the various landmarks of the skull, the contours of head and face could be filled in to proper levels. Of course, the all-important expression of the living face, as well as the amount of beard, head, and eyebrow hair and the shape and size of the nose, mouth, and ear, would remain conjectural.

Postcranial Skeleton

MEASUREMENTS AND INDICES

The postcranial skeleton includes the bones of the trunk and limbs. Measurements of these bones are used to determine the size of the individual, and comparisons between bones indicate body proportions. These Mokapu bones, like the skulls, were remarkably well preserved. Some individuals had characteristically light, "chalky" bones, but these were few. These variations of general bone preservation may reflect conditions and time of burial as well as individual constitution, sex and age.

Table 19 presents the measurements and indices for all of the postcranial bones with their statistical measures of variability. "Paired" refers to bones from the same individual; "total" includes the paired bones plus all the left and right bones that could not be paired. Typical sex differences are found in the gross measurements; yet the proportions of the bones, male and female, are often strikingly similar.

In general, the measurements and indices show these Hawaiians to have been of more than average size compared with other skeletal series, for example, ancient Greeks (Angel, 1946, p. 71) and most aboriginal groups (Martin, 1928, pp. 1098–1172). Probably the very favorable physical environment was a big factor in the growth and development of these Mokapuans to their full potential.

While the data in Table 19 are self-explanatory, some deserve special attention. In the first place, characteristics of the humeri and femora, the largest long bones of the body, are noteworthy. The ball-shaped heads of both of these bones are smaller than the large-jointed Europeans, but larger than the ancient Greeks (Angel, 1946, p. 71) and most of the aboriginal people listed by Martin (1928, p. 1150).

Second, when we were measuring the hip bones, we routinely measured both the maximum diameters and the greatest depths of the acetabulum of all intact left innominates, using coordinate calipers. Thieme and Schull (1957, p. 264) have shown in the case of Negro skeletons that the diameters of the femoral heads are the best single measure for determining the sex of the individual. I obtained sig-

nificant differences which parallel this singularly useful revelation. The acetabular measurements and the diameter depth index were useful in separating the hip bones of the two sexes at Mokapu. Moreover, it was obvious that the typical female had the classical smaller and shallower acetabulum.

Furthermore, the Mokapu humeral shafts are flattish beyond the usual square shape; the index for men is 75.4; for women, 73.9. Femora are platymeric with the subtrochanteric indices of 71.6 for males, 70.1 for females. At midshaft, the cross sections show greater anteroposterior diameters; pilasteric index, which is the reciprocal index of the midshaft diameters, is 118.2 for men, 115.7 for women. Similarly, the tibiae show remarkably thin shafts; the platycnemic shape is 66 for men, 68 for women. At midshaft the indices are virtually the same; men average 65.4, women, 69.2. The Polynesian shin bones listed by Martin (1928, p. 1159) tend to be even flatter than those of the Mokapuans. These are believed to reflect functional adaptations.

Torsion of the femur and tibia shafts is recorded by Martin (1928, pp. 928–1159) as 27.2° femoral and 18° tibial. Torsion in the Mokapu bones was observed, not measured, but most of the femora were noticeably twisted. The range of tibial shaft torsion (the most and the least torsion observed) was measured and photographed (see Fig. 44). The greatest shaft torsion was 40°–41°, the highest listed anywhere.

The condylodiaphysial angles of the humeri (carrying or cubital angles) were 82° for males, 82.5° for females. Very similar angles (82.1°) were measured for Alabama Indians (Snow, 1940, p. 14) and for early Kentucky Indians (Snow, 1948a, p. 455) (80.6° for men, 80.4° for women). All of these measures show similar sex differences. Martin (1928, p. 1103) notes that primitive peoples, because of more constant manual labor, have straighter arms (higher angles) than less active white-collar workers. It seems likely that functional adaptation is again involved here.

The Mokapu scapulae of both men and women tend to be narrower but better muscled than those of European and American whites.

The bones of the lower back—lumbar vertebrae—were measured in order to estimate the posture of the individual, which depends on the curvature of the small of the back and the tilt of the pelvis. The vertical diameters, front and back, of each vertebra tend to run a little smaller than those listed for

Fig. 44. Torsion of the tibial shaft associated with the squatting habit. The steel needles attached to centers of the head and lower ends indicate degree of twist.

Europeans, but are larger than the values for Japanese, Senoi, and other aboriginal people (Martin, 1928, p. 1080), and early Kentucky Indians (Snow, 1948a, p. 462).

The Mokapu Lumbar Index, which is the sum of the posterior diameters compared with the sum of the anterior diameters, is high (104.3 for males and 102.3 for females). It ranks near those of the Senoi (105.0), Bushmen (106.8), and Australian (106.0), and is high compared with the lower values for Europeans (95.8) (Martin, 1928, p. 1080). It is interesting to note that Martin lists a value of 104.0 for Sandwich Islanders (Hawaiians). Thus these Hawaiians had very little concavity compared to Europeans, who have a generous lordosis curvature.

The length and breadth diameters of the sacrum, the "key" bone at the base of the spine that transmits the torso weight through the hip bones to the legs, are average. The Sacral Index shows that the Hawaiian bones are of moderate proportions—neither long and narrow nor short and broad. It also reveals an important sex difference: the female sacrum is wider and shorter than that of the male. The values of the Lumbar Index are higher for the males, indicating a straighter lower back. This is in contrast to the Sacral Index, in which the values for the female are higher.

Certain measurements of the pelvis and of the left innominate bone were utilized to obtain additional sex determinants. The technique used was as follows: The right and left innominates and the sacrum were held in articulation by an assistant. Maximum breadth (bi-iliac) was measured on the osteometric board. All other diameters were measured with the sliding calipers. Since the ischiatic spines were broken in nearly all cases, the interspinous diameters were carefully estimated.

The base of the pelvis (biischiatic diameter) of both sexes was compared with the measurements of hip breadth across the crests (bi-iliac diameter). The resulting index shows that the females have significantly wider pelvic diameters. The female pelvis is much more rectangularly shaped (a basal section of a long cone) than the more sharply angled, wedge-shaped pelvis of the male (the conic base of a short cone). Clear-cut sex differences, six units between males and females, are revealed in this Biischiatic/Maximum Breadth Index, although there is a considerable overlap of the range. Also of interest are the important differences of the brim diameters (pelvic inlet).

The best means of determining the sex from the pelvis is by comparing the length of the pubic element with that of the ischium—the Ischiopubic (I-P) Index. Both right and left bones were measured and a clear-cut separation of the sexes obtained.

Measurements for Hawaiians were compared with those for other peoples (see Table 20). The Mokapu pubic length was the greatest, and the difference between male and female the least. Ischial lengths were the same as those for American white males and the greatest for females. The sex difference was less than that for American whites and Negroes, but slightly greater than for Bantus, Bushmen, and Kentucky Indians. The difference between male and female for the I-P Index was the least, which means that these Hawaiian men and women were more alike in the pelvic structure which separates the sexes.

Three dimensions of the calcaneus of right and left bones of both sexes were routinely measured according to methods described by Martin (1928, p. 1054). (See Table 19.) Although measurements of the heel bone are rare in skeletal reports, those of early Kentucky Indians, early Greeks, Irish Monks, and Americans of English extraction were available. As the length-breadth and breadth-height index shows, the Mokapu calcanei were very short, quite broad, and very high—quite different from the others. Talar bones were likewise measured and found to be fairly long, very broad, and fairly high compared with the other groups.

Two indices are of interest in assessing the skeleton as a whole: the Intermembral Index and the Index of Robustness. The Intermembral Index is a comparison between the bones of the arm (humerus plus radius) and those of the leg (femur plus tibia). This index shows that the Mokapu males have relatively longer arms than the Mokapu females; for males the arms are 70.0 percent, and for females 68.7 percent, of the length of the legs. For males this relationship is close to that determined for whites, Negroes, early Kentucky Indians, and Australians. On the other hand, we find higher values for this index among people of shorter stature—Eskimos, other American Indian series, and Chinese men. We find a significant difference of limb proportions between the sexes. The Mokapu females, like those of ancient Greece, appear to have shorter arms compared with legs than do Mokapu males and early Greek men.

The Index of Robustness is a comparison of the lengths of long bones with their midshaft girths. Examination of this index reveals distinct sex differences. It is also interesting as a measure of the relative bulk of the different long bones of the body. Going from the most to the least robust, the following order is found: clavicle, tibia, humerus, femur, ulna and radius, fibula.

Table 21 presents a comparison of paired bones. The Mokapu series follows the usual asymmetries which have been noted by other investigators. Like Schultz (1937, p. 325) and Angel (1946, p. 85), I can say that for the arm bones (humerus, ulna, and radius) the right members exceed in length and girth the corresponding opposite members. This was true among ancient Greeks, and among the very large series of American and European white bones listed by Schultz. On the other hand, the left collar bones are longer and straighter but smaller in girth than the bones of the right side. This is true for all the series, including Mokapu. Females from Indian Knoll and Mokapu have slightly larger hip bones on the left side than on the right, and the males have slightly larger right hip bones.

The leg bone asymmetries are just the opposite of those of the upper limbs in that the lengths of the femur, tibia, and fibula on the left side exceed those of the corresponding bones of the right side. Usually, however, the girth of the bones of the right leg is larger and the bones are better developed than the longer left bones. It is interesting to note that at Indian Knoll the females maintained a larger size of the head of the right femur, whereas the males were superior on the left side. This same difference exists for the Mokapu males wherein the left bone supported the larger head.

MORPHOLOGY

It is important in a study like this, which necessarily concerns itself with many details, to remember that the parts make up an active, integrated whole. The individual bones with their muscles and attachments, nourished by means of the circulatory system and stimulated by the nerves, are coordinated in the daily activities of the whole person. The parts are all interrelated, interdependent, and coordinated.

The morphological features of each bone in the Mokapu series are tabulated in Tables 22 and 23. What we hope to determine in this discussion is the relationship of the detailed observations to the whole body structure. The governing conditions which prevail are age changes, sex differences, muscularity, and other variations due to function. Pathology, an additional variation, is discussed in another chapter.

Those features affected by age changes are present in all adults; they are universal. A significant sex difference in the age categories of the Mokapuans was noted in the Census section, above. It has also been mentioned that the Mokapu population contained more younger women and more older men. The shoulders and hip girdles demonstrated this fact. The clavicle is the last long bone to complete its growth; the sternal epiphysis closes last. A higher percentage of the men had closed or united sternal epiphyses, indicative of advanced maturity, while the women had a greater number of open epiphyses. Similarly, the phases of the pubic symphysis (not tabulated), which formed the principal basis for age determination, revealed the same differences between men and women.

Inside the hip sockets (acetabulae) there were breaks in the smooth articular surfaces which denoted incomplete growth or development. This condition ran 16 to 19 percent in both sexes. The edges of the glenoid fossae of the shoulder joints in the older individuals showed arthritic lipping. Here again there were four times as many men as women with an advanced degree of border exostoses. In both sexes, the right shoulder appeared to have been more afflicted than the left. Finally, in the older people, the scapulae showed buckling, "wrinkling," and thinning of the flat-bone tissue.

While many regions of the body differentiate between the sexes, the pelvis is peculiarly and particularly important. Pelvic shapes and sizes show clear-cut sex distinctions. The shape as viewed from the front showed 97 percent of the males with flaring, wedge-shaped structures, and 77 percent of the females with more rectangular shapes (see Fig. 3). More important was the shape of the pelvic brim, or, in females, the opening into the bony birth canal. In this area, 81 percent of the male pelves were either heart-shaped or narrowly oval, and 75 percent of the females had either round or broadly oval brims. The contours of the sacrum were also important. Females generally had shorter, wider, and straighter sacra while those of the males were longer, narrower, and more curved. The subpubic angles were another very distinctive feature. Eighty-two percent of the male pelves had narrow angles (less than 90°) between the two pubic rami; eighty-seven percent of the females had wide angles (more than 90°).

Accessory sacral articulations were found in many of the older men and women. Here again the women showed a predominance which may have been associated with childbearing.

Another feature of decided importance is the preauricular sulcus (a deep sacroiliac groove on the medial anterior surface of the posterior inferior iliac spine). Average to deep forms occurred in 79 percent of the females, while 96 percent of the males had no grooves or very small ones.

The above features were utilized to assess the sex of the skeletons, in addition to the measurements and relationships of the pubic and ischial elements of the innominates (I-P Index).

The breast bone also showed a sex distinction. The body of the sternum in the male was long in comparison with the short, broad segment in the female breast bone. Males showed a frequency of seven rib attachments on each side of the sternum more than twice that of females, while the frequency of six rib attachments was 74 percent for females and only 54 percent for males. This variation may also be functionally linked.

Additional sex differences in the postcranial bones were found in the relative size and in muscle markings. The bones of the women were smaller, smoother, and more gracile, while the men had larger, rougher, more rugged bones. The percentage of males with a large degree of muscularity was greater for almost every bone (see Table 22), but there were also some females with great muscularity and some males with a lesser degree.

The presence of a third trochanter (gluteal tuberosity) on the femur of 10 percent of the females, an incidence two and one-half times that of the males, is another sex difference to be noted. The low frequency of this interesting anatomical tubercle has been noted before by Hrdlička (1937, p. 187). In some North American Indian series (Snow, 1948a, pp. 475–76; idem, 1943, pp. 608–09), this third trochanter was prevalent and is considered to be of genetic origin.

Other sex differences apparently stem from the distinctive activities of men and women.

I have referred several times to the large, heavy musculature of these Mokapuans. However, muscularity cannot be treated as a separate entity for it is dependent not only on genetic and sex influence, but on function; that is, on the manner in which the individuals use their bodies. Wolf's law (Bowers, 1966, p. 215) "postulates that bone structure is dependent upon function. Internal architectural formation depends on lines of stress, and even external configuration of bone depends on muscle pull or lines of weight-bearing." It is evident from the skeletal record that these people lived vigorous lives.

The relationships between the muscles and their bony origins and insertions are marked by bone-modeling. This modeling may be barely noticeable or it may be in deep relief, indicating extraordinary development of the muscle fibers occupying the area.

The degree of modeling for some of the Mokapu bones has been tabulated in Table 22; some of it was only observed in rating the muscularity. On the whole there were the usual sex differences—men were more muscular than women; but some of the women were more muscular than some of the men of this group and of some European and American Indian series. The following descriptions of ridges, knobs, and grooves on the arm bones, pectoral and pelvic girdles, and trunk and leg bones present the evidences for great muscularity.

Humerus: Intertubercular grooves, deltoid ridges, and radial grooves reached all-time highs for size and modeling. In addition, an unusual development of a lateral flare and crest at the distal extremities where the coracobrachialis muscles arise was present in both sexes and was greater in the larger men (see Fig. 45).

Ulna and Radius: Extensions of interosseus crests were well marked, and bones of the males showed more bowing and greater development of these crests. The muscle mark or ridge of the pronator teres on the radius was measured; the males showed uniformly larger development.

Clavicle: Sex differences were apparent. All of the men had well curved, robust clavicles while 10 percent of the women had almost straight, gracile bones. Left and right sides were nearly equally curved. In the males there was a predominance of more curvature on the right side, and women showed a five-fold preponderance on the left side. This may reflect the division of labor in the family.

Scapula: Extension of the teres major muscle attachment was present in 25 percent of the men, both left and right sides, and in the women, 11 percent on the left and 13 percent on the right. An unusually large degree of concavity of shoulder joints (glenoid fossae), signifying heavy back muscles, particularly those involved with shoulder movement, was noted for both sexes. Large, deeply modeled shoulder blades were observed in most persons.

Vertebrae: Although it was not possible to measure the muscle attachment areas of the various vertebrae, it was noted that many of the vertebral spines of males in particular showed great development, in both length and height, with deeply excavated processes, indicating well-developed trunk musculature.

Innominates: Many of the male pelves showed an unusual ruggedness of the iliac crests, the edges of the ischial and pubic rami, and ischial tuberosity; large, well-developed anterior and posterior iliac spines; and strong relief of muscle attachment on the well-curved lateral sides of the ilium. The origin of the gluteus maximus had an unusually large amount of bone extending posteriorly beyond the sacroiliac joint.

Femur: Almost all of these bones show well-developed pilastering of the linea aspera. This buttressing, reinforced bony ridge was strong evidence for well-developed flexor and extensor muscles (see Fig. 45). The bone relief of the trochanteric region was bold and showed extensive muscular areas. Likewise, in the popliteal region at the back of the knee, the adductor tubercle was very well developed.

Tibia: This lower leg bone showed unusual markings of the anterior tibial crest in both sexes. Instead of being the usual nearly straight, longitudinal shape (for the anterior tibialis muscle), it was strongly S-shaped and overlapped onto the medial surfaces of the anterior crest. Likewise, strong adductor muscle crests were seen on many of the bones of both sexes (see Fig. 45).

Fibula: The companion bone of the tibia had deep flutings and channels bounded by thick-walled muscular crests which usually ran the length of the slender bone.

I attempted to compare the overall musculature of the arm bones with those of the leg bones. In general it can be said that in both sexes the arms commonly showed greater muscular development than the corresponding legs of the same individual, again undoubtedly a functional adaptation.

Variations, those features that are different from the usual structure seen in anatomy books, are always of great interest and give rise to speculation. The variations discussed below may be the result of one or several processes: genetics, influences of sex hormones; certainly function and habitus have left their mark. I believe all of the following vari-

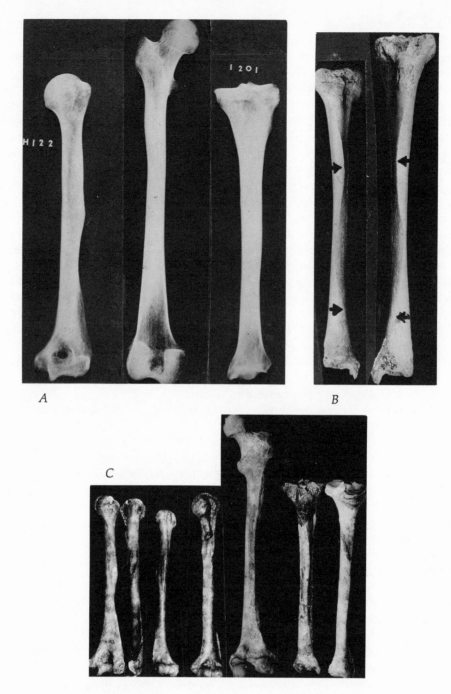

FIG. 45. Strong muscle marks on limb bones. *A*, X-rays show a great density where heavy bone exists. *B*, *C*, gross views, show various muscle attachments in the form of extended crests, rough ridges, grooves, and tubercles.

ations were due, at least in part, to function—that is, the manner in which the individual used that part of his body.

These Mokapu people lived vigorous, active lives; this is evident from both the muscular marks on their bones and the historic accounts of early Hawaiians. The men spent much of their time planting, fishing, hunting, paddling canoes, cutting and hauling wood from the mountains, and climbing. Their sports included swimming, wrestling, coasting, dancing, and contests of strength. Presumably they were responsible for the preparation and tending of the *imu* (earth oven) which necessitated hauling wood and rocks. Poi-pounding was doubtless another household responsibility of the men.

Women's work included the preparation of bark cloth (*kapa*), which required pounding the tough fibers into pliable sheets; cultivation of the plants in the fields; the collecting of shellfish, seaweed, and other food products of the shore; the preparation and serving of foods, and other household tasks. They were responsible for weaving the mats, and this in turn required gathering and preparing the fibers, such as *hala* and palm leaves. Bearing and rearing the children was no small task. Swimming and dancing were probably their principal recreations, although they doubtless participated in other sports.

Their life-style required strenuous effort, and tasks were divided among men, women, and children. Their work and play were factors in the development of their bodies and probably account for many of the variations which are described below.

Perforation of the olecranon fossae (septal apertures or supracondyloid foramina) on the distal end of the humerus was very common among most of the Mokapu females, but occurred in only 9 percent of the men, predominantly on the left side. Perforations of these elbow joint structures (olecranon fossae) of the humerus are definitely associated with primitive peoples, who performed much more arduous manual labor in their daily lives than do modern, civilized white-collar workers (Martin, 1928, p. 1103). The evidence indicates that the incidence of this septal aperture in modern European whites averages from 3 to 10 percent for both arms; and in Negroes, from 4 to 19 percent (Schultz, 1937, pp. 288–89). Angel (1946, p. 73) indicates that the ancient Greeks had a 24 percent average. The Mokapuans, on the other hand, had almost 50 percent, and early Kentucky Indians and some other primitive

groups had incidences as high as 58 percent (Snow, 1948a, p. 454).

Extra lateral articular surfaces at the elbow joint, plainly visible on both the olecranon process of the ulna and a matching facet in the humeral fossae, were present in a small group (see Fig. 46D). Only thirty-seven males and fifty-two females were examined for this feature. (See Table 24.) These extra joints were medium to large in size in 57 percent of the males and 59 percent of the females. These joint surfaces were brought into articulation only when the elbow joint was straightened (complete extension) and must have had some connection with lateral movement. Apparently these have never been observed before.[1]

Asymmetry of the sternomanubrial joint was found. Ninety-three percent of the males and 70 percent of the females had a sloping joint that angled from the right side down to the left. Thirty percent of the females, but only 7 percent of the males, showed a reverse slope, left side down to the right. This trait may be associated with handedness or involved with other functional unilaterality.

Anomalous articular patterns occurred in the thoracic lumbar transitional zone. In all there were twenty-four cases (15 percent of all the spines examined) in which these patterns were present, with the percentage of females higher by 1 percent. The twelfth thoracic vertebra, which is distinguished by lumbarlike facets to articulate with the first lumbar, varied in eleven cases in which the flat thoracic pattern prevailed. In five cases, the left side only was flat, and in three this occurred on the right side only. There were two cases, one of each sex, in which the eleventh thoracic vertebra as well as the twelfth had this lumbar pattern. Whitney (1926, pp. 451–55) indicates an incidence of 4 to 6 percent in both Negroes and whites, with 1 percent higher for whites. The incidence in this Mokapu series is three times as high.

Another variation in articular pattern was found in more than half of the lower back vertebrae of both sexes: V-shaped or sloping-sided inferior articular facets and articulating superior facets and processes of the lower thoracic and lumbar vertebrae. Ordinarily the articular processes and their receiving "sockets" show vertical sides so that movements are more or less up and down. These V-shaped processes, however, slope down and in-

1. M. Trotter, 1957, personal communication.

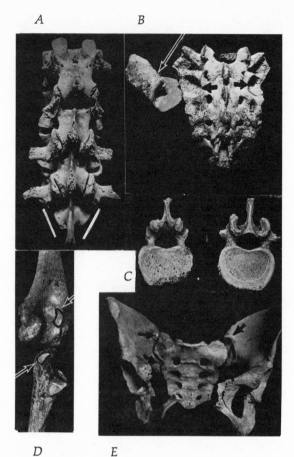

A   B

C

D   E

FIG. 46. Accessory joints. *A* (HX), a typical example of lumbar vertebrae with V-shaped inferior facets inclined obliquely and toward the midline. Also note the curved, "wrap-around" facets in the upper vertebrae. The facets interlock, preventing A-P movement. *B* (H-91), the arrows indicate accessory sacroiliac joints. *C* (H-76), lumbar vertebrae with "wrap-around" articulations; inferior aspect seen at left. *D* (H-182), accessory lateral elbow joints. *E* (C-2), an irregular S-shaped sacroiliac joint in a female pelvis.

ward so that considerable lateral motion is possible. (See Fig. 46*A*.) There were twenty-seven cases (17 percent) in all.

Even more peculiar were extra bone formations which I have called "wrap-arounds" (see Fig. 46*C*). The superior articular processes, usually of the lumbar vertebrae, extend posteriorly and medially to lock in place the inferior facets of the vertebra above. The articulated vertebrae can be separated only by lifting them one by one from above. Usually these extra articular extensions occurred in three vertebrae in the transitional zone of the thoracic and lumbar spine. This anomaly occurred in twenty-nine cases (18 percent; 7 percent men and 11 percent women). There were seven cases involving the twelfth thoracic, the remainder the lumbar, usually between the first, second, and third. In one male, four vertebrae were thus affected.

Both of these anomalous structures I believe to have been adaptations to either lateral movement or a combination of lateral movement and extreme flexion, as, for example, in paddling a canoe. Illustrations of paddlers in outrigger canoes (Buck, 1957, Fig. 192, p. 271) show peculiar humps or angles of the back at this location.

An unusual feature sometimes occurred on the sacrum in which the superior surface was cleft at the midline by a V-shaped groove (see Fig. 47). There were several examples of sacralization of the fifth lumbar vertebra on the wings with no fusion of the base in which the V-shaped groove was evident, and even one case of complete fusion. This feature occurred in 55 percent of the adults (59 percent of the males and 50 percent of the females). This is a feature that has not to date been reported in other skeletal series.[2] It may be of congenital origin or may represent a functional adaptation.

Unusual "distorted" posterior surfaces of the pubic bone were present on many of the Mokapu females but were not observed in the males. These surfaces appeared eroded with "eaten-out" pockets. Stewart (1957, pp. 16, 47) has indicated that these "abnormalities of the pubic symphysis confined to females must be connected with childbearing." Although no tabulation was made of these abnormal pubes at Mokapu, they were present. We can infer that these skeletal marks are eloquent evidence of the effects of frequent childbearing.

These functional pubic marks were coupled with

2. In 1959 I noted this V-shaped sacral cleft on adult Indian Knoll skeletons.

accessory sacroiliac articulations on the posterior aspect of the pelvis. The frequency of these extra joints was impressive. They occurred at the key-stone point of weight-transfer to the hip bones and thence to the legs. More women than men had these joints—78 out of 112 women (70 percent) compared to 40 out of 71 men (56 percent). (See Fig. 46B.) It seems clear that these are functionally but not exclusively linked with childbearing. Trotter (1937, p. 255) has indicated that age is an important factor in the incidence of these joints; in this series more older people than younger had them.

These extra sacroiliac articulations were most frequently found at the contacts between the wings of the sacrum and the iliac juncture on each side. The next location in frequency of occurrence was the first sacral segment. At the level of the second and third sacral segments additional extra contact joints occurred posteriorly and were evenly distributed between the sexes. One male had a reverse form wherein tubercles were formed on the sacrum and articulated with fossae-joints rather than the usual tubercle formation found on the hip bones. Sacralization of the fifth lumbar, either onto both wings of the sacrum or on one side only, occurred in nearly 6 percent of the men and 10 percent of the women.

Several features of the lower leg bones represented variations in degree rather than in structure and could definitely be related to sex or muscularity.

The angle of the femoral neck in women showed a higher proportion of larger angles. This was doubtless associated with the greater angulation of their knees (tendency to knock-knees), and, along with torsion of the leg bones and certain marks on the posterior surface of the pubic bones, may very well have been functionally linked with squatting and with parturition.

The male femurs showed three times as much anterior-posterior bowing as those of the females. Stresses of weight-bearing and muscle-pull were undoubtedly responsible, and the large pilaster was the response to these stresses. As for the tibia, more men than women showed a large degree of bowing; in fact, 10 percent of the women showed no bowing.

The torsion of the femoral shaft as seen between the plane of the head and neck in contrast to that of the condyles, reflected sex differences the opposite of those found with bowing; men had less than women. In both sexes the right bone showed the greater amount of torsion—65 percent for both

A

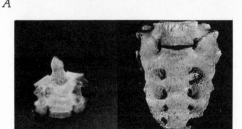

B

FIG. 47. A (H-183), X-ray and gross views showing the V base of sacrum. B (H-281), sacrum with a V base below a fused fifth lumbar vertebra.

sexes. This I interpret as a typical footedness asymmetry similar to handedness. There was additional evidence of right-sided asymmetry in the muscle development of arms, legs, and trunk.

Tibial torsion (the fibulae in accompaniment) is not recorded in Table 22, but a study was made of one group (H series) of ninety-seven pairs of tibiae (Table 25). A precise measure taken in degrees revealed extreme torsion. Figure 44 illustrates the maximum torsion present as indicated by the angle between the steel needles held in place through the transverse planes of the articular extremities. Martin (1928, p. 1165) presents such data and lists 18° as the maximum recorded. Some individuals from Mokapu exceeded this. Here, as with the femur, there were more females than males with a high degree of torsion.

Torsion is certainly related to the habitual posture of deep squatting for which the evidence is multiple. In squatting, the individual assumed a position of rest with the legs and feet in extreme flexion; he literally sat on his heels with the feet flat upon the supporting surface. The tibio-talus joint at the ankle was bent forward in a sharp angle so that the anterior surface of the shin bone rested

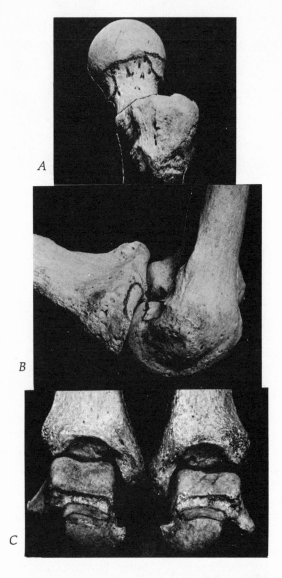

FIG. 48. Squatting facets shown on *A*, the head of the femur (double facets) (C series), *B*, the back of the knee joint (1201), and *C*, the ankle joints (H-273). Facets have been outlined in black in *A* and *B*; in *C* the facets are identified by indentations on the tibia and black outline on the upper surfaces of the heads of the tali.

upon the neck and head of the talus (see Fig. 48*C*). In some extreme cases the trochlear surfaces of the talus may have been extended forward by both malleoli of the leg bones. Additional evidences were to be found at the knee and hip joints.

In the case of the knee joint, the lateral posterior articular surfaces of the femoral condyles and the corresponding joint surfaces of the tibia met in a position of extreme flexion so that extra joint surfaces of dense bone were formed beyond the limits of the usual contact surfaces (see Fig. 48*B*).

In the femur, this squatting facet took the form of a triangular extension anteriorly and superiorly from the lateral condyle. A corresponding articular facet was formed on the posterior lateral surface of the tibial head. This consisted of a rounding over of the posterior edges of the articular facet into the vertical plane above and inside the facet for the fibula. (See Fig. 48*A*.)

Squatting also produced extra joint surfaces on the hip joint. Here, in extreme cases, the hard, dense joint bone of the femoral head was extended down onto the neck in a medial superior position, corresponding with an increase of bone in the acetabulum (see Fig. 48*A*).

Only five adults (four with clubfoot and one with a foot injury) showed no evidence of squatting facets at the ankles. Extra facets at the backs of the knee joints on both the femoral condyle and the tibial plateau marked more men than women, while those at the hip joint were fairly uncommon. In several cases double facets were found on the femoral necks (see Fig. 48*A*). It is interesting to note that the fully flexed position of the body was the characteristic burial position.

Barnett (1954, p. 511) reports that most fetuses in their tight dorsi-flexed position are born with these anterior extensions of the trochlear surfaces. It is clear, then, that when little children sit on their haunches, this squatting facet is maintained, but "civilized," chair-sitting peoples lose them soon after their preschool years. However, in many parts of the world where people do not use chairs habitually—Asia and Africa, particularly, and even parts of our own Deep South—squatting persists. In the course of identification of the unknown dead of World War II, squatting facets were found on both Negroes and whites who were later traced as coming from Southern homes (Snow, 1948b, p. 327).

Mrs. Pukui has written an interesting account of ways of sitting which documents the use of this posture among her own people of Ka'u, Hawaii. (See Appendix D, below.)

Another habitual posture of these early Hawaiians left its mark upon the bony frame. The backward slope of the articular surfaces of the shin bone (tilt or retroversion of the tibial plateau) formed a definite angle of flexure with the femur in what is commonly known as the "bent-knee gait"—a postural dynamic (Angel, 1946, p. 77). This habitual bending of the knees is said to characterize most peoples of the world who are not accustomed to walking on flat surfaces, such as pavement. It has been characteristic of vigorous outdoor people ever since the Pleistocene, and is present today among most of the world's rural peoples. This stance in which the thigh muscles are flexed provides a type of springy balance, allowing easy shifting to other positions. This crouching position is found currently in almost all sports from skiing to the boxing ring. It is easy to imagine the effectiveness of this posture in the activities of the Hawaiians—for example, dancing the hula, working in the taro fields, climbing the steep mountains, fishing, and surfboard-riding. Virtually all of the adults from Mokapu and most of the subadult skeletons where the tibial head was present showed the characteristic backward sloping surfaces of the knee-joint.

Finally, the two foot bones, the talus and the calcaneus, likewise showed some interesting sex differences, some of which may have been functionally acquired. The head and neck sections of the male tali showed more divergent and greater angles than those of the females. This bone gives rise to the structures which lead to a more medially spread great toe, the pollux, from which we infer a wide, muscular foot. Similarly, the heel bones showed a clear-cut difference in the development of the lateral and posterior tubercle. Females had many more upright bones which were stable and thus would sit on horizontal surfaces in anatomical position because of the greater size of the tubercle. More male bones, on the other hand, showed the more primitive condition of little development of the tubercle, and as a consequence the bones would roll over on their outsides. The male bones also showed a much greater ruggedness of structure and muscle marking. It was also noted that the hand and foot bones of many individuals had well-formed muscular ridges and channels, denoting strong musculature. This was particularly true of many of the foot bones found among the more rugged males.

Angel (1946, p. 77) related the functionally-associated bony characters of the ancient Greeks with the Greek countryside. He showed the dynamic relationship of the body to function. His description could well portray the Hawaiians described in this study, except that the Mokapuans were possibly better muscled, better nourished, and more consistently active throughout the year.

Certainly, as a group, the bones of the entire skeletons of these Hawaiian people exceeded, in evidence of muscle development and other forms of functionally related hypertrophies, the bones of American Indians, Negroes, and whites, and any other skeletal series heretofore described.

BODY SIZE AND BUILD

The skeletal framework forms the basis of body size and build. Measurements and observations of the bones, which are necessary to estimate stature, have been discussed in detail in the two preceding sections. Coordinating the results of these two methods of study permits us to approximate the physique of these Hawaiians at Mokapu. Stature estimations were computed, using the average as well as the minimum and maximum lengths of all the limb bones (humerus, radius, femur, tibia, fibula, the femur and tibia together), based on the formulae of Trotter and Gleser (1952, pp. 496–98). They are presented in Table 26, along with stature data of living Hawaiians obtained by Sullivan (1927, p. 281), and Dunn and Tozzer (1928, p. 102).

The early Hawaiian men from Mokapu averaged 5 feet 7 inches in height, ranging from 5 feet 2 inches to 6 feet, while the women averaged 5 feet 2½ inches, ranging from 4 feet 9 inches to 5 feet 9 inches. These figures are virtually identical with those obtained for twentieth-century Hawaiians regarded by Sullivan as racially unmixed. However, Tozzer measured a different sample of pure Hawaiians who were slightly taller than the old Hawaiians from Mokapu. The 3½- to 4-inch sex difference in stature is typical of most populations.

There were no exceptionally tall Hawaiians in the Mokapu series. However, the idea that all ancient Hawaiians were big and strong comes to us through the records of the early explorers. Undoubtedly, the basis for this impression was comparison with themselves, enhanced by the bulk and muscular development of the Hawaiians; certainly they were not measured with modern instruments and techniques. Another factor in this discrepancy may be found in the sociocultural distinction of lineage and rank. The *ali'i* (royalty) were a breed apart, in both size and privilege, and were not limited by the food taboos applied to the commoners (Miller, Appendix E, below). Modern Hawaiians of pure ancestry are among the world's heaviest people—170 lbs. average for 60 males, 153 lbs. for 16 females (Dunn and Tozzer, 1928, p. 106).

In an effort to assess the body proportions of the Mokapu people, a number of indices were calculated. Perhaps the first comparison that comes to mind is that of the largest gross dimension of the body, shoulder breadth (twice the clavicle) to stature. This index showed no significant variations in the populations compared (see Tables 27 and 28). Aware that stature estimates involve another variable, we tried the actual bone lengths involved; that is, twice the clavicle length in relation to the combined lengths of the femur and tibia. This index likewise failed to reveal a useful ratio to separate the groups. The truth appears to be that the proportions of these parts of the body are remarkably uniform for all the population groups at hand.

Table 27 presents the following indices: bi-iliac diameter with the length of (1) the femur, (2) the femur and tibia together, and (3) the estimated stature; the breadth of the shoulders (twice the clavicle) with bi-iliac diameter; and, finally, the shoulder-hip ratio with the length of the entire leg. These proportions for skeletal populations of various periods and ethnic extractions are compared with the Mokapu series.

The Mokapu hip bones compared with leg bones, singly or taken together, have the lowest index, indicating the narrowest hip diameters known to modern man. The comparison of clavicles with bi-iliac resembles that of the large series of early prehistoric Indians from Kentucky (Indian Knoll) more than any other group, which means their torsos are more nearly alike in shape. The indices for torsos and limbs are lowest for Mokapu and highest for the Japanese; in other words, the Japanese had the shortest limbs compared with body breadth, tending to be heavy-set, and the Mokapuans had long limbs compared with body breadth, or were slender.

Interbone comparisons for peoples of different ethnic extraction are presented in Table 28. The relationships between arm bones (humero-radial index) indicate that the Mokapu population approximated the ancient Greeks and Kentucky Indians and fell in an intermediate position with the other

groups. When the upper arm bones were compared with the collar bone (claviculo-humeral index) we found that Australians had the narrowest shoulders and short-armed Eskimos the broadest, with Mokapuans in an intermediate position. In comparing parts of the leg (tibio-femoral index), this series was again more nearly like the ancient Greeks and the Kentucky Indians, as they were in the relationships of arm bones—that is, the tibia was relatively short compared to the femur, while the tibiae of modern Negroes and Australians are relatively long compared to the femora. The intermembral index (entire arm compared with entire leg), when used to compare these various populations, showed that Mokapuans, with the highest value, were among the relatively long-armed, short-legged group, and the Eskimos were most like them.

These Hawaiians, then, had fairly long arms, moderately narrow shoulders, and very narrow hips; and the intermembral index suggests that their legs were relatively short compared with their arms. Overall, they would be judged slender for their height in spite of heavy musculature.

The validity of the impression of great size and bulk that has come down to modern times through the excellent Webber and Choris sketches, as well as through verbal reports, lies in the musculature of these people. A detailed description of the extraordinary muscle markings has been given above in the section of postcranial morphology, and the daily activities of the people that would develop such musculature have also been discussed.

If we could clothe the skeletal frame described above with muscle and tissue, we would see upper arm muscle-masses, biceps, triceps, and the deltoid, of vast size. Comparison of the upper and lower limb bones of the same individual revealed larger markings of arm and shoulder muscles. Their large and muscular hands (clenched in a fist) produced large cords (separate muscles) in the forearms which stood out in relief to the elbow. For the men, we can draw the great roll of tissue that marked the inguinal ligaments which extended from hip crest into the groin and delimited the roll of muscles above the hip bones. The lower torso (back) and hips likewise showed great muscular development. In the lower limbs there were massive muscle groups which produced, in the males, large cylindrical thighs, and vast muscle bellies of the soleus and gastrocnemius in the lower leg.

Although only two of the numerous foot bones

were measured and studied, it was observed that for the most part the metatarsals and phalanges of the feet of both sexes showed extraordinary development of muscular ridges and insertions. Modern Hawaiians have feet of great breadth and thickness compared with the skinny, long, narrow feet of most *haoles* (whites).

The female figurine in the frontispiece gives an impression of this sturdiness and muscular development quite beyond that of the usual European representation of the female body. Add to that the bent-knee posture, the cultural mark of head shaping, and the typical rocker-jaw contour of the lower face, and we have the typical Hawaiian.

Carey D. Miller, in her report on the influence of foods on the ancient Hawaiians (Appendix E, below), states, "Although heredity may determine the potential stature of an individual, food to furnish the needed nutrients in the right proportions at the proper time is the chief factor in determining whether or not the individual will achieve his potential." This suggests the following comparison.

The Hawaiian-born Japanese studied by Shapiro (1939) with Fred Hulse demonstrated remarkable increase in size and changes in proportions as compared to their relatives born and bred in Japan but resident in Hawaii, and to their antecedents resident in Japan. Similar changes in body form were reported by Lasker in his study of American-born Chinese (1946, p. 296). However, the modern Hawaiians measured by Dr. Sullivan in 1920–1921 did not show any appreciable increase in size over their predecessors from Mokapu. The Mokapuans apparently achieved virtually a maximum size, or at least the great bulk of their hereditary potential. This probably means that the native diet, *kapu* restrictions and all, was as adequate for growth as the diet of their modern descendants—a mixture of old Hawaiian and modern American foods.

TOOLS FROM HUMAN BONES

At Mokapu evidence was found of mutilation of the shafts of limb bones on nine individuals, two of them clearly females; only the broken-off ends of the bones were found in the graves (Figs. 49–51). In some cases, other bones of the skeleton or the smashed, splintered fragments of the shafts were present. These appeared to have been intentional rather than accidental mutilations. The following is a list of such finds and the bones present:

FIG. 49. The broken, split, and cut-up bones of a young woman (H-252). The shafts of all but two long bones were missing when the burial was excavated. The ends of each long bone show typical breakage occurring with burials whose bones have been taken for manufacture of artifacts.

1) CX–12, adult male; ends of femur and tibia with cut marks on femoral necks.

2) HX, adult male; ends of limb bones.

3) N–3, young adult male; ends of both femur and tibia with cut marks.

4) H–196, male, about 35; head of right tibia, skull, four vertebrae (cervical, thoracic, and lumbar).

5) H–218, male, 35; large ends of all long bones (humeral head = 54 mm., femoral head = 52 mm.) with cut marks on tibia and femur; pelvis.

6) CX–13, adult female; ends of femur and tibia.

7) H–117, male, 35–40; both femoral heads, pelvis, sacrum, vertebrae, ribs, and four long bones.

8) C–23A, male, 25; ends of all major long bones with splintered shafts, bones of feet and hands.

9) H–252, female, 22–24; ends of all limb bones with splintered shafts, skull, vertebrae.

Incision marks, interpreted as being the result of the cutting action necessary to sever the ligament attachments, were visible on the joint pieces of three individuals. Usually the cutting marks were at right angles to the long axes of the bone indicating that cutting extended directly across the axial fibers of the ligaments and tendons.

In the literature of Polynesian peoples there are numerous references to the use of human bones and teeth to fashion useful or ornamental objects (Buck, 1957). Bone was one of the materials used to make fishhooks and the hooks on cowrie shell squid-lures. The clavicle and humerus were sometimes fashioned into handles for shark-tooth weapons. The most

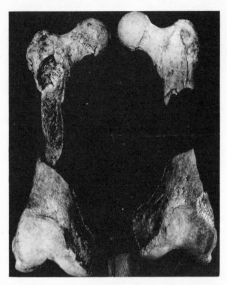

A

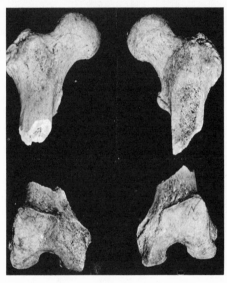

B

Fig. 50. Femoral joint ends of *A*, a female (CX-13), and *B*, a male (N-3).

honored use was for *kahili* (feather standard) handles. Disks were fashioned from leg bones and strung on a slender core of *kauila* wood or whalebone to make such handles. Kamehameha honored some of the lesser chiefs killed in the famous battle of Nuuanu in 1795 by using their bones in this manner. One such *kahili* may be seen in the Bishop Museum collection (Buck, 1957, p. 579). (See Fig. 52.)

Teeth from enemies slain in battle or otherwise were often used to ornament the scrap bowls of chiefs (Buck, 1957, pp. 53–54). They were also used on drums and to decorate feathered sashes. One necklace of human teeth exists with a worked whale tooth as a pendant. (See Fig. 53.)

A fisherman's kit, also in Bishop Museum, from the island of Kahoolawe, contains sections of human femora. Some sections had been split and the bone pieces left in various steps of manufacture. The material was worked with coral files from a central perforation. A detailed description of this process is given by Buck (1957, pp. 324–25). (See Fig. 54.)

William Ellis, writing in the early nineteenth century, shed an interesting sidelight on this subject. He says, "When they searched the field of battle for the bones of the slain, to use them in the manufacture of chisels, gimlets, or fish hooks, they always selected those whose skins were dark, as they supposed their bones were strongest" (1832, 1:83). Buck (1957, p. 325) says, "Hawaiians believed that fishhooks made from the bones of people without hair on their bodies . . . were more attractive to fish than hooks from normal bones."

From these facts it seems probable that the mutilated bones with missing shafts found at Mokapu were used for such purposes. As for the shattered, splintered shafts of two individuals of different sexes and from different burial sites, there is at present no conclusive or hypothetical explanation. Buck (1957, p. 567) refers to intentional mutilation of the bodies of chiefs as part of burial honor. The incomplete remains of some of the skeletons from Mokapu are a mystery; it may be that some of these individuals were of chiefly rank.

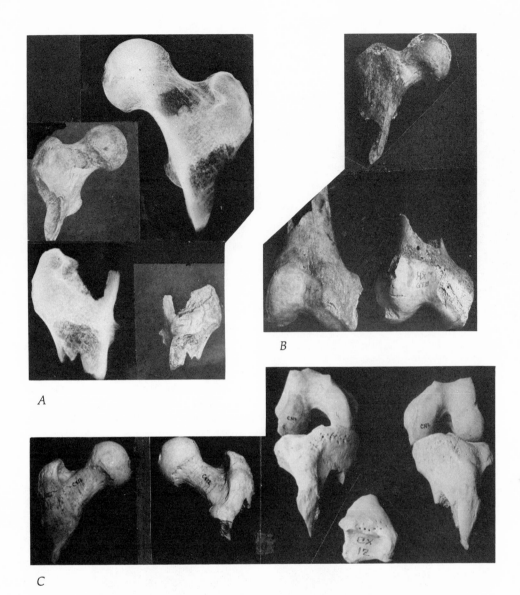

A

B

C

FIG. 51. Joint ends of leg bones. *A*, X-rays and gross pictures of male femoral heads (C-23) showing cut marks and broken area on necks. *B*, right head and both knee joints of male femora (HX). *C*, femoral heads, condyles, tibial heads, and lower end of right tibia (CX-12).

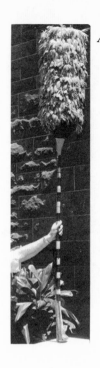

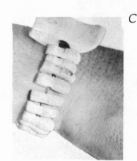

Fig. 52. Human bone handle and bracelet. *A, kahili* with handle made of sections of human limb bones. The upper section of a right tibia (male) is at the lower end. *B, kahili* handle end in anatomic position. *C,* human finger bones drilled and modified for a bracelet, with the tooth of an animal (pig or whale) as the "jewel." Photos courtesy of Bernice P. Bishop Museum, Honolulu.

Fig. 53. Human teeth as ornaments. *A,* long-rooted adult teeth—incisors, canines, and premolars—strung in a necklace with the tooth of a sperm whale as the pendant. *B,* top and bottom sides of a wooden bowl decorated with adult teeth, primarily molars and premolars. *C,* human adult teeth in Umi's feather sash (Malo). Photos courtesy of Bernice P. Bishop Museum, Honolulu.

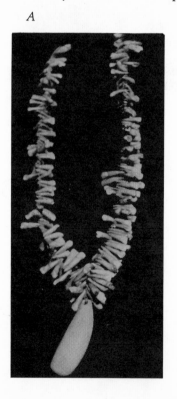
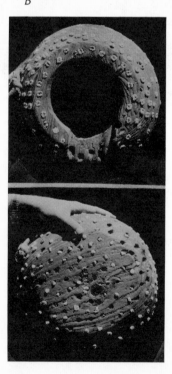

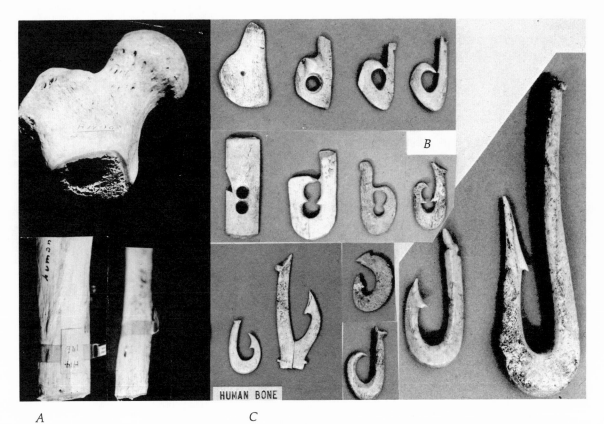

A   C

Fig. 54. Human bone fish hooks. *A*, the upper end of a right femur and upper bone shafts of right tibia and fibula showing cut sections of the bone-tubes. *B*, types of fish hooks and steps in their manufacture. *C*, fish hooks from human bones. Photos courtesy of Bernice P. Bishop Museum, Honolulu.

Pathology and Anomalies
of the Skeleton

An account documenting and illustrating the outstanding forms of bone pathology which have been positively identified in the Mokapu skeletal material has been published by Warner F. Bowers (1966). Much of the material in the following section is repetitious of that covered by Bowers, but it is offered here from the viewpoint of an anthropologist who recognizes deviation from the normal without necessarily knowing the causative factors known to the medically trained person, such as Bowers. For that reason, all deviations are included, no matter what the possible or probable causative agent. Conditions that are probably congenital anomalies are also included. The variations in structure that can be linked to function are discussed in the section on postcranial morphology, above.

CRANIUM

A curious bone condition of the crania of young and old alike of both sexes was observed and tabulated. This consisted of extra deposits of vault bone along the borders of the sutures in areas not covered by musculature, that is, high upon the parietals and frontal above the temporal lines, and on the occipital above the nuchal musculature. In addition, porosities appeared, usually in symmetrical patches, over much of these thickened bone areas. These porous patches appeared on the roofs of the orbits and on the palate; and sometimes large perforations, a millimeter or more in diameter, were found on the lower portions of the great wings of the sphenoid and adjoining portions of the pterygoid plates. Several outstanding examples are illustrated in Figure 55A, B, C. Nearly 96 percent of the male skulls and 88 percent of the female had such porosities somewhere, as indicated in Table 29. In the subadults there were fifty-two cases (35 percent) in which this condition occurred in the orbits, and twenty-eight cases (19 percent) in which other bones of the vault were afflicted.

In anthropological literature, this common bone condition has been termed osteoporosis (McKern

and Stewart, 1957, p. 15; Brues, 1959, pp. 67–68; Williams, quoted by Hooton, 1930, p. 317; Briggs, 1955, pp. 86–87; Snow, 1948a, p. 498). In medicine this term is used to describe a disease entity. Bowers (1966, p. 214) discusses the condition as found in the Mokapu material. Here, the term simply means porosities of the bone.

The cause of this peculiar condition, confined mostly to the bones of the head and face in the Mokapu series, is actually unknown. It may reflect dietary deficiencies. Ackerknecht (1953, p. 124) suggests avitaminosis along with possible mechanical causes as etiological factors. Such porosity was also noted in the remains of Americans imprisoned in the Korean War, who suffered privations for up to one and one-half years (McKern and Stewart, 1957, p. 15).

Fractures and injuries to the skull were found (see Fig. 56). Broken noses (healed fractures) were more common than broken long bones. They were found in 33 percent of the men and 29 percent of the women, some seventy individuals in all (see Fig. 57). This high rate of fracture of the nose is ascribed to fighting and perhaps marital difficulties, as well as accidents. Scalp wounds were recorded on 24 percent of the men and 15 percent of the women, a sex difference probably associated with the more strenuous male activities or occupational hazards. Seven men and three women had long styloid spines (temporal) which had been broken and healed during their lifetimes. This must have involved neck constrictions, such as strangling or blows along the side and under the jaw. Among the males there were also three cases in which the lower jaw was broken. Two involved the left condyle and one was an unhealed fracture of the right ramus where ordinarily it joins the horizontal body. This last, an extraordinary specimen, is shown in Figure 58A, B. The one broken lower jaw among the females displayed a fracture of the right ramus of the right side of the body which had healed smoothly near the position of the first molar.

Evidence of middle-ear infection was found in three men and one child (see Fig. 59). Exostoses of the ear hole occurred in one male and one female, with one completely occluded.

Peculiar subnasal pits or enlarged fossae were found on seven individuals, two females and five males; one occurred bilaterally, one on the right side, and five on the left. Although the fossae are all similar in appearance, the etiology may well be different. Cysts, apical abscesses, or even hereditary origin may explain their presence. Figure 60 presents six examples of this strange feature. *A* (H–253): A young man with a bilateral occurrence that appears to have had no pathological origin associated with dental disturbance. *B* (H–1362): Here the subnasal pit on the left appears to be associated with possible breakage of the left central incisor and the subsequent exposure of the pulp cavity and apical abscess; it is doubtful that a cyst was involved here. *C* (N–19): The only pit on the left side appears to have involved necrosis, possibly caused by either a cyst or an abscess, which in turn affected the tip of the central incisor immediately below it. *D* (H–91): Another young man shows a left fossa with pittings that may be evidence of bone reaction to disease, but no associated dental pathology. Two other examples (not illustrated), again young men, showed absorption of overlying alveolar tissue and of the root tips of the first three teeth on the upper left side, possibly caused by a cyst. *E* (H–121A): A female shows, in addition to the small pit on the left and left asymmetry, a thinning of the alveolar tissue covering the roots of the upper left front teeth. *F* (C–2 series): An adult male with a left subnasal pit and three teeth whose root-covering bone has become lost to the degree of exposure. Note again the left asymmetry.

Lopsided skulls were present in twenty individuals—eleven females and nine males. In each case one side of the occipital base was elevated unilaterally. This affected the normal carriage of the head by tipping it to either the left or the right. In three adult females and one boy the asymmetry was extreme and caused the individuals to incline their heads to the side, one to the left, and three to the right. The brief descriptions which follow give in some detail the structures affected by this asymmetry.[1]

H–2, a young adult female of 19–20 years, whose head droops to the right side. Figure 61 shows X-ray as well as gross views. The face (front) view is oriented so as to approximate the position during life. There may have been a unilateral failure of the neck muscles to function, particularly the sternocleidomastoid. The whole occiput is involved, with the base and the condyles markedly twisted to the right (clockwise), leaving the left occipital con-

1. I am indebted to Dr. Edward E. Hunt, Jr., for his guidance in the interpretation of these abnormalities during his visit in January 1957.

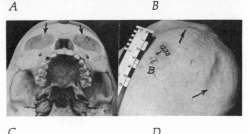

FIG. 55. Porosities of cortical bone of individuals of various ages. *A*, a 15-year-old female (85A); *B*, an adult male (1313); *C*, characteristic perforations of the orbital roof in a child of 6 to 7 years (C-37); *D*, a middle-aged female (1273) with depressed areas on the top side of the skull suggestive of healing.

dyle high (inferiorly low), and with it the left occipital base is enlarged. This head-droop involves many muscles and structures, most of which show a decided response to the force of gravity. The marked left facial asymmetry and twist to the right side can be seen plainly in the photographs showing the facial and oblique base views. The right mastoid process is the more massive, but the masseter area as well as the zygomatic arch are both smaller on the right side. This size difference is reflected in the thinness of the bone as well as the reduced area of muscle attachments. The coronoid process of the mandible is more spikelike (sharper and more elongated) on the affected side and shows more muscular grooving than on the left side.

It would appear here that the position of the head, tilted to the right, may have been accompanied by failure of the structures of the condyle and skull base and of the various muscles of the neck. The external pterygoid muscles show much less development on the right side, judging from the size of the plate and the sphenoid base. This fact is plainly revealed in the truncated gonial margin on the right side. The depressed right side of the skull base

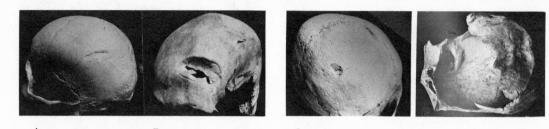

| A | B | C | D |

FIG. 56. *A* (H-180) and *B* (C-2 misc. 13) show old healed skull fractures. The failure to regenerate completely and bridge the gap in *B* is typical of many fractures of membranous bone. *D*, inner aspect of B, shows the degree of depression, probably asymptomatic because this is over a "silent" area. *C* (1369) shows a depressed fracture which is fresh, without any evidence of healing; possibly this fracture contributed to death.

FIG. 57. Healed fractures of the nose and cheek bones; the arrows point to the areas of healed injury. *A,* a female (1258); *B,* a male (1337); *C,* a female (1351); *D,* a male (H-258); *E,* a male (N-6); and *F,* a male (N-27).

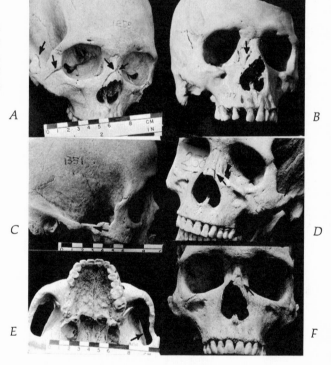

affected virtually all of the structures in proximity, including the petrous portion of the right temporal. The foramen magnum is likewise twisted and, as mentioned above, the skull base lateral to it is the point of lowest elevation. In particular, the sheath in front of the styloid is bent curiously forward and the ear hole is more circular than that on the left side.

1321 (Fig. 62B, D). This female, like H–2, inclined her head markedly to the right side with similar morphological adaptations. Perhaps the greatest difference may be noted in the marked left facial asymmetry and in the structure of the right ascending ramus. This side of the jaw is smaller but noticeably thicker than the left, and shows larger relief for muscle attachments. The right coronoid process is likewise longer, more spiked, and thicker. Looking at the base of the skull (base up), we note the very marked depression (elevation) of the right condyle and the region just lateral and posterior to it. Indeed, the skull vault in its posterior aspect presents a very marked left asymmetry which may have been caused or reinforced somewhat by the individual's habits during her lifetime. Whatever the cause of this deforming asymmetry (failure of the neck muscles to function properly or some similar cause), this girl probably had to sleep with the head tilted toward the right shoulder and drawn downward so that the habitual sleeping position was also an important factor in the shaping of her head. We note in the right temporal fossa considerable relief running from a deep groove diagonally across the temporal bone at the zygomatic process and extending up onto a rounded ridge or low mound which gives way anteriorly to a deepened sphenoid depression. Like H–2, the right mastoid process is larger, longer, and more massive than that on the left. Unlike H–2, it is the left external pterygoid plate which is the smaller in size and development. In Figure 62D the facial view shows the tilted position of the head.

It should be noted that although the permanent dentition is complete (all thirty-two teeth) and functional without any sort of disease, the lower right second molar is rotated 90 degrees counterclockwise (lingually-buccally). Whether or not this has any association with the marked forces of asymmetries cannot now be determined.

N–40 (Fig. 62A, C). This young adult female presents a marked droop of the head to the left side with accompanying morphological asymmetries.

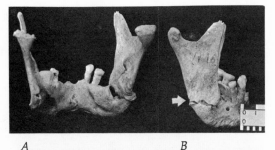

A   B

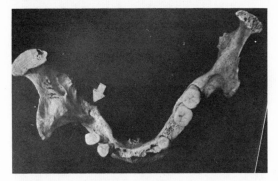

C

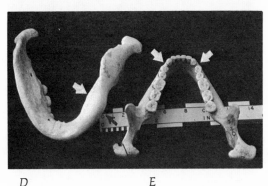

D   E

FIG. 58. Fractured jaws and an anomaly. *A*, back, and *B*, right side views of unhealed fracture of the right ascending ramus near its base and the resulting foreshortening of the right side of the jaw (N-16). *C*, top view shows the ramus advanced forward onto the molar tooth area; the mandibular canal was preserved. *D*, a healed fracture, right side, center of the body (1314). *E*, an anomalous gap between canines and first molars (H-40).

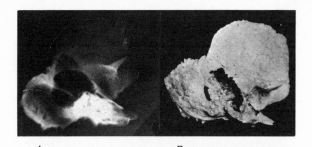

A   B

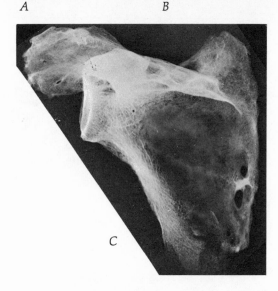

C

FIG. 59. *A*, this right temporal bone (HX) shows evidence of middle ear infection with osteosclerosis and erosion of bone; the remaining bone structure in this X-ray view is normal. *B*, gross view of the same specimen. *C*, X-ray view of a right scapula shows osteomyelitis with gross deformity of the acromial process, areas of increased and decreased density, and areas of bone destruction. Osteomyelitis of the scapula is rare.

Figure 62*C* shows the lopsidedness of the face as well as that of the right side of the skull base. In looking at the base the malformed foramen magnum is very apparent along with the depression centering around the left condyle. As in the others described, but on the opposite side, we find that the skull base shows a contrast in development on the left side with that on the right. In the first place the left mastoid process is two or three times larger than that of the right. This specimen shows very large dehiscences of both auditory floors, which may or may not be associated with the neck condition. The left temporal fossa is smaller than that of the right side. Its

diminution may be ascribed to greater muscle relief, which consists of the same diagonal groove above the zygomatic process with an accompanying bulge along the inferior margin of the temporal squamous and a deeper "lopsided" groove to the sphenoid. Note in passing that the upper left third molar is carious. Unfortunately, the pterygoid plates are all broken and cannot be observed and described. The face is twisted toward the deformed side.

H–291 (Fig. 61*D*). This is a female child with a dental age of 6 to 7 years, the only one in the series in which the asymmetries associated with a crooked neck can be observed during the prepuberty period of growth. The facial and cranial asymmetries are not as marked as in the adult cases, although the skull base does present an elevated area (depressed, right side up) centered about the right occipital condyle—that is, the head was tilted to the right. Even at this early age the bending of the right temporal petrous portion along with a smaller foramen ovale and the skewing of the skull base as well as that of the face are noticeable. We know that during growth these lopsided contours increase and become more marked, as revealed by the adult specimens. The mandible and its relationship to the skull present a lower and possibly defective articular eminence on the left side (which may represent an adaptation to the underthrust jaw). Perhaps because the left side of the face is "stretched out"—that is, twisted toward the right side—the mandible has been thrust forward thus in its function. In addition, there is a crossbite present on the right side. Here on the affected side, the buccal surfaces of the lower deciduous molars occlude on the outside of the same surfaces of the upper deciduous molars, an altogether abnormal condition.

In addition to these cases of extreme asymmetry, both sexes showed noticeable left nasal and left facial asymmetries, common to all people.

Arthritis affected the bones of the skull as well as the long bones and the spine. Evidence of it was found on temperomandibular joints and at the base of the skull where it articulates with the neck vertebrae.

There was one subadult, five or six years old, with a baby-sized skull. This condition, termed microcephaly, is usually due to premature closure of the sutures which prevents cranial growth so necessary to normal development. There were two other cases of arrested growth of the skull—a seven-year-old with premature closure of the sagittal and left coro-

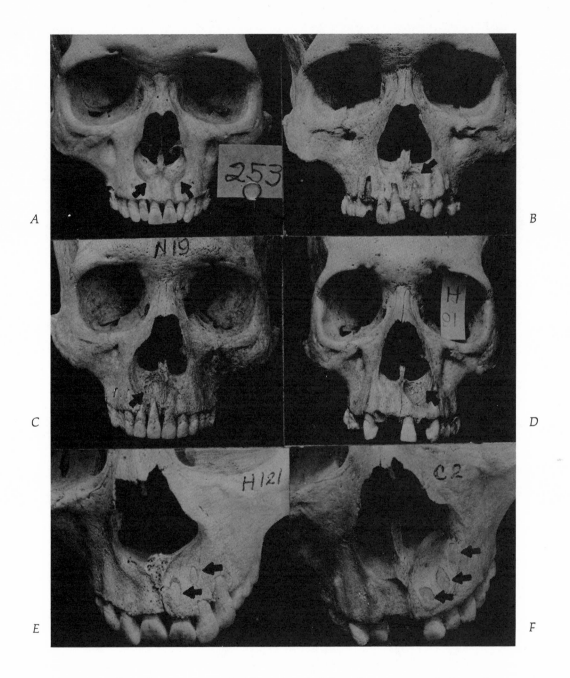

FIG. 60. Subnasal pits. *A*, a male (H-253) with bilateral occurrence of pits and no dental involvement. *B*, another male (H-1362) with a left pit and an upper incisor apical abscess. *C*, a male (N-19) with a large right pit and a central incisor abscess; note asymmetry of the right nasal opening. *D*, a male (H-91) with a large left pit and resulting asymmetry. *E*, a female (H-121A), and *F*, a male (C-2 series) with left fossae and asymmetries, exposed, eroded root tips of the incisors and, in *F*, of the canine as well. Photo *E* and *F* courtesy of Dr. Samuel B. Rabkin.

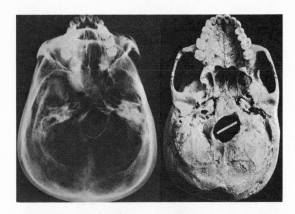

A   B

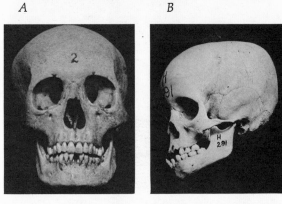

C   D

FIG. 61. "Tilt" heads. X-ray (A) and gross view (B and C) of a young woman (H-2) with a crooked neck, vault, and face. Her head tilted to the right side. Bar indicates degree of asymmetry. D, side view of a 6- or 7-year-old girl (H-291) with a right side tilt of the head and malocclusion of the jaws. Note the underthrust lower jaw and a right crossbite.

nal sutures, and an eleven- to twelve-year-old with closure of the sagittal and right side of the lambdoidal sutures. Normally these sutures do not begin to unite until the early twenties and after.

Dental pathology was prevalent among these Mokapuans. Alveoclasia, or periodontal infection, was widespread; indeed, on early manifestations, some evidence of bone recession and necrosis could be found in most adults (see Fig. 63). These pathological alveolar conditions appear to be the very ones that result from vitamin C deficiency of the diet. Summerson (1954, p. 1227) reports that profound pathological changes of the teeth and gums, especially the vascular pulp, periodontal and gingival tissues, occur as a result of this deficiency. Bleeding and sore gums are clinical symptoms which

accompany gum recession and finally bone deterioration, such as is seen in various stages in these Hawaiian jaws. According to Miller (Appendix E, below), the Hawaiians apparently had no fruit other than the mountain apple and plantain as possible sources of vitamin C.

The effects of this deficiency are present in both jaws (see Fig. 29 and Appendix C, Fig. C6), but the lower jaws seem to exhibit more extensive destruction of the bony alveolar tissues in which the teeth are maintained. Obviously when this bone foundation with the gums is destroyed the otherwise sound teeth are freed and fall out.

Dental abscesses were present in 66 percent of the men and 49 percent of the women. It is probable that these abscesses were associated with alveoclasia. Some of the worst cases included necrotic perforations of the maxillary sinuses (4 percent of the men and 6 percent of the women had such painful conditions).

The occurrence of dental decay as reported in the section on dentition, above, was as follows: of the 144 men, only 27 (19 percent), and of the 134 women, 19 (14 percent) had caries. While these figures destroy the tradition of perfect dentition among the native Hawaiians, the proportions do not seem excessive when compared with present-day rates found in North American whites and Europeans in general.

Broken teeth in the form of either chipped edges or loss of a cusp or even of a whole tooth were a common occurrence, particularly among the women (18 percent, contrasted with but 6 percent of the men). This is a significant sex and occupational (functional) difference.

Mrs. Pukui, when questioned about the way in which Hawaiians might have used their teeth in the performance of manual tasks, responded that the women in particular used their teeth in many ways while going about their daily work. In the twisting and making of cord and in the cutting of various fibers, including cord; in the cutting and stripping of the midribs of the hala (Pandanus) and the ti plant leaves; in holding all manner of things, as well as in cracking nuts, we have a variety of activities in which the teeth would have been exposed to such stresses as would cause fracture. Upon two or three individuals, marks of unusual wear—concave surfaces into the edges of the incisor teeth—were noted. Perhaps this involved the habitual biting of some object in the same place throughout a lifetime.

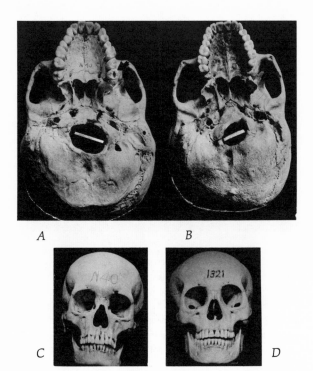

A   B

C   D

FIG. 62. "Tilt" heads of two young women. *A*
and *C* (N-40) tilted to the left, and *B* and *D*
(1321) tilted to the right. Note the twisted, lopsided base, vault, and face. Black arrow in *A*
shows a decayed third molar. Bars indicate degree of asymmetry.

Extra bone deposits (exostoses) were found along
the facial borders of the maxillary alveoli in 23
percent of the women and 16 percent of the men;
mandibular exostoses were present in only 4 percent
of the women and 3.6 percent of the men.

Other bone deposits or tori on the palate or along
the inside surfaces of the mandibular alveolus were
uncommon. No large mass, either ridge or mound
form, was found. However, some 6.4 percent of
women and 5.6 percent of the men showed small
torus formations. These deposits of extra bone may
have been functionally associated with mastica-
tion (Hooton, 1918; Lasker, 1946, p. 296).

POSTCRANIAL SKELETON

Just as porosities of the skull and alveoclasia of the
dental arches were impressive by their frequency
and extent, so was the evidence of arthritis in the
postcranial skeleton. Arthritic changes in bone appeared in 53 percent of the adult skeletons. A tabulation of joints affected (see Table 30) includes the

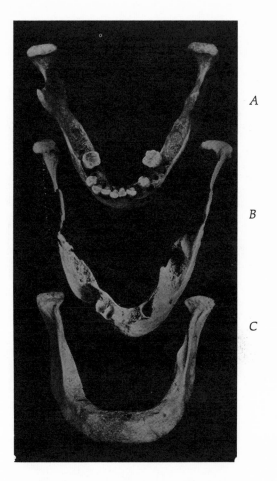

A

B

C

FIG. 63. Last stages in tooth loss. *A* (H-95)
shows abscess pockets (necrosis); *B* (H-
142) gives evidence of healing following
loss of molars; *C* (H-146) is edentulous.

shoulder, elbow, wrist, hip, knee, and ankle, and
joints of the hands and feet. Eburnation of some of
these arthritic joints was evidence of destruction of
the cartilages (see Figs. 64 and 65). Where movement of bone on bone occurred the articulating surfaces were both polished and grooved. Table 31
shows the occurrence of eburnation.

But the most dramatic evidence of arthritis was
found along the backbone. In typical cases of arthritis deformans (osteoarthritis), the lumbar vertebrae show bony spurs (osteophytes) first. These
outgrowths may develop into interfingering rough
borders which make movement limited and painful.
In the most extreme cases the arthritic outgrowths
join each other, literally fusing one vertebra to the
next, above and below—that is, ankylosis (see Figs.

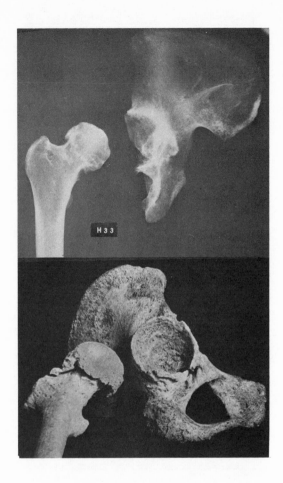

FIG. 64. This 30-year-old female (H-33) had marked traumatic osteoarthritis of the right femoral head and acetabulum with increase in bone density, spur formation, loss of cartilage, and eburnation of the weight-bearing surfaces; top, X-ray; bottom, gross view.

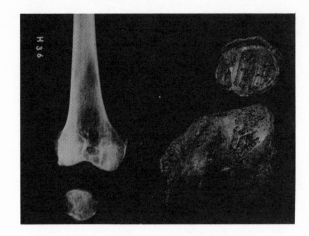

FIG. 65. Osteoarthritis at the knee (H-36) is shown with marked eburnation and actual scratch marks on the bone surfaces in the direction of motion. The lateral femoral condyle shows marked increase in density on X-ray (left). With the cartilage obviously destroyed, this must have been a very painful knee.

66, 67, 68). The joints of the vertebrae appear to be fused together, as if by candle wax which in melting has flowed down over the candle and candlestick. This fusion prevents movement, the bony "wax" holding the joints in bondage. This condition was evident in the Mokapu skeletons. In addition there were two cases of "bamboo" spine in which the ligaments became calcified and the vertebrae were joined so as to give the appearance of one segmented bone, an indication of rheumatoid arthritis (see Fig. 69).

Altogether, 164 spinal columns were examined. Of this number, 66 were male and 98 female. In 127, or 77 percent, there was evidence of some degree of arthritis; 73 were judged as representing beginning arthritis, 39 as moderate, and 15 as advanced or extreme. Thirty-five, or 21 percent, had arthritis in

all areas of the spine—cervical, thoracic, lumbar, and sacral—usually in varying degrees, with an advanced stage in the lumbar region. It is significant that 52 percent were afflicted in the lumbar region. (See Fig. 70.)

The location of the lumbar region as the first area of arthritic affliction appears to be connected with function. In the initial stages the upper rims of the bodies of the vertebrae (centra) usually show the first spurs. Many of the known activities of the Hawaiian people—for example, planting, climbing, paddling canoes, and hula dancing—require motion of the middle and low back. Stewart (1931, pp. 51–61) has found that Eskimos, who do a great deal of their work bending sharply from the waist, become afflicted first in the lumbar region. Early prehistoric Indians from Kentucky (Snow, 1948a, p. 498) likewise were found to have more arthritis in the lumbar section, whereas the thoracic and cervical regions were relatively free of arthritic lipping. In contrast, among our contemporary white-collar workers, the first evidence of arthritis is more commonly found in the neck vertebrae.

In addition to these arthritic changes, fifteen cases of vertebral collapse were found, evenly distributed between the sexes. Here the anterior height of the vertebra was reduced as far as possible, leaving a wedge-shaped centrum in the anteroposterior plane. This collapse usually occurred in the first or second

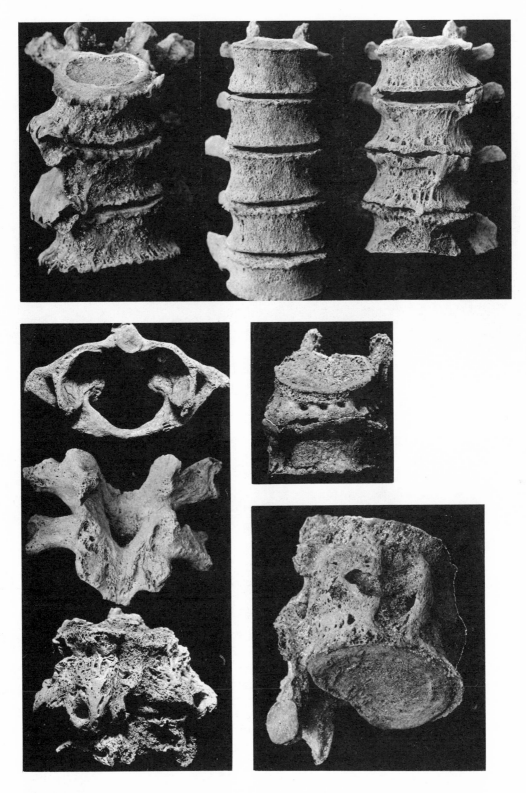

FIG. 66. These spinal segments from various individuals show degrees of osteoarthritic changes with bridging osteophytes, ankylosis, and collapse of body in some instances.

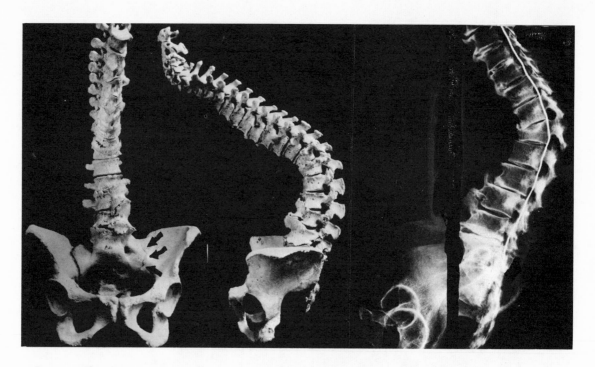

FIG. 67. This spine (H-50) shows extreme osteoarthritic involvement with bridging osteophytes and actual collapse of the body of the first lumbar vertebra. The X-ray on the right shows these changes in architectural detail.

FIG. 68. Front and side views of a male spine (C-2 series, U-8) showing extreme osteoarthritis.

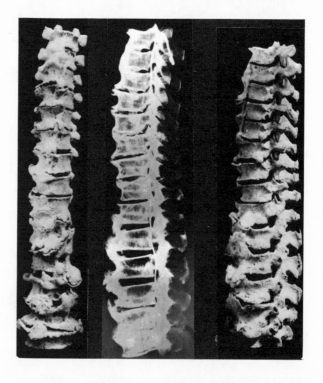

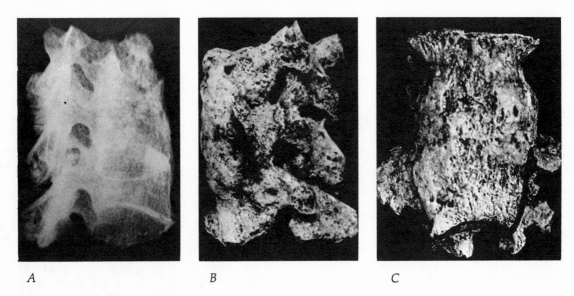

A   B   C

FIG. 69. An example (H-86) of "bamboo spine" or rheumatoid arthritis, a rare occurrence in the series. Ossification of the spinal ligaments is shown in X-ray view *A,* and in gross views of left side *B,* and front *C.*

lumbar vertebra, or in the dorsal-lumbar zone of transition. There was one case in a female of the tenth thoracic collapse; three cases, two females and one male, involving the twelfth thoracic. In eleven cases, two vertebrae were involved, both first and second lumbars; three cases involved three lumbar vertebrae; and in one case the fourth lumbar, along with the third, had given way under weight-bearing and lifting stresses. These people in life were what we call hunchbacks, and in several extreme cases these unfortunate people were so bent over that they walked with their faces toward the ground (see Fig. 71). Mrs. Pukui, from her knowledge of Hawaiian folkways, gave them the name "rat-eyed," which her people used. Hormonal and decalcification changes were the probable causes of these spine deformities. The functional stresses placed on the back by the activities peculiar to these people were doubtless a final contributory agent.

Spondylolisthesis, a congenital separation of the vertebral arch from the body, was found in seventeen cases—eight adult males, eight adult females, and one teen-aged female. Most of these separate neural arches occurred bilaterally in the fifth, or last, lumbar vertebra. One case, a male, involved the third lumbar, and two cases involved the fourth. In one man the separation was on the left side only. The occurrence of this hereditary feature was 10.5 percent for the total adult population. This is about half the rate of occurrence found among the earliest

Kentucky Indians at Indian Knoll (18 percent of the males and 22 percent of the females) and also less than the incidence found among Eskimos by Stewart (1931, pp. 51–61). (See Fig. 72.)

Action in the lower spine (the lumbars) involving these particular joints is primarily anteroposterior (bending over) with some movement sideways when combined with torsion (twisting). The Hawaiians in their very active and often strenuous pursuits subjected their bodies and backs to just these types of movement in bending over to plant, cultivate, and harvest crops of taro, yam, and sweet potato, and in climbing coconut palms. This last activity requires the flexion and extension of the legs, plus movement of the lower spine and pelvis. The warrior in wrestling, grappling, and parrying his opponent's blows of the staff would use back muscles in varied states of contraction and extension; and in paddling the outrigger canoes, warriors and fishermen alike would pivot at the lower waist. In all these activities separate neural arches would tend to afford their unaware owners a greater amount of supple flexibility.

Another spinal abnormality was observed—spina bifida, which is a congenital anomaly (see Fig. 72C). In this condition the spinous processes fail to unite and in extreme cases allow herniation of the spinal cord. There were seven cases in which the spinous process of the sixth or seventh cervical vertebra, or both, showed separation either as an eyelet or as a completely open slit. In the sacral region five cases,

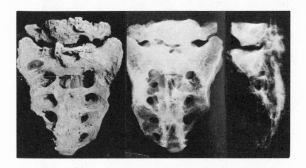

FIG. 70. Osteoarthritis of the lumbosacral area (H-9) is shown with destruction of the anterior inferior lip of the lumbar body and osteophytes on the sacrum; gross view and front and side views in X-ray.

FIG. 71. Dr. and Mrs. Snow assist "Mrs. Bent-back" to "stand." H-50, an old woman, was crippled by arthritis, had a collapsed vertebra, and only one (front) tooth.

three men and two women, were recorded. Taber's *Cyclopedic Medical Dictionary* (1944, p. 576) lists the lumbar region as the site of 50 percent of all contemporary cases of spina bifida. The absence of the condition in this region at Mokapu may be explained by natural death or infanticide of babies so afflicted, or it may represent a genetic strain free of this weakness. Spina bifida is listed by Snyder as a semidominant lethal gene (Montagu, 1951, p. 415).

Other abnormalities of the spine found among the Mokapuans included a fused sacroiliac joint on the left side of one female with extreme osteoarthritis (Fig. 67) and six males and two females with sacra of six segments.

Additional characteristics of the spine and pelvis that deviated from the normal were discussed in the section on postcranial morphology, above, because they appear to have been linked to function rather than to pathology or congenital anomalies. The causes cannot be definitely determined, of course, so the choice was arbitrary, based on my judgment.

The late Dr. J. Warren White, orthopedic surgeon of the Shriners' Hospital in Honolulu, was interested in the incidence of certain congenital deformities present or absent in this series as compared to the incidence in the present-day Hawaiian or part-Hawaiian population. The two cases with dislocation of the hip—one subadult female, bilateral (Fig. 73), and one old adult—he believed were "unquestionably postnatal in origin and are the result of slipped capital epiphyses, coxa plana, or trauma." Congenital dislocation of the hip is absent now in pure-

blooded Polynesians, as far as the records of patients examined at Shriners' Hospital, Honolulu, reveal.

Congenital clubfoot (*kukuʻe*) was present in three individuals, bilateral in one instance. The incidence of seven per thousand reported by the Territorial Board of Health in 1958 is precisely the same as that in this series. However, the incidence of cleft palate in the Board of Health report is the same as that of clubfoot, but no evidence of cleft palate was found in the total skeletal population of Mokapu.

The only other major pathological condition observed was fracture. The incidence of postcranial bone fracture is as follows: ulna, 9; radius, 7; humerus, 6; tibia and fibula, 5; fibula alone, 2; femur, 2; metacarpals, 3; ribs, 5; pelvis, 2; patella, 2; coccyx and sacrum, 2; clavicle, 1; arch, fourth lumbar vertebra, 1. (See also Fig. 74.) In an active, vigorous, war-club-wielding population such as these early

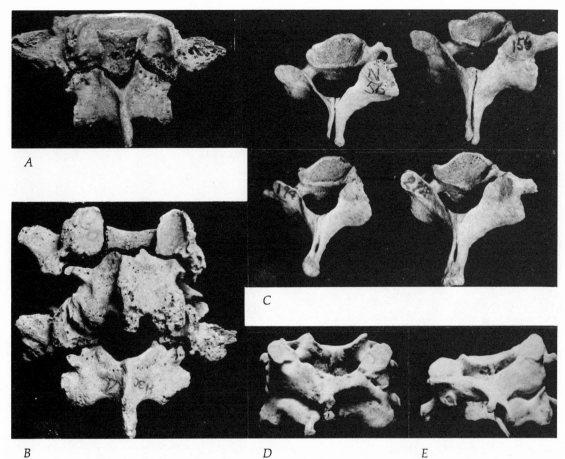

A

B

C

D

E

FIG. 72. Congenital spine anomalies. *A*, spondylolisthesis in lumbar 5, and *B*, the same in lumbar 4 and 5. *C*, open spinous processes of lower cervical vertebrae. Absence of spinous process of *D*, right, and *E*, left sides in cervical vertebrae and fusion of the bodies.

A

B

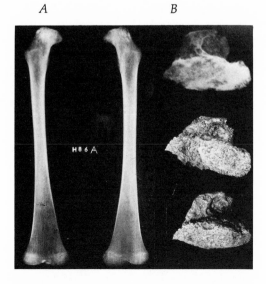

FIG. 73. *A* (H-86), anteverted femoral necks represent congenital dislocation of the hip of a 15-year-old female. *B*, X-ray and gross views of an old dislocation (left femoral head) with eburnation.

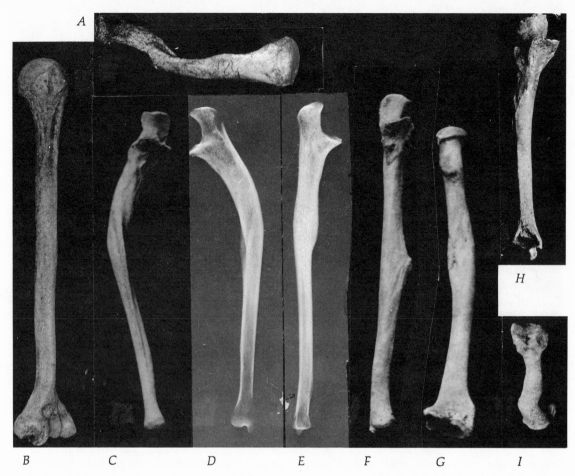

FIG. 74. *A*, fracture of the clavicle in this series is very rare, this being one of three. *B*, fracture of the lower humeral shaft is an area where deformity is common and in this left humerus there is posterior angulation of the distal end following fracture. *C, D* (X-ray), marked bowing has followed fracture of the shaft of the right ulna; even this degree of deformity may not interfere with function. *E*, healing in excellent position and alignment is demonstrated in this left ulna (X-ray). *F, G*, both bones of the left forearm were fractured and such a fracture often causes cross-union of the bones; in this case, it can be seen how such a deformity might eventuate. *H*, right ulna shows an unhealed fracture of the shaft. *I*, fracture of the right second metacarpal.

Hawaiians represent, it is remarkable that the incidence of broken bones is so low. No fractures whatever were found in the subadult group.

Most fractures encountered showed remarkably good unions. Not only was there good alignment of the parts but there were no evidences of undue torsion. Usually the sites of bone healing were remarkably small, compact, and well-formed. It seems reasonable to believe that these Mokapuans had the care of skilled bone-setters (*kahunas*), whose knowledge of anatomy and the physiological processes of bone repair was extensive and time-proven. In addition to the development of techniques in setting broken bones they must also have had remedies which were effective in reducing swelling and bringing the separated bone ends into line so that they would heal properly. In any event, we can conclude from the excellent bone healing found that good care under skilled practitioners was available to these people of Mokapu.

To complete the discussion, the presence of three females with sharply angled rib cages, termed "pigeon breasted," must be noted, as well as a single case of a man with amputation of the left humerus, well healed at midsection. (See Fig. 75.)

As an addition to this section on pathology and anomalies of the skeleton, the complete report on selected specimens by Lent C. Johnson of the Armed Services Institute of Pathology will be found as Appendix B, below. It is a valuable addition to this book because the conclusions are the result of detailed study.

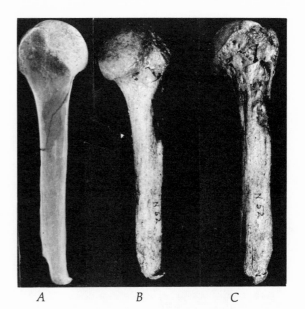

A   B   C

FIG. 75. These X-ray (*A*) and gross views of *B*, posterior, and *C*, anterior surfaces reveal the only evidence of major amputation in the series (N-52). Clean healing without osteomyelitis is demonstrated.

Conclusions

The purpose of this study was to determine what the Mokapu skeletal remains could tell us about the lives of these prehistoric Hawaiians. Now, in concluding, I can give partial answers and indicate many more unanswered questions.

Although it was not possible to determine an exact date for all the people of Mokapu, we do know that they lived before the Europeans came to the islands, 200 or more years ago. These Hawaiians were remarkably homogeneous according to various statistical measures. Stature and body build have been determined; detailed characteristics of the skull, jaws, and dentition have been described; length of life, both the average and the range, is known; their diseases and injuries have been diagnosed and described as correctly as is possible at this time. We have found the marks and changes on the bony skeleton that give evidence of their way of life, such as extraordinary musculature, shaped or deformed skulls, and facets which could have been acquired only from squatting and from backward tilt of the tibial head associated with the bent-knee gait. There are many more characteristics less obvious.

From my own observations and those of other experts, I believe the Mokapuans represent part of an isolated breeding group, forming its own distinctive genotypes and the expressed phenotype—a case of microevolution, as it were. This group must have contained many of the genes which linked it to its origins (Synder, 1949), and yet its isolated geographical location caused it to evolve into a kind apart. These people were Polynesian by immediate relationship, but separation from their kind by the waters of the Pacific caused them to become unique.

Hulse (1957, p. 43) says,

A physical type is not a racial stock, but selection and isolation may transform what was simply a type into a stock, just as hybridization may eliminate a stock, but leave types. Whenever, either inadvertently or by design, migrants are a select group rather than a random sample of the population from which they were derived, the possibility for the emergence of a new racial stock is created. Should the migrant group remain genetically isolated, such a stock will come into existence. If circumstances lead to a considerable increase in the numbers of such a group it will even be recognized as a racial stock. In the course of human history, many such groups have had only a brief existence, but others have flourished. I suspect that both American Indians and Polynesians originated in this manner.

Other studies by Sullivan (1924), Buck (1945), Shapiro (1943), Birdsell (1951), and Howells (1959) have indicated the strong probability that these Pacific island populations are a racial blend, resulting from both their place of origin and their later contacts with other populations.

Certain physical features that I observed appear to have been genetic characters influenced more or less by environment. These are listed below and I venture to infer that they are useful units of the Hawaiian genetic pool represented at Mokapu.

CHARACTERS OF THE MOKAPUANS, POSSIBLY GENETIC IN ORIGIN

1) Nose bone anomalies (absence of one, both, or parts thereof).

2) Large-sized teeth with sex differences.

3) Shovel-shaped incisors with midline twist and marginal enamel ridges.

4) Absence of M_3—especially mandibular.

5) Cusp patterns including: (a) Carabelli's cusps; (b) protostylids.

6) Rocker jaws, with both prominent chins and subchin arches and a tendency for absence of M_3.

7) Septal perforations of olecranon fossae.

8) Interlocked lower thoracic and lumbar vertebral articulations (perhaps functional).

9) V-cleft A. P. grooves of sacral bases.

10) Spondylolisthesis.

11) Club feet.

12) Brow ridges, glabellar development, and regions of nasion depression.

13) Inca bone (divided occiput).

14) Occipital tori and hook (neck peg) (perhaps functional).

15) Canine fossae.

16) Prenasal fossae (nasal sill region).

17) Palate predominantly hyperbolic in shape and straight sided.

18) Palatal tori (perhaps functional).

19) Mental foramen, position in area of premolars 1 and 2, direction oblique, posterior-superior.

20) Supernumerary teeth.

21) Size sequence in mandibular molars 1 > 2 > 3 or 2 < 3.

22) Y–5 pattern on lower molars.

23) Premaxillary suture to incisive canal persistent in infants and children.

Many other features were obviously acquired by each individual and were not transmitted through heredity to their descendants. Those physical traits formed by occupational and other functional activities are listed below.

FEATURES OF THE MOKAPUANS, POSSIBLY ACQUIRED

1) Large-sized bones with extensive areas of rugged muscles which helped mold the cross-section shapes.

2) Shaped heads (deformation).

3) Chipped and broken teeth.

4) Extra elbow joints on lateral surfaces (possibly associated with septal aperture).

5) V-shaped inferior articular facets and "wraparounds" in lower-back vertebrae.

6) Accessory sacroiliac joints.

7) Squatting facets at hips, knees, and ankles.

8) Torsion of thigh and shin bones (from squatting).

9) Retroversion of tibial plateaus (bent-knee gait and stance).

10) Location of arthritis in the spine (lumbar region affected first).

The probable origins of these early Hawaiians and, for that matter, of Polynesians as a whole, are intriguingly obscure. The vast problem of human population origins is a complex one and beyond the scope of this report. Very few facts revealed by this study definitely link the Polynesian population to any original homeland. Some of the findings—for instance, shovel-shaped teeth and large prominent cheek bones—bespeak Mongoloid connections; large brow ridges are similar to the Australoids; prominent chins are commonly found in most Europeans; physical types among the crania point to Australoid, Negroid, and Mongoloid types. All of these facts add credence to the belief of most anthropologists that the Polynesians originated in Southeast Asia. The burden of proof can better be found in the cultural baggage of the far-flung migrators of Polynesia (Spoehr, 1957, pp. 176–82).

This study, which is primarily an objective description of the people of Mokapu based on their skeletal remains, has attempted to assess the role of function, culture, and physical environment in the shaping of certain features. It shows that much of importance lies in this vast area of human ecology.

Obviously this study is only a beginning. We suffer from a dearth of information on the living descendants of the early Hawaiians. A few of the particular areas that merit investigation are body weight (Roberts [1953] indicates that Hawaiians outweigh all other groups), surface area, fat folds (distribution of tissue), dentition and its pattern today, serology (an attempt was made to study serology of the Mokapu population by means of techniques devised for dry bones, but technical difficulties prevented its completion), genetic patterns, and the factors that produce the rocker jaw. Such studies should be initiated before more admixture of the population brings additional complexities.[1]

The people who lived at Mokapu in earlier times have given us a hazy glimpse into their era, telling us much of how they lived and challenging us to learn more about their descendants.

1. Dr. Snow initiated such a study in 1964–1965, but the data remained unanalyzed at the time of his death. The data are now in the keeping of Dr. William M. Bass, Department of Anthropology, University of Tennessee, Knoxville, and are available for study.

Tables

Note: All measurements, with the exception of those of the teeth, were made with standard anthropometric instruments of the Martin design and recorded to the nearest millimeter.

In the tabulation, compilation, and statistical treatment of the data, the following method was used for determining the significant decimal values. All results were carried out to two decimal places. To evaluate the significance of the first decimal, the size of the second was considered. For both even and odd first decimals, second decimals through 4 were ignored; second decimals 6 and above raised the first decimal to the next higher digit. Where the second decimal was 5 and the first was an even number, the 5 was ignored, the first decimal remaining the same (for example, .25 = .2). When the second decimal was 5 and the first was an odd number, the latter was raised to the next digit (for example, .35 = .4).

Table 1
Mokapu Census, Totals

Series	Total Series		Subadults		Adults	
	No.	% of Total	No.	% of Total	No.	% of Total
H Series	668	57.0	246	21.0	422	36.0
W Series	169	14.4	23	2.0	146	12.5
N Series	98	8.4	31	2.6	67	5.7
C-1 Series	97	8.3	16	1.4	81	6.9
C-2 Series	139	11.9	17	1.4	122	10.4
Total	1,171	100.0	333	28.4	838	71.6

Table 2

Mokapu Census, Adults in Series by Sexes

Total Series

Age in Years	Both Sexes No.	%	Males No.	%	Females No.	%
20.6 - 30.5	454*	54.2	172	43.2	281	64.0
30.6 - 40.5	338	40.3	200	50.3	138	31.4
40.6 - 50.5	43	5.1	24	6.0	19	4.3
50.6 - Over	3	0.4	2	0.5	1	0.3
Total	838*	100.0	398	100.0	439	100.0
		100.0		47.6		52.4

H Series

Age in Years	Both Sexes No.	%	Males No.	%	Females No.	%
20.6 - 30.5	206	48.8	68	37.0	138	58.0
30.6 - 40.5	191	45.3	105	57.1	86	36.2
40.6 - 50.5	23	5.4	10	5.4	13	5.4
50.6 - Over	2	0.5	1	0.5	1	0.4
Total	422	100.0	184	100.0	238	100.0
		100.0		43.6		56.4

W Series

Age in Years	Both Sexes No.	%	Males No.	%	Females No.	%
20.6 - 30.5	96	65.8	43	55.1	53	77.9
30.6 - 40.5	47	32.2	33	42.3	14	20.6
40.6 - 50.5	3	2.0	2	2.6	1	1.5
50.6 - Over	0	0.0	0	0.0	0	0.0
Total	146	100.0	78	100.0	68	100.0
		100.0		53.5		46.5

N Series

Age in Years	Both Sexes No.	%	Males No.	%	Females No.	%
20.6 - 30.5	45	67.1	26	63.4	19	73.0
30.6 - 40.5	20	30.0	13	31.7	7	27.0
40.6 - 50.5	2	2.9	2	4.9	0	0.0
50.6 - Over	0	0.0	0	0.0	0	0.0
Total	67	100.0	41	100.0	26	100.0
		100.0		61.2		38.8

C-1 Series

Age in Years	Both Sexes No.	%	Males No.	%	Females No.	%
20.6 - 30.5	44*	53.7	17	43.6	26	63.4
30.6 - 40.5	34	42.5	19	48.7	15	36.6
40.6 - 50.5	3	3.7	3	7.7	0	0.0
50.6 - Over	0	0.0	0	0.0	0	0.0
Total	81*	100.0	39	100.0	41	100.0
		100.0		48.2		51.8

C-2 Series

Age in Years	Both Sexes No.	%	Males No.	%	Females No.	%
20.6 - 30.5	63	51.6	18	32.1	45	68.2
30.6 - 40.5	46	37.7	30	53.6	16	24.2
40.6 - 50.5	12	9.9	7	12.5	5	7.6
50.6 - Over	1	0.8	1	1.8	0	0.0
Total	122	100.0	56	100.0	66	100.0
		100.0		53.5		46.5

*Sex unknown in one case, C-1 Series.

Table 3

Mokapu Census, Subadults in Series,
Sexes Combined

Age	Total Series		H Series		W Series		N Series		C-1 Series		C-2 Series	
	No.	%	No.	%	No.	%	No.	%	No.	%	No.	%
Fetus	8	2.4	8	3.2	0	0.0	0	0.0	0	0.0	0	0.0
N.B. - 3 mo.	18	5.4	16	6.5	1	4.4	1	3.2	0	0.0	0	0.0
4 - 6 mo.	11	3.3	11	4.5	0	0.0	0	0.0	0	0.0	0	0.0
7 - 11 mo.	22	6.6	19	7.7	0	0.0	1	3.2	0	0.0	2	11.8
1 - 3.5 yrs.	95	28.5	77	31.3	0	0.0	9	29.0	7	43.8	2	11.8
3.6 - 5.5 yrs.	38	11.4	24	9.8	8	34.8	3	9.7	1	6.2	2	11.8
5.6 - 6.5 yrs.	27	8.1	16	6.5	3	13.0	6	19.4	0	0.0	2	11.8
6.6 - 8.5 yrs.	25	7.5	19	7.7	1	4.4	1	3.2	3	18.8	1	5.9
8.6 - 10.5 yrs.	13	3.9	9	3.7	2	8.7	0	0.0	1	6.2	1	5.9
10.6 - 12.5 yrs.	26	7.8	17	6.9	2	8.7	3	9.7	2	12.5	2	11.8
12.6 - 16.5 yrs.	24	7.2	15	6.1	2	8.7	2	6.4	1	6.2	4	23.5
16.6 - 20.5 yrs.	26	7.8	15	6.1	4	17.4	5	16.1	1	6.2	1	5.9
Total	333	100.0	246	100.0	23	100.0	31	100.0	16	100.0	17	100.0

Table 4

Average Age of Adults at Death,
Mokapu and Other Series

Series	Sex	No.	Average Age in Years	Average, Sexes Combined
Mokapu	M	295	31.91	30.45
	F	336	28.99	
Indian Knoll*	M	260	31.1*	27.1*
	F	191	23.1*	
Modern American	M		67.3	70.4
Whites†	F		73.6	

*Snow, 1948a. As a result of a reevaluation of age criteria
made in 1959-1960, the ages of both sexes averaged higher than
originally estimated, 32 years for males and 30 years for females,
for a combined average of 31 years.

†Krogman, 1958, p. 246.

Table 5

Measurements (in mm.) and Indices, Mokapu and Other Hawaiian Crania*

Measurement	No.	Mean + S.E.	S.D. + S.E.	V.	Range	No.	Mean + S.E.	S.D. + S.E.	V.	Range
		Males					**Females**			
Glabello-occipital length	134	184.3 + 0.6	6.6 + 0.4	3.6	167 - 210	165	174.5 + 0.5	6.0 + 0.3	3.5	160 - 190
	56	182.5 + 1.0	7.8 + 0.7	4.3	--	46	172.7 + 1.0	6.7 + 0.7	3.9	--
Maximum breadth	139	145.0 + 0.5	5.4 + 0.3	3.7	130 - 160	172	140.5 + 0.4	5.4 + 0.3	3.8	126 - 154
	56	143.1 + 0.7	5.2 + 0.5	3.6	--	46	138.8 + 0.8	5.1 + 0.5	3.6	--
Basion-bregma height	128	143.0 + 0.4	4.7 + 0.3	3.3	131 - 158	158	136.9 + 0.4	4.4 + 0.2	3.2	125 - 148
	56	141.2 + 0.6	4.4 + 0.4	3.1	--	46	135.4 + 0.6	3.8 + 0.4	2.8	--
Auricular-vertex height	128	127.7 + 0.4	4.1 + 0.3	3.2	112 - 142	159	122.4 + 0.3	4.1 + 0.2	3.4	112 - 132
	56	122.0 + 0.6	4.4 + 0.4	3.6	--	46	117.6 + 0.5	3.7 + 0.4	3.1	--
Porion-basion height	125	22.2 + 0.3	2.9 + 0.2	15.4	15 - 32	145	20.6 + 0.2	2.9 + 0.2	14.2	13 - 30
	56	20.8†	--	--	--	46	19.5†	--	--	--
Average thickness of left parietal	135	5.7 + 0.1	0.9 + 0.1	16.5	3.8 - 7.8	172	5.1 + 0.1	1.0 + 0.1	20.0	3 - 9
	--	--	--	--	--	--	--	--	--	--
Minimum frontal diameter	132	95.6 + 0.4	4.4 + 0.3	4.6	85 - 108	168	91.6 + 0.3	4.1 + 0.2	4.5	75 - 100
	56	94.1 + 0.6	4.1 + 0.4	4.4	--	46	91.9 + 0.5	3.1 + 0.3	3.4	--
Maximum frontal diameter	136	117.6 + 0.4	4.4 + 0.3	3.8	106 - 136	169	112.3 + 0.3	4.2 + 0.2	3.7	103 - 125
	55	115.3 + 0.5	3.9 + 0.4	3.4	--	46	112.5 + 0.7	4.7 + 0.5	4.2	--
Biorbital diameter	128	98.9 + 0.2	2.3 + 0.2	2.3	91 - 108	153	94.9 + 0.2	3.1 + 0.2	3.3	86 - 103
	56	98.5 + 0.5	3.5 + 0.3	3.6	--	46	94.9 + 0.4	2.9 + 0.3	3.1	--
Bizygomatic diameter	136	138.3 + 0.4	5.1 + 0.3	3.7	124 - 151	163	129.1 + 0.3	4.5 + 0.2	3.5	115 - 143
	55	135.6 + 0.6	4.8 + 0.4	3.6	--	43	127.4 + 0.8	5.1 + 0.6	4.0	--
Nasion-menton height	104	119.8 + 0.7	6.9 + 0.5	5.8	100 - 136	124	110.4 + 0.5	4.5 + 0.3	5.0	91 - 123
	--	--	--	--	--	--	--	--	--	--
Nasion-prosthion height	125	71.9 + 0.4	4.2 + 0.3	5.8	60 - 82	157	67.5 + 0.3	3.7 + 0.2	5.5	54 - 77
	49	70.4 + 0.5	3.5 + 0.4	4.9	--	45	66.4 + 0.6	3.7 + 0.4	5.6	--
Nasal height	127	55.0 + 0.3	3.2 + 0.2	5.8	47 - 62	157	51.2 + 0.2	2.9 + 0.2	5.7	43 - 58
	55	53.5 + 0.4	3.1 + 0.3	5.8	--	46	50.1 + 0.4	2.9 + 0.3	5.8	--
Nose bone length	88	23.0 + 0.3	3.0 + 0.2	13.1	14 - 31	121	22.5 + 0.2	2.6 + 0.2	11.6	15 - 32
	54	19.3†	--	--	--	45	18.6†	--	--	--
Lower nasalia breadth	116	16.2 + 0.2	2.0 + 0.1	12.1	11 - 21	141	15.7 + 0.2	2.1 + 0.1	13.4	12 - 26
	45	16.9 + 0.3	1.8 + 0.2	10.3	--	34	15.9 + 0.4	2.0 + 0.2	12.8	--
Nasal diameter	131	26.4 + 0.2	2.0 + 0.1	7.4	22 - 34	157	25.0 + 0.2	1.8 + 0.1	7.3	17 - 30
	55	26.2 + 0.2	2.0 + 0.2	7.6	--	45	24.6 + 0.2	1.4 ± 0.2	5.8	--

*Mokapu data are given first, with K. A. Wagner (1937) data below.
†Calculated from means; possible differences of technique involved.

Measurement	No.	Males Mean + S.E.	S.D. + S.E.	V.	Range	No.	Females Mean + S.E.	S.D. + S.E.	V.	Range
Anterior inter-orbital breadth (MF)‡	122	20.3 + 0.2	2.1 + 0.1	10.4	16 - 27	154	19.0 + 0.2	2.0 + 0.1	10.4	14 - 26
	56	18.4 + 0.3	2.0 + 0.2	11.0	--	46	17.9 + 0.3	2.1 + 0.2	11.5	--
Nasal bridge height	84	20.8 + 0.3	2.9 + 0.2	13.9	14 - 30	113	17.9 ± 0.2	2.4 + 0.2	13.5	13 - 23
	--	--	--	--	--	--	--	--	--	--
Nasal bridge breadth (maxillo-malar suture)	120	59.3 + 0.4	4.5 + 0.3	7.6	49 - 74	105	56.1 + 0.5	4.7 + 0.3	8.4	45 - 68
	--	--	--	--	--	--	--	--	--	--
Minimum nasal diameter	119	7.8 + 0.2	1.8 + 0.1	19.9	3 - 12	151	7.8 + 0.2	1.9 + 0.1	24.2	2 - 14
	52	7.6 + 0.2	1.7 + 0.2	21.9	--	44	7.4 + 0.2	1.6 + 0.2	22.2	--
Minimum nasal subtense (nasal bone height)	119	3.6 + 0.1	1.7 + 0.1	31.6	1 - 7	151	2.9 + 0.1	1.0 + 0.1	35.5	1 - 6
	54	3.4	--	--	--	45	2.8	--	--	--
Left orbital breadth (MF)‡	127	42.9 + 0.2	2.0 + 0.1	4.5	32 - 48	155	41.3 + 0.1	1.5 + 0.1	3.7	38 - 44
	56	43.0 + 0.2	1.7 + 0.2	4.0	--	46	41.1 + 0.2	1.3 + 0.1	3.1	--
Left orbital height	125	35.0 + 0.2	2.3 + 0.2	6.7	31 - 46	155	34.5 + 0.1	1.6 + 0.1	6.4	30 - 39
	56	34.8 + 0.2	1.7 + 0.2	4.9	--	46	34.7 + 0.2	1.2 + 0.1	3.5	--
External palatal length	121	55.6 + 0.4	4.3 + 0.3	7.8	49 - 66	156	52.6 + 0.2	2.7 + 0.2	5.1	46 - 60
	46	54.0 + 0.4	2.6 + 0.3	4.9	--	44	51.7 + 0.5	3.1 + 0.3	6.0	--
External palatal breadth	120	65.8 + 0.3	3.6 + 0.2	5.5	58 - 76	146	61.8 + 0.2	2.8 + 0.2	4.5	55 - 69
	43	64.9 + 0.5	3.4 + 0.4	5.2	--	40	60.4 + 0.5	3.4 + 0.4	5.7	--
Basion-prosthion length	112	104.4 + 0.5	5.4 + 0.4	5.2	94 - 123	143	99.7 + 0.3	4.1 + 0.2	4.1	88 - 110
	50	102.2 + 0.6	4.3 + 0.4	4.2	--	46	98.2 + 0.5	3.4 + 0.4	3.5	--
Basion-nasion length	121	106.8 + 0.4	4.1 + 0.3	3.9	97 - 117	150	101.6 + 0.3	3.6 + 0.2	3.5	93 - 118
	56	105.0 + 0.6	4.5 + 0.4	4.3	--	46	99.8 + 0.5	3.2 + 0.3	3.2	--
Horizontal circumference	132	523.2 + 1.2	14.1 + 0.9	2.7	492 - 590	161	501.9 + 1.0	12.4 + 0.7	2.5	459 - 529
	56	525.8 + 1.8	13.2 + 1.2	2.5	--	46	501.6 + 1.7	11.6 + 1.2	2.3	--
Nasion-opisthion arc	127	380.2 + 1.2	13.5 + 0.8	3.6	346 - 442	161	363.9 + 0.9	11.2 + 0.6	3.1	335 - 393
	56	375.0 + 2.1	15.4 + 1.4	4.1	--	46	356.9 + 1.8	12.2 + 1.3	3.4	--
Nasion-bregma arc	131	135.9 + 0.5	6.1 + 0.4	4.5	121 - 164	166	128.8 + 0.4	5.5 + 0.3	4.3	116 - 145
	56	133.0 + 0.9	6.7 + 0.6	5.0	--	46	125.0 + 0.8	5.7 + 0.6	4.6	--
Nasion-lambda arc	129	262.0 + 1.0	11.4 + 0.7	4.4	233 - 315	163	250.6 + 0.8	10.0 + 0.6	3.9	225 - 279
	56	258.1 + 1.0	14.2 + 0.7	6.0	--	46	246.5 + 1.9	13.5 + 0.8	6.4	--
Transverse arc	131	333.4 + 0.9	10.3 + 0.6	3.1	306 - 376	160	320.2 + 0.8	10.6 + 0.6	3.8	288 - 343
	56	324.2 + 1.5	11.2 + 1.0	3.4	--	46	313.2 + 1.5	10.0 + 1.0	3.2	--

‡Landmark maxillofrontale

Table 5 *(continued)*

	Males					Females			
Measurement	*No.*	*Mean + S.E.*	*S.D. + S.E.*	*V.*	*Range*	*No.*	*Mean + S.E.*	*S.D. + S.E.*	*V.*	*Range*
Total facial angle	106	84.2 + 0.3	3.4 + 0.2	4.1	68 - 94	141	83.9 + 0.2	2.7 + 0.2	3.2	77 - 90
	49	83.9 + 0.4	3.0 + 0.3	--	--	43	83.0 + 0.4	2.7 + 0.3	--	--
Alveolar angle	102	65.0 + 0.6	6.1 + 0.4	9.4	50 - 83	138	63.5 + 0.2	2.4 + 0.2	3.9	42 - 79
	49	72.6 + 0.8†	5.8 + 0.6	--	--	41	69.6 + 0.9†	5.5 + 0.6	--	--
Mandible length	119	108.9 + 0.5	5.7 + 0.4	5.2	94 - 125	143	102.9 + 0.4	4.8 + 0.3	4.6	90 - 115
		107.0@	--	--	--	--	101.7@	--	--	--
Height to condyles	129	59.9 + 0.6	6.8 + 0.4	11.3	40 - 80	142	53.2 + 0.4	5.4 + 0.6	10.0	40 - 66
		61.0@	--	--	--	--	54.0@	--	--	--
Bicondylar diameter	125	128.1 + 0.6	6.1 + 0.4	4.8	109 - 143	150	121.1 + 0.5	5.9 + 0.4	4.9	110 - 136
	--	--	--	--	--	--	--	--	--	--
Bigonial diameter	129	104.4 + 0.5	5.8 + 0.4	5.5	89 - 119	157	96.0 + 0.4	4.4 + 0.2	4.6	85 - 112
	--	--	--	--	--	--	--	--	--	--
Height of symphysis	127	32.8 + 0.2	2.8 + 0.2	8.5	27 - 42	153	29.6 + 0.2	2.4 + 0.1	8.0	22 - 36
	--	--	--	--	--	--	--	--	--	--
Minimum diameter, left ramus	133	36.7 + 0.2	2.9 + 0.2	7.9	30 - 48	159	34.3 + 0.2	2.5 + 0.1	7.4	29 - 41
	--	--	--	--	--	--	--	--	--	--
Thickness body premolar$_2$	116	12.4 + 1.2	1.3 + 0.9	10.6	9 - 15	145	11.3 + 1.0	1.2 + 0.7	10.2	8 - 14
	--	--	--	--	--	--	--	--	--	--
Gonial angle	129	119.1 + 0.6	6.9 + 0.4	5.7	104 - 145	159	122.8 + 0.4	5.5 + 0.3	4.5	110 - 142
		117.0@	--	--	--	--	120.8@	--	--	--
Cranial capacity	--	--	--	--	--	--	--	--	--	--
	56	1464.6 ± 13.4	100.1 ± 9.45	6.83						
Indices										
Module	125	157.1 + 0.4	3.9 + 0.2	2.5	141 - 176	158	150.8 + 0.3	3.7 + 0.2	2.5	139 - 162
	56	155.6@	--	--	--	46	149.0@	--	--	--
Cranial	135	79.2 + 0.4	4.4 + 0.3	5.5	70 - 97	171	80.5 + 0.3	4.3 + 0.2	5.3	68 - 96
	56	78.5 + 0.6	4.8 + 0.4	6.2	--	46	80.5 + 0.7	4.5 + 0.5	5.5	--
Length-height	124	77.7 + 0.3	3.0 + 0.2	3.9	69 - 85	161	78.7 + 0.3	3.4 + 0.2	4.3	72 - 96
	56	77.5 + 0.4	3.4 + 0.3	4.4	--	46	78.5 + 0.6	3.8 + 0.4	4.9	--
Breadth-height	126	98.3 + 0.4	4.4 + 0.3	4.5	84 - 112	163	97.5 + 0.4	4.2 + 0.2	4.4	87 - 110
	56	98.9 + 0.6	4.1 + 0.4	4.2	--	46	97.7 + 0.6	4.0 + 0.4	4.2	--
Mean-height	129	87.3 + 0.3	3.5 + 0.2	4.0	78 - 98	161	86.9 + 0.2	2.8 + 0.2	3.2	79 - 94
	46	86.9@	--	--	--	46	86.9@	--	--	--
Basion-porion-bregma	124	16.0 + 0.2	1.8 + 0.1	10.2	11 - 21	148	15.1 ± 0.2	1.9 ± 0.1	12.7	9 - 21
	--	--	--	--	--	--	--	--	--	--
Fronto-parietal	130	66.3 + 0.3	3.5 + 0.2	5.3	57 - 79	171	65.4 + 0.3	3.4 + 0.2	5.3	55 - 74
	56	65.9 + 0.5	3.7 + 0.3	5.6	--	46	66.3 + 0.4	2.5 + 0.3	3.8	--

@Approximated averages based on reorientation of rocker jaws (see pp. 13-14).

Measurement		Males					Females			
	No.	Mean + S.E.	S.D. + S.E.	V.	Range	No.	Mean + S.E.	S.D. + S.E.	V.	Range
Transverse frontal	135	81.8 + 0.3	3.5 + 0.2	4.3	74 - 98	176	81.3 + 0.4	3.0 + 0.3	4.3	72 - 89
	55	81.8 + 0.5	3.6 + 0.3	4.4	--	46	81.8 + 0.4	2.7 + 0.3	3.3	--
Total facial	104	86.4 + 0.5	5.0 + 0.4	5.8	74 - 98	127	85.4 + 0.4	4.8 + 0.3	5.6	71 - 98
	--	--	--	--	--	--	--	--	--	--
Upper facial	120	52.1 + 0.3	3.2 + 0.2	6.1	44 - 61	169	52.7 + 0.2	3.2 + 0.2	6.0	42 - 59
	47	52.2 + 0.4	2.9 + 0.3	5.5	--	42	52.1 + 0.5	3.0 + 0.3	5.8	--
Cranio-facial	134	95.6 + 0.3	3.8 + 0.2	4.0	87 - 109	169	92.2 + 0.3	3.5 + 0.2	3.8	86 - 101
	55	95.0 + 0.6	4.5 + 0.4	4.7	--	43	91.9 + 0.6	3.6 + 0.4	4.0	--
Zygo-frontal	131	69.8 + 0.3	3.2 + 0.2	4.6	61 - 78	166	71.0 + 0.2	3.0 + 0.2	4.2	60 - 79
	55	69.5 + 0.4	3.3 + 0.3	4.7	--	43	71.9 + 0.5	3.3 + 0.4	4.6	--
Nasal	128	48.0 + 0.4	4.2 + 0.3	8.8	41 - 64	159	49.1 + 0.3	4.0 + 0.2	8.2	38 - 65
	55	49.0 + 0.6	4.1 + 0.4	8.4	--	45	49.4 + 0.6	4.0 + 0.4	8.1	--
Interorbital	120	20.4 + 0.2	1.8 + 0.1	8.8	16 - 25	158	20.0 + 0.2	1.9 + 0.1	9.7	14 - 26
	56	18.7 + 0.3	1.9 + 0.2	10.4	--	46	18.9 + 0.3	1.9 + 0.2	10.1	--
Nose bone (nasalia/length)	86	71.4 + 1.1	10.5 + 0.8	14.7	50 - 100	124	69.9 + 1.1	12.4 + 0.8	17.7	29 - 104
	45	87.5†	--	--	--	34	85.9†	--	--	--
Nose height subtense/min. br.	118	48.8 + 1.4	15.0 + 1.0	30.8	20 - 100	155	36.6 + 0.9	11.0 + 0.6	30.0	14 - 71
	52	44.8†	--	--	--	43	37.9†	--	--	--
Left orbital	124	81.0 + 0.5	5.2 + 0.3	6.4	70 - 96	159	82.7 + 0.3	4.0 + 0.2	4.8	71 - 93
	56	81.0 + 0.6	4.2 + 0.4	5.2	--	46	84.5 + 0.4	2.8 + 0.3	3.4	--
External palatal	112	17.9 + 0.7	7.4 + 0.5	6.9	80 - 138	147	117.9 + 0.5	6.4 + 0.4	5.4	100 - 132
	40	19.9 + 1.0	6.2 + 0.7	5.2	--	38	116.3 + 1.3	8.0 + 0.9	6.9	--
Cranial base/ face height	99	67.3 + 0.7	6.6 + 0.5	7.5	62 - 182	149	67.1 + 0.4	5.2 + 0.3	7.7	55 - 95
	49	66.9	--	--	--	45	66.5	--	--	--
Face projection/ face height	89	68.7 + 0.8	7.5 + 0.6	8.7	58 - 99	148	68.4 + 0.4	5.4 + 0.3	7.9	54 - 94
	49	68.8†	--	--	--	45	67.7†	--	--	--
Zygo-gonial	111	76.4 + 0.5	4.9 + 0.4	6.4	57 - 90	136	74.4 + 0.3	3.4 + 0.2	4.5	66 - 83
	--	--	--	--	--	--	--	--	--	--
Fronto-gonial	109	109.5 + 0.8	7.8 + 0.5	7.2	80 - 127	142	105.0 + 0.5	6.0 + 0.4	5.7	94 - 128
	--	--	--	--	--	--	--	--	--	--
Mandibular 1, length/breadth	124	85.3 + 0.6	6.1 + 0.4	7.2	72 - 114	139	85.2 + 0.4	5.1 + 0.3	6.0	73 - 99
	--	--	--	--	--	--	--	--	--	--
Mandibular 2, height/breadth	121	47.1 + 0.5	5.2 + 0.3	11.0	32 - 69	139	43.9 + 0.4	4.5 + 0.3	10.3	31 - 56
	--	--	--	--	--	--	--	--	--	--

Table 6

Classified Skull Features, Mokapu

A = age changes; C = cultural, i.e., acquired; H = hereditary Hawaiian phenotype; S = sex differences.

Feature	Males No.	%	Females No.	%
Skull in General				
Skull Size (S)	133*		178*	
Small	6	4.5	96	54.0
Medium	89	66.9	79	44.5
Large	38	28.6	3	1.5
Muscularity (S)	133*		179*	
Small	8	6.0	117	65.4
Medium	67	50.4	58	32.4
Large	58	43.6	4	2.2
Weight (S)	132*		177*	
Light	29	22.0	53	30.0
Medium	60	45.4	74	41.8
Heavy	36	27.3	47	26.5
Very Heavy	7	5.3	3	1.7
Deformation (C)	129*		169*	
None	15	11.6	20	11.8
Slight	55	42.6	75	44.4
Medium	42	32.6	59	35.0
Pronounced	17	13.2	15	8.8
Shape (horizontal) (S)	133*		177*	
Oval	68	51.1	83	46.9
Long oval	5	3.8	5	2.8
Broad oval	23	17.3	44	24.9
Round	4	3.0	5	2.8
Pentagonal or rhomboid	17	12.8	28	15.8
Elliptical	16	12.0	12	6.8
Shape (vertical) (S)	132*		177*	
Pentagonal	45	34.1	60	33.9
Low pentagonal	5	3.8	20	11.3
High pentagonal	52	39.4	37	20.9
Rounded pentagonal	13	9.9	49	27.7
Wedge	17	12.9	11	6.2
Suture pattern (H; S?)	125*		179*	
Simple	67	53.6	106	59.2
Average	51	40.8	72	40.2
Complex	7	5.6	1	.6
Pterion shape (H)	127*		172*	
Straight line	3	2.4	4	2.3
K	113	88.9	144	83.7
H	3	2.4	12	7.0
X	5	3.9	4	2.3
Combination	3	2.4	8	4.7
Wormians (H; S)	123*		183*	
None	28	22.8	61	33.3
Few	49	39.8	52	28.4
Average	28	22.8	47	25.7
Many	18	14.6	23	12.6
Frontal				
Forehead height (H; S; C)	131*		174*	
Low	10	7.6	14	8.0
Medium	63	48.1	102	58.7
High	58	44.3	58	33.3
Bosses (H; S)	92*		177*	
None	4	4.4	0	--
Small	46	50.0	23	13.0
Medium	22	23.9	90	50.8
Large	20	21.7	64	36.2
Postorbital construction (S; H)	131*		185*	
Very Small	1	.8	0	--
Small	14	10.7	29	15.7
Medium	46	35.1	108	58.4
Large	70	53.4	48	25.9
Browridge size (H; S)	131*		180*	
Small	10	7.6	141	78.4
Medium	48	36.6	33	18.3
Large	67	51.2	6	3.3
Very large	6	4.6	0	--
Browridge type (S)	97*		174*	
Divided	62	63.9	105	60.4
Median	15	15.5	54	31.0
Continuous	20	20.6	15	8.6
Glabella size (H; S)	129*		177*	
Very small	0	--	25	14.1
Small	7	5.4	97	54.8
Medium	61	47.3	50	28.3
Large	56	43.4	5	2.8
Very large	5	3.9	0	--
Nasion depression (H; S)	126*		167*	
None	1	.8	13	7.8
Very small	0	--	40	23.9
Small	13	10.3	77	46.1
Medium	74	58.7	34	20.4
Large	34	27.0	3	1.8
Very large	4	3.2	0	--
Forehead slope (H; S)	128*		178*	
None	2	1.6	21	11.8
Small	17	13.3	62	34.8
Medium	55	43.0	76	42.7
Large	50	39.0	19	10.7
Very large	4	3.1	0	--
Frontal flattening (C)	128*		171*	
None	9	7.0	16	9.4
Small	41	32.0	75	43.8
Medium	61	47.7	62	36.3
Large	17	13.3	18	10.5
Parietal				
Sagittal crest (S; H)	132*		179*	
Small	40	30.3	115	64.3
Medium	63	47.7	57	31.8
Large	29	22.0	7	3.9
Bosses (H; S)	133*		177*	
Small	35	26.3	24	13.6
Medium	75	56.4	90	50.8
Large	23	17.3	63	35.6
Occipital				
Projection (C)	133*		136*	

*Individuals observed.

Feature	Males No.	%	Females No.	%
Very small	3	2.3	5	3.7
Small	41	30.8	49	36.0
Medium	69	51.9	67	49.3
Large	20	15.0	15	11.0
Flattening (C)	133*		137*	
None	16	12.0	19	13.9
Very small	11	8.3	24	17.5
Small	55	41.4	41	29.9
Medium	45	33.8	43	31.4
Large	6	4.5	10	7.3
Position of lambda (H; C)	131*		175*	
Low	1	.8	2	1.1
Medium	24	18.3	23	13.2
High	106	80.9	150	85.7
Inca bone (H; S?)	129*		157*	
Present	25	17.0	10	6.4
Torus size (S; H?)	132*		173*	
None	8	6.1	20	11.5
Small	48	36.4	111	64.2
Medium	56	42.4	37	21.4
Large	20	15.1	5	2.9
Torus type (S; H?)	132*		173*	
Ridges	81	61.4	37	21.4
Mounds	32	24.2	106	61.3
Lateral bulges	29	22.0	22	12.7
Extentions	82	62.1	93	53.8
External protuberance (hook) (S; H?)	131*		178*	
None	40	30.5	130	73.0
Small	36	27.5	44	24.7
Medium	39	29.8	4	2.3
Large	16	12.2	0	--
Basilar size (S; H)	130*		150*	
Small	17	13.1	14	9.3
Medium	86	66.1	123	82.0
Large	27	20.8	13	8.7
Basilar lateral mass (H)	124*		161*	
None	4	3.2	11	6.8
Small	51	41.1	75	46.6
Medium	42	33.9	54	33.5
Large	27	21.8	21	13.1
Condyle elevation (S)	123*		162*	
Flat	9	7.3	17	10.5
Medium	74	60.2	124	76.5
Large	40	32.5	21	13.0
Condyle shape (S; H?)	121*		163*	
Oval	38	31.4	72	44.2
Kidney	47	38.8	55	33.7
Elliptical	36	29.8	36	22.1

Temporal

Feature	Males No.	%	Females No.	%
Flatness (H; S?)	133*		178*	
None	1	.7	0	--
Small	57	42.9	79	44.4
Medium	67	50.4	97	54.5
Large	8	6.0	2	1.1
Mastoid size (H; S)	132*		178*	
Small	3	2.3	103	57.8
Medium	66	50.0	69	38.8

Feature	Males No.	%	Females No.	%
Large	60	45.4	6	3.4
Very large	3	2.3	0	--
Supramastoid crest (H; S)	132*		174*	
Small	6	4.6	49	28.2
Medium	40	30.3	92	52.8
Large	65	49.2	32	18.4
Very large	21	15.9	1	.6
Auditory meatus shape (H; S?)	124*		175*	
Oval	57	46.0	92	52.5
Elliptical	64	51.6	77	44.0
Round	3	2.4	6	3.5
Tympanic plate thickness (H)	134*		177*	
Thin	32	23.9	38	21.5
Medium	73	54.5	96	54.2
Thick	25	18.7	35	19.8
Very thick	4	2.9	8	4.5
Glenoid fossa depth (H; S)	132*		178*	
Shallow	17	12.9	41	23.1
Medium	79	59.8	99	55.5
Deep	36	27.3	38	21.4
Postglenoid process (S; H)	128*		179*	
Absent	1	.8	13	7.3
Very small	11	8.6	35	19.6
Small	52	40.6	77	43.0
Medium	51	39.8	47	26.2
Large	13	10.2	7	3.9
Height of articular eminence (S)	133*		177*	
Small	8	6.0	32	18.1
Medium	83	62.4	124	70.0
Large	42	31.6	21	11.9
Zygomatic process thickness (S)	131*		176*	
Thin	27	20.6	143	81.2
Medium	88	67.2	32	18.2
Thick	16	12.2	1	.6

Face

Feature	Males No.	%	Females No.	%
Size (S)	129*		167*	
Small	1	.8	2	1.2
Medium	9	6.9	54	32.4
Large	106	82.3	109	65.2
Very large	13	10.0	2	1.2
Shape (S; H?)	115*		137*	
Short	10	8.7	8	5.8
Long	15	13.0	11	8.1
Rectangular	80	69.6	117	85.4
Triangular	10	8.7	1	.7
Orbital shape (H; S?)	128*		163*	
Oval	1	.8	1	.6
Rectangular	39	30.5	57	35.0
Rhomboid	67	52.3	77	47.2
Square	21	16.4	28	17.2
Orbital slant (down) (S; H?)	129*		167*	
None	5	3.9	19	11.4
Very slight	5	3.9	14	8.4
Slight	31	24.0	65	38.9
Average	69	53.5	63	37.7
Large	19	14.7	6	3.6

Table 6 *(continued)*

Feature	Males No.	%	Females No.	%
Infraorbital suture (H?; A; S)	116*		160*	
Absent	61	52.6	58	36.3
Open, both	20	17.2	55	34.4
Open, left only	14	12.1	15	9.4
Open, right only	9	7.8	24	15.0
Closing, both	7	6.0	6	3.7
Closing, left only	1	.9	1	.6
Closing, right only	4	3.4	1	.6
Superior orbital edge (S)	127*		170*	
Sharp	8	6.3	84	49.4
Small	5	3.9	27	15.9
Medium	72	56.7	56	32.9
Rounded	42	33.1	3	1.8
Inframaxillary notch (S?; H)	121*		167*	
Small	14	11.6	25	15.0
Medium	49	40.5	84	50.3
Deep	58	47.9	58	34.7
Canine fossae (H; S)	126*		168*	
Small	38	30.2	89	53.0
Medium	69	54.8	67	39.8
Deep	19	15.0	12	7.2
Maxillary-malar suture (A; S?)	125*		160*	
Open	39	31.2	116	72.5
Closing	36	28.8	29	18.1
Closed	50	40.0	15	9.4
Cheek Bone				
Size (H; S)	130*		168*	
Small	4	3.1	35	20.8
Medium	37	28.5	97	57.7
Large	89	68.4	36	21.5
Anterior projection (H)	131*		169*	
Small	9	6.8	15	8.9
Medium	33	25.2	44	26.1
Large	89	68.0	110	65.0
Lateral projection (S; H)	131*		169*	
Small	3	2.3	37	21.9
Medium	75	57.2	116	68.6
Large	53	40.5	16	9.5
Anterior jut (S; H)	132*		168*	
None	25	18.9	43	25.6
Small	33	25.0	68	40.5
Medium	65	49.3	53	31.5
Large	9	6.8	4	2.4
Malar tuberosity (H; S)	131*		167*	
None	28	21.4	141	84.4
Small	42	32.0	23	13.8
Medium	47	35.9	3	1.8
Large	14	10.7	0	--
Malar process (S; H)	131*		165*	
None	15	11.4	30	18.2
Small	55	42.0	72	43.6
Medium	49	37.4	52	31.5
Large	12	9.2	11	6.7
Nose				
Profile (H)	94*		135*	
Concavoconvex	79	84.0	114	84.4
Concave	10	10.7	10	7.4
Straight	5	5.3	11	8.2
Shape of nose bones (H)	106*		159*	
Hour glass	75	70.8	114	71.7
Divergent (triangular)	29	27.4	43	27.1
Parallel	2	1.8	2	1.2
Nasal suture (A)	117*		156*	
Open	56	47.9	94	60.2
Closing	47	40.2	84	30.8
Closed	14	11.9	14	9.0
Nasal sill edge (H)	127*		168*	
None	3	2.4	5	3.0
Dull	70	55.1	84	50.0
Medium	40	31.5	65	38.7
Sharp	14	11.0	14	8.3
Double sill (H; S)	127*		164*	
Present	13	10.2	7	4.3
Nasal spine size (H; S)	125*		167*	
None to very small	11	8.8	13	7.8
Small	94	75.2	134	80.2
Medium	20	16.0	20	12.0
Nasal gutter (prenasal sulcus) (H; S?)	127*		169*	
None	15	11.8	21	12.4
Very small	15	11.8	43	25.5
Small	43	33.9	57	33.7
Medium	36	28.3	35	20.7
Large	18	14.2	13	7.7
Palate				
Size (see Table 5) (H; S)	121*		164*	
Small	0	--	6	3.7
Medium	35	28.9	92	56.0
Large	78	64.5	66	40.3
Very large	8	6.6	0	--
Shape (H; S)	115*		150*	
Parabolic	23	20.0	19	12.7
Hyperbolic	84	73.0	106	70.7
Elliptical	5	4.4	14	9.3
U	3	2.6	11	7.3
Straight sided (H; S?)	100*		143*	
Present	71	71.0	87	60.8
Absent	29	29.0	56	39.2
Height (see Table 5) (S)	117*		158*	
Low	21	17.9	51	32.3
Medium	85	72.7	100	63.3
High	11	9.4	7	4.4
Pterygoids (S)	113*		152*	
Small	31	27.4	55	36.2
Medium	59	52.2	86	56.6
Large	23	20.4	11	7.2
Palatal spine (H; S)	124*		143*	
Small	23	18.5	42	29.4
Medium	61	49.2	74	51.7
Large	24	19.4	21	14.7
Divided	16	12.9	6	4.2
Torus (H)	104*		164*	
None	69	66.4	102	62.2

Feature	Males No.	%	Females No.	%
Small	28	26.9	51	31.1
Medium	7	6.7	11	6.7
Type of torus (H)	47*		63*	
Ridge	25	53.2	35	55.6
Mound	22	46.8	28	44.4
Maxillary teeth				
Size (see Table 12) (S; H)	107*		158*	
Medium	35	32.7	93	58.9
Large	65	60.8	61	38.6
Very large	7	6.5	4	2.5
Condition (A; H)	117*		161*	
Perfect	18	15.4	58	36.0
Excellent	25	21.4	41	25.5
Good	35	29.9	29	18.0
Fair	21	17.9	19	11.8
Poor	18	15.4	14	8.7
Wear (A; H)	115*		155*	
Very small	9	7.8	39	25.2
Small	31	27.0	63	40.6
Medium	68	59.1	50	32.3
Large	7	6.1	3	1.9
Incisors				
Shovel shaped (H)	78*		132*	
None	10	12.8	9	6.8
Slight	52	66.7	92	69.7
Medium	16	20.5	31	23.5
Mesiopalatal torsion (H)	100*		139*	
Absent	33	33.0	51	36.7
Present	67	67.0	88	63.3
Marginal ridges (H; S?)	75*		128*	
Absent	30	40.0	44	34.4
Small	31	41.3	50	39.1
Medium	11	14.7	33	25.8
Large	3	4.0	1	.7
Crown shape (H; S?)	81*		120*	
Short	2	2.5	7	5.8
Medium	57	70.4	77	64.2
Long	22	27.1	36	30.0
Molars				
Molars with Carabelli's cusp (H)	83*		136*	
Absent	56	67.5	94	69.0
Present	27	32.5	42	31.0
Maxillary M₃ (third molars) (H; S?)	105*		155*	
Absent	24	22.9	34	22.0
Both present	77	73.3	106	68.4
Left only present	4	3.8	10	6.4
Right only present	0	--	5	3.2
Cusp pattern for maxillary molars (H; S?)	51*		82*	
4 - 3 - 3	2	3.9	3	3.7
4 - 4 - 1	1	2.0	0	--
4 - 4 - 2	0	--	1	1.2
4 - 4 - 3	19	37.2	36	43.9
4 - 4 - 4	26	51.0	37	45.1
4 - 4 - 5	2	3.9	3	3.7

Feature	Males No.	%	Females No.	%
4 - 4 - 6	1	2.0	1	1.2
5 - 5 - 3	0	--	1	1.2
Mandible				
Size (H; S)	123*		160*	
Small	2	1.6	87	54.4
Medium	66	53.7	73	45.6
Large	55	44.7	0	--
Rocker jaw (H; S)	123*		160*	
Absent	36	29.3	19	11.9
Small	32	26.0	55	34.4
Medium	42	34.2	52	32.5
Large	13	10.5	34	21.2
Rocker jaw with arch (H)	123*		159*	
Present	59	48.0	75	47.1
Absent	64	52.0	84	52.9
Chin type (S; H)	124*		159*	
Median	74	59.7	95	59.6
Median with sharp point	27	21.8	56	35.2
Mediobilateral	23	18.5	8	5.2
Chin projection (H)	122*		158*	
Receding	40	32.8	51	32.3
Small	17	13.9	16	10.1
Medium	35	28.7	51	32.3
Large	30	24.6	40	25.3
Jowl eversion (H; S)	125*		162*	
Absent	3	2.4	11	6.8
Small	29	23.2	63	38.9
Medium	72	57.6	80	49.4
Large	21	16.8	8	4.9
Jowl musculature (H; S)	125*		162*	
Small	5	4.0	42	25.9
Medium	51	40.8	99	61.2
Large	69	55.2	21	12.9
Mental foramen direction (H; S?)	126*		158*	
Superior	8	6.4	17	10.8
Oblique post.-sup.	109	86.4	117	74.0
Posterior	2	1.6	9	5.7
Direct	7	5.6	15	9.5
Mental foramen position below (H)	106*		140*	
Premolar ₁ and ₂	6	5.6	6	4.3
Premolar ₂	55	51.9	80	57.1
Premolar ₂ - molar ₁	36	34.0	47	33.6
Molar ₁	9	8.5	7	5.0
Genial tubercles size (H; S)	125*		160*	
Very small	17	13.6	43	26.9
Small	60	48.0	80	50.0
Medium	42	33.6	37	23.1
Large	6	4.8	0	--
Mylohyoid ridge size (S; H)	126*		159*	
Small	23	18.2	34	21.4
Medium	65	51.6	91	57.2
Large	38	30.2	34	21.4
Torus (H; S?)	124*		157*	
Absent	117	94.4	143	91.1
Small	7	5.6	10	6.4
Medium	0	--	4	2.5

Table 6 (continued)

Feature	Males No.	Males %	Females No.	Females %
Supernumerary (H)	123*		160*	
Present	1	.8	1	.6
Absent	122	99.2	159	99.4
Tooth wear (A; H)	106*		147*	
Very small	10	9.4	17	11.6
Small	30	28.3	75	51.0
Medium	61	57.6	53	36.0
Large	5	4.7	2	1.4
Mandibular Teeth				
Incisors				
Shovel shaped (H; S)	69*		108*	
None	34	49.3	27	25.0
Small	22	31.9	55	50.9
Medium	13	18.8	26	24.1
Mesiopalatal torsion (H; S?)	91*		133*	
Present	40	44.0	72	54.1
Absent	51	56.0	61	45.9
Molars				
Size (see Table 12):				
M_1 compared to M_2 (H)	78*		123*	
1 > 2	68	87.2	106	86.2
1 < 2	1	1.3	2	1.6
1 = 2	9	11.5	15	12.2
Size: M_2 compared to M_3 (H; S?)	55*		75*	
2 > 3	31	56.4	39	52.0
2 < 3	17	30.9	17	22.7
2 = 3	7	12.7	19	25.3
Mandibular third molar (H; S?)	82*		106*	
Absent	24	29.3	39	36.8
Present, both	53	64.6	58	54.7
Present, left only	3	3.7	6	5.7
Present, right only	2	2.4	3	2.8

Feature	Males No.	Males %	Females No.	Females %
Protostylid (H)	93*		133*	
Absent	75	80.7	101	75.9
Present on:				
M_1	4	4.3	11	8.3
M_2	3	3.2	7	5.3
M_3	11	11.8	14	10.5
Dryopithecus pattern (Y5) (H; S?)	86*		126*	
M_1 only	32	37.2	46	36.5
M_1 and M_2	12	14.0	33	26.2
M_1 and M_3	21	24.4	20	15.9
All 3 Ms	19	22.1	27	21.4
M_3 only	2	2.3	0	--
Bite (occlusion) (H; A)	85*		124*	
Small over	54	63.5	97	78.2
Medium over	5	5.9	8	6.5
Large over	0	--	2	1.6
Under	2	2.4	0	--
Edge	24	28.2	17	13.7
Alveolar exostosis (H; A)	100*		139*	
Absent	73	73.0	112	80.6
Maxillae	23	23.0	22	15.8
Mandible	4	4.0	5	3.6
Physical type (H; S?)	127*		175*	
Hawaiian	47	37.0	77	44.0
Hawaiian mixture	56	44.1	71	40.6
Mongoloid	5	3.9	9	5.2
Caucasoid	8	6.3	6	3.4
Negroid	3	2.4	6	3.4
Australoid	2	1.6	0	--
Other mixture	6	4.7	6	3.4

Table 7

Mokapu Maxillary Dental Arch Dimensions and Indices (in Mm.)

		Males					Females			
Measurement	No.	Mean ± S.E.	S.D. ± S.E.	V.	Range	No.	Mean ± S.E.	S.D. ± S.E.	V.	Range
Arch length	24	46.4 - 0.65	3.1 - 0.46	6.7	40 - 52	28	45.4 - 0.52	2.7 - 0.37	6.0	40 - 50
Bicanine diameter	69	41.8 - 0.25	2.1 - 0.18	5.0	36 - 47	109	39.9 - 0.19	2.0 - 0.14	5.0	34 - 47
Bi-PM$_1$ diameter	69	49.3 - 0.30	2.4 - 0.20	5.0	46 - 56	105	46.8 - 0.19	2.0 - 0.14	4.2	41 - 52
Bi-M$_1$ diameter	71	61.7 - 0.37	2.7 - 0.26	4.4	56 - 68	102	58.8 - 0.24	2.4 - 0.17	4.0	50 - 64
Height of palate (from M$_1$)	69	22.0 - 0.33	2.7 - 0.23	12.3	15 - 28	105	19.7 - 0.24	2.4 - 0.17	12.4	13 - 25
Occlusal diameter M$_1$ fissure	68	51.2 - 0.34	2.8 - 0.24	5.4	46 - 57	105	48.8 - 0.23	2.4 - 0.16	4.9	42 - 54
Bi-M$_2$ diameter	52	66.4 - 0.35	2.7 - 0.25	3.9	61 - 72	94	63.5 - 0.30	2.6 - 0.20	4.2	57 - 70
Indices										
Arch (length/breadth)	16*	68.8 --	6.2 --	--	56 - 78	26	70.1 - 0.8	4.1 - 0.6	5.9	64 - 79
Bi-C/Bi-PM$_1$	60	84.8 - 0.38	2.9 - 0.23	3.5	79 - 92	89	85.1 - 0.3	3.0 - 0.3	3.6	72 - 93
Bi-C/Bi-M$_1$	60	68.2 - 0.51	3.9 - 0.36	5.7	61 - 78	99	68.0 - 0.3	3.0 - 0.2	4.4	56 - 74
Bi-C/Bi-M$_2$	43	63.2 - 0.50	3.2 - 0.35	5.1	56 - 70	90	63.0 - 0.3	3.0 - 0.2	4.7	52 - 69
Ht. M$_1$/Occl. M$_1$	71	43.1 - 0.65	5.5 - 0.46	12.7	31 - 60	105	40.4 - 0.52	5.4 - 0.37	12.9	28 - 52

*Statistics limited to 20 and more.

Table 8

Maxillary Dental Arch Dimensions, Mokapu and North Americans* (in Mm.)

			Males			Females	
Arch Lengths		No.	Average	Range	No.	Average	Range
I$_1$ - M$_1$	Mok.†	24	(35.7)	(29 - 42)	28	(35.2)	(30 - 40)
	Amer.	65	32.9	(28 - 38)	62	31.3	28 - 37
I$_1$ - M$_2$	Mok.	24	46.4	40 - 52	28	45.4	40 - 50
	Amer.‡	65	(43.3)	39 - 48	62	(41.1)	(38 - 47)
Palatal Height from M$_1$ Surface							
	Mok.	69	22.0	15 - 28	105	19.7	13 - 25
	Amer.	67	20.4	15 - 26	65	19.2	14 - 22
Arch Breadths							
Bicanine	Mok.	69	41.8	36 - 47	109	39.9	34 - 47
Max.	Amer.@	45	(40.7)	(32 - 46)	45	(37.0)	(31 - 43)
Bi-PM$_1$	Mok.	69	49.3	46 - 56	105	46.8	41 - 52
Max.	Amer.@	42	(48.8)	(43 - 53)	41	(45.1)	(40 - 50)
Bi-M$_1$	Mok.	71	61.7	56 - 68	102	58.8	50 - 64
Max.	Amer.@	37	(58.7)	(52 - 64)	37	(54.5)	(49 - 60)

*Moorrees, 1959.

†Actual measurements minus mesiodistal diameter of M$_2$ = M$_1$.

‡Actual measurements plus mesiodistal diameter of M$_2$ = M$_2$.

@In order to compare these dental arch dimensions with data on American whites by Moorrees (1959), an estimated standard of difference was added which adjusted the values. These values are recorded in parentheses.

Table 9

Maxillary Dental Arch Dimensions,
Mokapu, Aleut,* and North American,†
Sexes Combined (in Mm.)

	No.	Mean	$SE_m.$	S.D.	V.	Range
Arch Length (I_1 - M_2)						
Aleut	29	43.5	0.6	3.5	8.0	38.0 - 50.5
Mokapu	52	45.9	0.6	3.1	6.7	40 - 52
No. American‡	127	(42.1)	0.3	2.0	6.5	(37 - 58)
Arch Breadth (M_2 - M_2)						
Aleut	32	62.7	0.8	4.3	6.9	56.5 - 74.5
Mokapu	146	64.9	0.4	2.7	4.2	57 - 72
(M_1 - M_1 [occlusal])						
Aleut	35	47.8	0.5	2.8	5.9	41.5 - 53.5
Mokapu	173	50.0	0.3	2.8	5.4	42 - 57
Palatal Height@						
Aleut	35	18.8	0.3	1.8	9.6	16.0 - 23.5
Mokapu	174	20.9	0.3	2.7	12.4	13 - 28
No. American	132	19.8	0.2	2.1	10.4	14 - 26
Dental Arch Index (M_2 - M_2 x 100 [breadth] ÷ I_1 - M_2 [length])						
Aleut	28	145.9	2.1	11.2	7.7	123 - 167
Mokapu‖	52	141.4	--	--	--	--
Berger's Index (M_1 - M_1 x 100 ÷ bizygomatic diam.)						
Aleut	33	33.2	0.4	2.0	6.0	29 - 38
Mokapu‖	173	37.5	--	--	--	--
Izard's Index (M_2 - M_2 x 100 ÷ bizygomatic diam.)						
Aleut	31	44.8	0.7	3.9	8.7	39 - 55
Mokapu‖	146	48.7	--	--	--	--

*Moorrees, 1957, 1959.
†Eighteen-year-old North American males and females, Moorrees, 1959.
‡Use of I_1 - M_1, length plus mesiodistal size of M_2.
@Different techniques used.
‖Calculated from the means.

Table 10
Mokapu Tooth Crown Dimensions (in Mm.)

	Males					Females			
	No.	Mean ± S.E.	S.D. ± S.E.	V.	Range	No.	Mean ± S.E.	S.D. ± S.E.	V.	Range
Maxillary Teeth										
Central incisor	25	8.47 - 0.15	0.74 - 0.12	8.7	7.3 - 10.2	25	8.24 - 0.11	0.54 - 0.08	6.5	7.2 - 9.5
Length*	25	7.50 - 0.06	0.30 - 0.04	4.0	6.8 - 8.3	25	7.26 - 0.10	0.48 - 0.07	6.6	6.1 - 8.2
Canine										
Length	26	8.13 - 0.07	0.34 - 0.05	4.2	7.2 - 8.9	25	7.69 - 0.11	0.53 - 0.08	6.9	6.6 - 8.7
Breadth	26	8.81 - 0.11	0.55 - 0.08	6.2	7.9 - 10.4	25	8.26 - 0.13	0.65 - 0.09	7.8	7.2 - 9.4
First premolar										
Length	26	7.31 - 0.08	0.39 - 0.06	5.3	6.6 - 8.0	25	6.99 - 0.08	0.38 - 0.06	5.5	6.1 - 7.6
Breadth	26	10.24 - 0.11	0.55 - 0.08	5.3	9.4 - 11.5	25	9.59 - 0.09	0.45 - 0.06	4.7	8.7 - 10.5
First molar										
Length	26	11.11 - 0.13	0.67 - 0.09	6.0	8.9 - 12.2	25	11.04 - 0.11	0.52 - 0.08	4.7	9.9 - 11.9
Breadth	26	11.92 - 0.13	0.65 - 0.09	5.5	10.4 - 13.0	25	11.34 - 0.11	0.55 - 0.08	4.8	10.2 - 12.1
Second molar										
Length	25	10.69 - 0.19	0.93 - 0.13	8.7	9.1 - 12.1	25	10.16 - 0.14	0.67 - 0.10	6.6	8.9 - 11.6
Breadth	25	12.09 - 0.15	0.74 - 0.11	6.2	10.4 - 13.5	25	11.13 - 0.13	0.63 - 0.09	5.6	9.8 - 12.9
Mandibular Teeth										
Central incisor										
Length	23	5.37 - 0.10	0.47 - 0.07	5.4	4.7 - 6.7	25	5.32 - 0.08	0.38 - 0.05	7.1	4.5 - 6.0
Breadth	23	6.41 - 0.09	0.44 - 0.07	6.9	5.7 - 7.7	25	6.15 - 0.07	0.34 - 0.05	5.5	5.6 - 6.7
Lateral incisor										
Length	23	6.11 - 0.12	0.54 - 0.08	8.9	4.9 - 7.1	25	5.91 - 0.07	0.36 - 0.05	6.0	5.2 - 6.5
Breadth	23	6.82 - 0.08	0.39 - 0.06	5.7	6.1 - 7.9	25	6.43 - 0.08	0.38 - 0.05	5.9	5.6 - 7.4
Canine										
Length	24	7.15 - 0.08	0.42 - 0.06	5.9	6.3 - 8.1	25	6.62 - 0.10	0.47 - 0.07	7.1	5.5 - 7.3
Breadth	24	8.32 - 0.07	0.35 - 0.05	4.2	7.7 - 9.1	25	7.51 - 0.11	0.55 - 0.08	7.4	6.5 - 8.6
First premolar										
Length	25	7.39 - 0.10	0.48 - 0.07	6.6	6.7 - 8.5	25	6.91 - 0.08	0.40 - 0.06	5.8	6.1 - 7.7
Breadth	25	8.56 - 0.11	0.55 - 0.08	6.4	6.8 - 9.4	25	8.14 - 0.10	0.51 - 0.07	6.2	7.3 - 9.6
First molar										
Length	25	11.55 - 0.13	0.65 - 0.09	5.6	10.4 - 13.7	25	11.11 - 0.09	0.46 - 0.07	4.2	10.2 - 12.1
Breadth	25	11.13 - 0.08	0.40 - 0.06	3.6	10.5 - 11.9	25	10.56 - 0.11	0.54 - 0.08	5.1	9.4 - 11.4
Second molar										
Length	25	11.12 - 0.18	0.86 - 0.12	7.8	9.6 - 13.1	24	10.69 - 0.15	0.71 - 0.11	6.7	9.2 - 12.1
Breadth	25	10.88 - 0.11	0.54 - 0.08	5.0	9.7 - 12.1	24	10.15 - 0.11	0.54 - 0.08	5.4	8.7 - 10.9

*Mesiodistal diameter.
†Faciolingual diameter.

Table 11
Mokapu Tooth Crown Index and Module (in Mm.)

		Males					Females			
	No.	Mean ± S.E.	S.D. ± S.E.	V.	Range	No.	Mean ± S.E.	S.D. ± S.E.	V.	Range
Maxillary Teeth										
Index										
Central incisor	25	88.9 - 1.3	6.2 - 0.9	7.0	76.5 - 98.7	25	88.4 - 0.9	4.6 - 0.7	5.2	81.5 - 100.0
Canine	26	108.4 - 0.9	4.7 - 0.7	4.4	100.0 - 122.4	25	107.6 - 1.1	5.6 - 0.8	5.2	97.4 - 118.3
1st premolar	26	140.1 - 1.5	7.3 - 1.0	5.2	130.0 - 153.4	25	137.3 - 1.4	6.7 - 1.0	4.9	123.7 - 150.0
1st molar	26	107.3 - 1.4	7.3 - 1.0	6.8	86.7 - 130.0	25	103.0 - 1.1	5.3 - 0.8	5.1	91.6 - 115.4
2nd molar	25	112.8 - 1.5	7.4 ± 1.1	6.5	90.0 - 128.0	25	110.4 - 1.7	8.1 - 1.2	7.4	96.5 - 126.6
Module										
Central incisor	25	7.9 - 0.1	0.5 - 0.1	6.0	7.15 - 9.0	25	7.8 - 0.1	0.5 - 0.1	6.1	6.7 - 8.8
Canine	26	8.5 - 0.1	0.4 - 0.0	4.4	7.55 - 9.3	25	7.9 - 0.1	0.6 - 0.1	7.6	6.9 - 9.1
1st premolar	26	8.9 - 0.1	0.5 - 0.1	5.7	8.15 - 9.8	25	8.3 - 0.1	0.4 - 0.0	4.4	7.5 - 8.9
1st molar	26	11.5 - 0.1	0.6 - 0.1	5.1	10.26 - 12.7	25	11.2 - 0.1	0.5 - 0.1	4.1	10.3 - 12.0
2nd molar	25	11.3 - 0.2	0.8 - 0.1	6.6	9.75 - 12.6	25	10.7 - 0.1	0.6 - 0.1	5.3	9.6 - 11.7
Mandibular Teeth										
Index										
Central incisor	23	120.0 - 1.8	8.3 - 1.3	7.0	101.5 - 138.3	25	116.1 - 1.2	5.9 - 0.9	5.1	106.7 - 126.0
Lateral incisor	23	111.4 - 1.7	8.0 - 1.2	7.1	100.0 - 132.0	25	109.2 - 1.3	6.1 - 0.9	5.6	96.9 - 118.2
Canine	24	116.0 - 0.1	4.6 - 0.1	3.9	107.9 - 123.9	25	113.2 - 1.1	5.4 - 0.8	4.8	101.4 - 121.0
1st premolar	25	117.5 - 1.6	7.8 - 1.1	6.6	106.0 - 135.7	25	117.7 - 1.8	8.8 - 1.3	7.5	98.7 - 137.4
1st molar	25	96.9 - 1.0	5.0 - 0.7	5.2	86.9 - 113.5	25	95.2 - 0.7	3.4 - 0.7	3.5	90.0 - 102.6
2nd molar	25	98.2 - 1.2	5.7 - 0.8	5.8	87.9 - 113.9	24	94.5 - 0.9	4.4 - 0.6	4.7	86.1 - 104.4
Module										
Central incisor	23	5.90 - 0.1	0.4 - 0.1	7.2	5.35 - 7.2	25	5.8 - 0.1	0.3 - 0.0	5.2	5.1 - 6.2
Lateral incisor	23	6.48 - 0.1	0.4 - 0.1	6.1	5.75 - 7.4	25	6.2 - 0.1	0.3 - 0.0	5.4	5.5 - 7.0
Canine	24	7.73 - 0.1	0.4 - 0.1	4.8	7.06 - 8.6	25	7.1 - 0.1	0.5 - 0.1	6.7	5.9 - 8.0
1st premolar	25	7.98 - 0.1	0.4 - 0.1	5.4	7.35 - 8.8	24	7.6 - 0.1	0.4 - 0.1	5.1	6.8 - 8.3
1st molar	25	11.35 - 0.1	0.4 - 0.1	4.0	10.66 - 12.8	25	10.8 - 0.1	0.4 - 0.1	4.1	9.7 - 11.5
2nd molar	25	11.08 - 0.1	0.6 - 0.1	5.9	9.75 - 12.5	24	10.4 - 0.1	0.5 - 0.1	4.9	9.4 - 11.3

Table 12

Sex Differences in Mokapu Tooth Crown Dimensions
and Proportions (in Mm.)

	Mean, Males	Mean, Females	Difference	Difference by t test
Diameters				
Maxillary				
Central incisor				
Length	8.47	8.24	0.23	0.23*
Breadth	7.50	7.26	0.24	0.05
Canine				
Length	8.13	7.69	0.44	0.01
Breadth	8.81	8.26	0.55	0.01
1st premolar				
Length	7.31	6.99	0.32	0.01
Breadth	10.24	9.59	0.65	0.01
1st molar				
Length	11.11	11.04	0.07	0.69*
Breadth	11.92	11.34	0.58	0.01
2nd molar				
Length	10.69	10.16	0.53	0.04
Breadth	12.09	11.13	0.96	0.01
Mandibular				
Central incisor				
Length	5.37	5.32	0.05	0.01
Breadth	6.41	6.15	0.26	0.03
Lateral incisor				
Length	6.11	5.91	0.20	0.17*
Breadth	6.82	6.43	0.39	0.01
Canine				
Length	7.15	6.62	0.53	0.01
Breadth	8.32	7.51	0.81	0.01
1st premolar				
Length	7.39	6.91	0.48	0.01
Breadth	8.56	8.14	0.42	0.01
1st molar				
Length	11.55	11.11	0.44	0.01
Breadth	11.13	10.56	0.57	0.01
2nd molar				
Length	11.12	10.69	0.43	0.05
Breadth	10.88	10.15	0.73	0.01
Indices				
Maxillary				
Central incisor	88.9	88.4	0.5	0.01
Canine	108.4	107.6	0.8	0.01
1st premolar	140.1	137.3	2.8	0.19*
1st molar	107.3	103.0	4.3	0.05
2nd molar	113.3	110.4	2.9	0.19*
Mandibular				
Central incisor	120.0	116.1	3.9	0.08*
Lateral incisor	111.4	109.2	2.2	0.31*
Canine	116.0	113.2	2.8	0.08*
1st premolar	117.5	117.7	-0.2	
1st molar	96.9	95.2	1.7	0.18*
2nd molar	98.2	94.5	3.7	0.05

*No significant difference.

Table 13

Mesiodistal Crown Diameters of Permanent Teeth of Different Populations (in Mm.)*

Population Group	Males No.	Mean	S.E.$_M$	Females No.	Mean	S.E.$_M$
Maxillary						
Central incisor						
Mokapu	25	8.47	0.15	25	8.24	0.11
Aleuts	97	8.45	0.05	65	8.07	0.05
Chinese	267	8.68	0.03	--	--	--
Japanese	132	8.5	0.03	45	8.2	0.04
Javanese	129	8.6	0.06	35	8.2	0.12†
American whites	87	8.78	0.05	87	8.40	0.06†
Swedes	483	8.84	0.03	490	8.62	0.02†
Tristanites	152	8.78	0.05	131	8.60	0.05†
Norwegian Lapps	73	8.37	0.05	85	8.34	0.05
Canine						
Mokapu	26	8.13	0.07	25	7.69	0.11
Aleuts	81	8.03	0.04	57	7.67	0.05
E. Greenland Eskimos	9	8.09	0.06	7	7.59	--
Chinese	210	8.06	0.03	--	--	--
Japanese	142	7.8	0.03	52	7.4	0.04†
Javanese	136	8.0	0.05	42	7.7	0.08
American whites	87	7.95	0.05	85	7.53	0.04†
Swedes	463	8.10	0.02	473	7.73	0.02
Tristanites	132	7.93	0.04	112	7.74	0.04
Norwegian Lapps	194	7.74	0.03	177	7.47	0.03†
1st premolar						
Mokapu	26	7.31	0.08	25	6.99	0.08
Aleuts	77	7.15	0.04	37	6.96	0.05
E. Greenland Eskimos	10	7.65	0.18	5	7.26	--
Chinese	209	7.21	0.03	--	--	--
Japanese	140	7.3	0.03	46	7.2	0.05†
Javanese	133	7.5	0.05	39	7.3	0.07
American whites	87	7.01	0.04	84	6.85	0.05†
Swedes	135	7.18	0.03	124	7.04	0.04
Tristanites	132	6.96	0.04	112	7.02	0.07
Norwegian Lapps	221	6.75	0.03	205	6.55	0.03†
1st molar						
Mokapu	26	11.11	0.13	25	11.04	0.11
Aleuts	53	10.37	0.10	36.	10.05	0.07
E. Greenland Eskimos	27	10.84	0.10	30	10.53	0.10†
Chinese	88	10.02	0.06	--	--	--
Japanese	151	10.2	0.03	60	10.0	0.05
Javanese	129	10.8	0.06	41	10.5	0.09†
American whites	83	10.81	0.06	85	10.52	0.06†
Swedes	164	10.69	0.04	135	10.47	0.05†
Tristanites	145	10.69	0.05	122	10.45	0.04†
Norwegian Lapps	256	10.23	0.04	223	9.93	0.03
2nd molar						
Mokapu	25	10.69	0.19	25	10.16	0.14
Aleuts	51	10.00	0.10	41	9.84	0.09
E. Greenland Eskimos	38	10.23	0.08	17	10.08	0.15†
Chinese	70	9.36	0.06	--	--	-- †
Japanese	142	9.8	0.03	56	9.4	0.06†
Javanese	125	10.0	0.06	39	9.6	0.11
American whites	65	10.35	0.08	50	9.81	0.06
Swedes	151	10.47	0.05	176	10.05	0.04†
Tristanites	109	10.03	0.08	96	9.78	0.07
Norwegian Lapps	267	9.34	0.04	225	8.93	0.04†
Mandibular						
Central incisor						
Mokapu	23	5.37	0.10	25	5.32	0.08

*Data for all groups other than Mokapu are from Moorrees, 1957.
†Significant differences between Aleuts and other groups in both males and females.

Population Group	Males			Females		
	No.	Mean	S.E.$_M$	No.	Mean	S.E.$_M$
Aleuts	98	5.23	0.04	73	5.08	0.05
Chinese	216	5.56	0.03	--	--	--
Japanese	129	5.4	0.03	44	5.2	0.04†
Javanese	128	5.5	0.04	37	5.4	0.08†
American whites	85	5.42	0.03	87	5.25	0.04†
Swedes	507	5.51	0.02	491	5.42	0.02†
Tristanites	154	5.54	0.04	132	5.49	0.04†
Norwegian Lapps	76	5.36	0.03	83	5.22	0.03
Lateral incisor						
Mokapu	23	6.11	0.12	25	5.91	0.07
Aleuts	100	6.09	0.03	72	5.90	0.04
Chinese	187	6.15	0.03	--	--	--
Japanese	136	6.0	0.03	51	5.9	0.04†
Javanese	133	6.2	0.05	39	6.1	0.09†
American whites	85	5.95	0.04	87	5.78	0.04†
Swedes	507	6.13	0.02	493	5.94	0.02
Tristanites	152	6.08	0.05	135	6.08	0.04
Norwegian Lapps	123	5.98	0.04	124	5.85	0.04†
Canine						
Mokapu	24	7.15	0.08	25	6.62	0.10
Aleuts	91	7.20	0.04	74	6.71	0,04
E. Greenland Eskimos	4	7.28	--	3	6.93	--
Chinese	209	7.31	0.03	--	--	--
Japanese	146	7.0	0.02	48	6.6	0.04
Javanese	139	7.2	0.04	42	6.8	0.08†
American whites	84	6.96	0.04	87	6.47	0.04†
Swedes	503	7.12	0.02	493	6.69	0.02†
Tristanites	136	7.15	0.04	120	6.87	0.04
Norwegian Lapps	219	6.82	0.03	186	6.50	0.03†
1st premolar						
Mokapu	25	7.39	0.10	25	6.91	0.08
Aleuts	94	7.01	0.06	64	6.85	0.04
E. Greenland Eskimos	7	7.15	--	5	7.04	--
Chinese	232	7.18	0.03	--	--	--
Japanese	143	7.1	0.05	49	7.0	0.03†
Javanese	133	7.3	0.05	42	7.1	0.07†
American whites	85	7.07	0.04	87	6.87	0.04
Swedes	160	7.27	0.03	146	7.16	0.03†
Tristanites	135	7.07	0.06	120	7.10	0.05†
Norwegian Lapps	226	6.72	0.03	191	6.59	0.03†
1st molar						
Mokapu	25	11.55	0.13	25	11.11	0.09
Aleuts	47	11.56	0.08	20	11.20	0.11
E. Greenland Eskimos	18	12.02	0.11	11	11.47	0.18†
Chinese	95	11.33	0.06	--	--	--
Japanese	137	11.2	0.03	52	10.9	0.05†
Javanese	114	11.5	0.06	36	11.2	0.09
American whites	76	11.18	0.05	84	10.74	0.06†
Swedes	145	11.24	0.05	123	10.98	0.06†
Tristanites	143	11.22	0.05	112	11.01	0.05†
Norwegian Lapps	228	10.95	0.04	192	10.64	0.04†
2nd molar						
Mokapu	25	11.12	0.18	24	10.69	0.15
Aleuts	43	11.19	0.14	36	11.16	0.10
E. Greenland Eskimos	22	11.52	0.12	12	11.29	0.17
Chinese	82	10.73	0.08	--	--	--
Japanese	141	11.0	0.04	45	10.6	0.08†
Javanese	132	10.9	0.06	38	10.4	0.12†
American whites	53	10.76	0.10	53	10.34	0.08†
Swedes	241	11.15	0.04	275	10.70	0.04†
Tristanites	108	10.77	0.07	92	10.51	0.07†
Norwegian Lapps	254	10.51	0.04	203	10.06	0.04†

Table 14
Faciolingual Crown Diameters of Permanent Teeth of Different Populations (in Mm.)

Population Group	Males No.	Mean	$S.E._M$	Females No.	Mean	$S.E._M$
Maxillary						
Canine						
Mokapu	26	8.81	0.11	25	8.26	0.13
Aleuts	65	8.47	0.05	44	8.15	0.06
E. Greenland Eskimos	13	8.59	0.05	8	8.40	--
Chinese	210	8.31	0.03	--	--	--
Japanese	142	8.4	0.04	52	7.9	0.04
Javanese	136	8.5	0.05	43	7.8	0.07
Tristanites	82	9.38	0.06	47	8.87	0.08*
Norwegian Lapps	197	8.18	0.04	167	7.67	0.04*
1st premolar						
Mokapu	26	10.24	0.11	25	9.59	0.09
Aleuts	81	9.31	0.07	29	9.18	0.04
E. Greenland Eskimos	14	9.65	0.18	6	8.13	--
Chinese	209	9.39	0.03	--	--	--
Japanese	140	9.5	0.03	46	9.3	0.06*
Javanese	132	9.8	0.05	39	9.4	0.09*
Tristanites	75	9.81	0.06	49	9.65	0.09*
Norwegian Lapps	203	8.91	0.04	189	8.64	0.04*
1st molar						
Mokapu	26	11.92	0.13	25	11.34	0.11
Aleuts	45	11.34	0.09	20	11.21	0.10
E. Greenland Eskimos	30	11.80	0.06	30	11.44	0.12*
Chinese	88	11.19	0.05	--	--	--
Japanese	151	11.4	0.03	60	11.0	0.04
Javanese	130	11.8	0.05	41	11.2	0.08*
Tristanites	104	12.14	0.06	70	11.77	0.06*
Norwegian Lapps	231	11.24	0.04	208	10.74	0.04*
2nd molar						
Mokapu	25	12.09	0.15	25	11.13	0.13
Aleuts	42	11.36	0.13	27	11.28	0.12
E. Greenland Eskimos	38	11.56	0.10	17	11.49	0.17
Chinese	70	11.0	0.05	--	--	--
Japanese	142	11.6	0.03	56	10.9	0.04
Javanese	125	11.7	0.06	39	10.9	0.12
Tristanites	84	12.33	0.09	47	11.97	0.09*
Norwegian Lapps	258	10.96	0.09	198	10.26	0.05*
Mandibular						
Canine						
Mokapu	24	8.32	0.07	25	7.51	0.11
Aleuts	74	7.93	0.07	57	7.58	0.06
E. Greenland Eskimos	11	7.86	0.14	3	7.13	--
Chinese	209	7.89	0.03	--	--	--
Japanese	146	7.7	0.03	48	7.3	0.04*
Javanese	139	7.9	0.04	42	7.2	0.07
Tristanites	54	8.97	0.09	43	8.45	0.10*
Norwegian Lapps	211	7.55	0.03	190	6.95	0.03*
1st premolar						
Mokapu	25	8.56	0.11	25	8.14	0.10
Aleuts	86	7.82	0.06	49	7.58	0.06
E. Greenland Eskimos	8	7.90	0.21	7	7.42	--
Chinese	232	8.07	0.03	--	--	--
Japanese	143	7.9	0.03	49	7.8	0.04*
Javanese	132	8.2	0.06	42	7.7	0.06*
Tristanites	64	8.81	0.06	61	8.69	0.07*

*Significant differences between Aleuts and other groups, in both males and females.

Population Group	Males			Females		
	No.	Mean	S.E.$_M$	No.	Mean	S.E.$_M$
Norwegian Lapps	226	7.39	0.03	197	7.13	0.03*
1st molar						
Mokapu	25	11.13	0.08	25	10.56	0.11
Aleuts	49	10.56	0.08	16	10.29	0.11
E. Greenland Eskimos	19	11.63	0.15	14	10.90	0.13*
Chinese	95	10.67	0.03	--	--	--
Japanese	137	10.8	0.03	52	10.7	0.04*
Javanese	117	11.0	0.06	35	10.7	0.10*
Tristanites	110	11.22	0.05	100	11.08	0.07*
Norwegian Lapps	246	10.40	0.04	207	10.05	0.04*
2nd molar						
Mokapu	25	10.88	0.11	24	10.15	0.11
Aleuts	45	10.58	0.10	37	10.29	0.10
E. Greenland Eskimos	22	11.01	0.15	13	10.59	0.17*
Chinese	82	10.37	0.04	--	--	--
Japanese	141	10.5	0.03	45	10.2	0.06
Javanese	133	10.5	0.06	38	10.2	0.10
Tristanites	80	11.16	0.07	72	10.94	0.07*
Norwegian Lapps	259	10.07	0.04	218	9.62	0.04*

Table 15
Crown Indices of Permanent Teeth of Different Populations

Population Group	Males			Females		
	No.	Mean	S.E.$_M$	No.	Mean	S.E.$_M$
Maxillary						
Canine						
Mokapu	26	108.4	0.9	25	107.6	1.1
Aleuts	65	105.6	0.8	44	105.9	0.7
Tristanites	82	118.8	0.9	46	116.0	1.6*
Norwegian Lapps	160	105.6	0.4	153	102.6	0.4
1st premolar						
Mokapu	26	140.1	1.1	25	137.3	1.4
Aleuts	79	130.4	0.6	27	133.4	1.4
Tristanites	75	140.7	1.2	47	139.3	1.4*
Norwegian Lapps	186	131.5	0.4	180	132.1	0.4
1st molar						
Mokapu	26	107.3	1.4	25	103.0	1.1
Aleuts	42	109.3	0.6	18	110.2	1.3
Tristanites	99	114.3	0.6	59	113.9	0.8*
Norwegian Lapps	217	109.5	0.3	191	108.4	0.4
2nd molar						
Mokapu	25	112.8	1.5	25	110.4	1.7
Aleuts	41	114.6	1.1	26	115.0	1.0
Tristanites	77	125.8	1.1	43	124.3	1.2*
Norwegian Lapps	253	117.4	0.4	194	115.2	0.5
Mandibular						
Canine						
Mokapu	24	116.0	0.1	25	113.2	1.1
Aleuts	72	110.1	1.0	57	112.4	0.7
Tristanites	51	125.7	1.4	43	123.0	1.0*
Norwegian Lapps	181	110.4	0.5	156	107.3	0.5*
1st premolar						
Mokapu	25	117.5	1.6	25	117.7	1.8
Aleuts	82	111.3	0.9	45	111.4	0.9
Tristanites	63	126.5	0.8	59	122.3	1.2*
Norwegian Lapps	203	110.1	0.4	177	108.7	0.5*
1st molar						
Mokapu	25	9.69	1.0	25	95.2	0.7
Aleuts	47	91.5	0.6	16	92.4	1.2
Tristanites	113	99.3	0.5	90	100.1	0.6*
Norwegian Lapps	215	94.7	0.3	185	94.5	0.3*
2nd molar						
Mokapu	25	98.2	1.2	24	94.5	0.9
Aleuts	44	93.7	0.8	36	91.9	0.4
Tristanites	78	103.9	0.8	71	104.4	0.7*
Norwegian Lapps	245	95.8	0.3	195	95.8	0.3*

*Significant differences between Aleuts and other groups, in both males and females.

Table 16

Crown Areas of Permanent Teeth
of Different Populations (in Mm.)

	Males		Females		Total	
Population Group	*No.*	*Mean*	*No.*	*Mean*	*No.*	*Mean*
Maxillary						
Central incisor						
Mokapu	25	63.5	25	59.8	50	61.7
Canine						
Mokapu	25	71.6	25	63.4	50	67.5
Aleuts	65	68.1	44	62.9	109	66.0
Tristanites	80	74.5	47	68.7	127	72.3
1st premolar						
Mokapu	25	74.8	25	67.0	50	70.9
Aleuts	79	66.9	27	63.7	106	66.1
Tristanites	73	68.6	47	67.4	120	68.2
1st molar						
Mokapu	25	132.4	25	125.2	50	128.8
Aleuts	43	116.4	18	115.6	61	116.1
Tristanites	94	129.5	66	123.4	160	127.0
2nd molar						
Mokapu	25	129.2	25	113.1	50	121.2
Aleuts	41	112.7	26	110.9	67	112.0
Tristanites	76	125.1	43	116.5	119	122.0
Mandibular						
Central incisor						
Mokapu	25	34.4	25	32.7	50	33.6
Lateral incisor						
Mokapu	25	41.7	25	38.0	50	39.8
Canine						
Mokapu	25	59.5	25	49.7	50	54.6
Aleuts	72	57.2	57	51.2	129	54.5
Tristanites	51	64.0	45	57.2	96	60.8
1st premolar						
Mokapu	25	63.3	25	56.2	50	59.8
Aleuts	81	55.4	45	52.1	126	54.2
Tristanites	64	61.4	58	62.7	122	62.0
1st molar						
Mokapu	25	128.6	25	117.3	50	122.9
Aleuts	47	122.4	16	114.6	63	120.6
Tristanites	105	126.1	91	123.8	196	125.0
2nd molar						
Mokapu	25	121.0	25	108.5	50	114.7
Aleuts	44	120.1	36	115.3	80	117.9
Tristanites	79	119.6	71	115.0	150	117.4

Table 17

Morphological Characteristics of Mokapu and Modern Hawaiian* Teeth

	Mokapu			Modern	
Characteristic	*% Males*	*% Females*	*% Subadults*	*% Males*	*% Females*
Shovel-shaped† maxillary incisors (central and lateral)	20	24	16	25	28
Carabelli's cusps, maxillary molars	32	31	20	17‡	9‡
Protostylid cusps, mandibular molars	19	24	29	--	--
+4 cusp on mandibular 2nd molar	77	90	--	44	53
Y5 cusp on mandibular 2nd molar	23	10	--	56	47
Y5 cusp on all 3 molars	22		--	--	--
Y5 cusp on mandibular 1st molar	37				
Absence of 3rd molar, maxillary and mandibular	26@	29‖		24#	

*Sullivan, 1927, pp. 294-95.   ‡1st molar only recorded.   ‖22% upper, 37% lower.
†To medium and marked degree.   @23% upper, 29% lower.   #Dahlberg, 1951, p. 171.

Table 18
Mokapu Skulls Compared with Other Hawaiian Heads (in Mm.)

Measurement or Index	Males					Females				
	Mokapu Skulls	Mokapu* Restored by Caucasoid Data	Mokapu† Restored by Japanese Data	Living Hawaiians‡	Living Hawaiians@	Mokapu Skulls	Mokapu* Restored by Caucasoid Data	Mokapu† Restored by Japanese Data	Living Hawaiians‡	Living Hawaiians@
Number	135			206	74	171			175	34
Head lg.	184.3	193.2	191.6	187.8	182.4	174.5	183.3	181.2	180.2	178.8
Head br.	145.0	(153.5)	154.4	157.7	152.0	140.5	148.5	147.7	152.5	150.3
Cephalic index	79.2	79.5	80.7	84.0	83.4	80.5	81.0	81.4	84.7	84.2
Forehead br.	95.6	(106.6)‖	101.2‖	107.8‖	121.4‖	91.6	100.6‖	95.6‖	106.1‖	115.7‖
Fronto-parietal index	66.3	69.5	65.4	68.4	---	65.4	67.8	64.8	69.6	---
Face br.	138.3	149.8	144.9	144.5	140.2	129.1	142.6	134.9	137.0	136.7
Zygo-frontal index	69.8	71.3	69.9	74.7	---	71.0	70.7	70.9	77.4	---
Cephalo-facial index	95.6	97.5	93.8	91.7	92.2	92.2	96.0	91.2	89.9	91.0
Total face ht.	119.8	125.8	123.3	124.4	122.7	110.4	116.9	113.2	118.0	116.2
Facial index	86.4	84.0	85.3	86.7	87.7	85.4	82.0	83.9	86.2	85.1
Nasal ht.	55.0	56.0	---	55.6	53.6	51.0	52.0	---	52.1	51.2
Bigonial	104.4	128.6‖	116.4	111.2	131.2	96.0	119.0‖	105.8	104.8	119.6
Zygo-gonial index	76.4	86.0	80.4	77.1	---	74.4	83.5	78.6	76.5	---

*Stewart, 1957, Table XXV, p. 446; Wilder, 1912, p. 418.

†Suzuki, 1948.

‡Sullivan, 1927, pp. 281-85. Age group 20-59 years, over half from Hawaii, remainder from Kauai, Lanai, Maui, Molokai, and Oahu.

@Dunn and Tozzer, 1928, pp. 107-18 and Table 22. Hawaiians in and near Honolulu.

‖In most anthropometry some compression of tissues ordinarily takes place; the values in columns 2 through 5 for each sex probably should be larger by 2-3 mm.

Table 19
Measurements (in Mm.) and Indices, Mokapu Postcranial Bones

Measurement	Males					Females				
	No.	Mean ± S.E.	S.D. ± S.E.	V.	Range	No.	Mean ± S.E.	S.D. ± S.E.	V.	Range
Humerus										
Maximum length										
Paired L.	47	317.8 ± 1.8	12.3 ± 1.3	3.9	289 - 347	82	289.9 ± 1.3	11.9 ± 0.9	4.1	257 - 319
R.	47	317.8 ± 1.9	12.9 ± 1.3	4.1	290 - 348	82	291.9 ± 1.3	11.8 ± 0.9	4.0	264 - 323
Total L.	73	320.2	--	--	289 - 347	116	291.0 ± 1.2	12.4 ± 0.8	4.3	257 - 322
R.	71	320.8 ± 1.6	13.4 ± 1.1	4.2	290 - 351	109	291.3 ± 1.1	11.6 ± 0.8	4.0	264 - 323
Physiological length										
Paired L.	44	312.0 ± 1.8	11.8 ± 1.3	3.8	285 - 342	81	286.3 ± 1.4	12.1 ± 1.0	4.2	257 - 317
R.	44	312.9 ± 2.1	13.5 ± 1.5	4.3	284 - 343	81	288.2 ± 1.4	12.2 ± 1.0	4.2	260 - 319
Total L.	59	314.6	--	--	285 - 345	114	287.3 ± 1.1	12.0 ± 0.8	4.2	257 - 317
R.	64	315.9 ± 1.6	12.8 ± 1.1	4.1	284 - 349	108	287.5 ± 1.1	11.3 ± 0.8	3.9	260 - 319
Diameter of head										
Paired L.	52	46.2 ± 0.3	2.1 ± 0.2	4.7	41 - 52	83	39.6 ± 0.2	1.9 ± 0.2	4.9	35 - 44
R.	52	46.7 ± 0.3	2.1 ± 0.2	4.6	42 - 52	83	40.2 ± 0.2	2.0 ± 0.2	5.1	36 - 44
Total L.	71	46.3 ± 0.3	2.2 ± 0.2	4.8	41 - 52	109	40.6 ± 0.2	2.0 ± 0.1	4.9	35 - 44
R.	81	46.8 ± 0.2	2.1 ± 0.2	4.5	42 - 52	114	40.3 ± 0.2	2.0 ± 0.1	4.8	36 - 44
Minimum diameter of midshaft										
Paired L.	68	16.8 ± 0.2	1.3 ± 0.1	7.7	14 - 20	96	13.6 ± 0.1	1.1 ± 0.1	8.1	11 - 17
R.	68	17.4 ± 0.2	1.2 ± 0.1	7.1	15 - 20	96	13.7 ± 0.1	1.1 ± 0.1	8.0	11 - 18
Total L.	80	17.3	--	--	14 - 20	124	13.6 ± 0.1	1.1 ± 0.1	8.4	11 - 17
R.	86	17.4	--	--	15 - 20	122	13.8 ± 0.1	1.1 ± 0.1	8.1	11 - 18
Maximum diameter of midshaft										
Paired L.	68	22.3 ± 0.2	1.7 ± 0.1	7.8	19 - 27	96	18.3 ± 0.1	1.4 ± 0.1	7.7	15 - 22
R.	68	23.1 ± 0.2	1.7 ± 0.1	7.4	19 - 27	96	18.8 ± 0.2	1.4 ± 0.1	7.6	16 - 22
Total L.	80	22.2	--	--	19 - 27	133	18.5 ± 0.1	1.5 ± 0.1	8.3	15 - 23
R.	104	23.6	--	--	19 - 27	122	18.8 ± 0.1	1.5 ± 0.1	7.9	16 - 24
Midshaft circumference										
Paired L.	65	64.0 ± 0.5	4.2 ± 0.4	6.6	53 - 74	93	52.2 ± 0.4	3.6 ± 0.3	6.8	45 - 59
R.	65	66.3 ± 0.5	4.2 ± 0.4	6.4	55 - 75	93	53.5 ± 0.4	3.7 ± 0.3	7.0	46 - 64
Total L.	77	63.8	--	--	52 - 74	124	52.5 ± 0.3	3.8 ± 0.2	7.2	45 - 63
R.	83	66.2	--	--	54 - 74	120	53.7 ± 0.4	3.9 ± 0.3	7.3	46 - 67
Condylodiaphysial angle										
Paired L.	59	83.0 ± 0.4	2.7 ± 0.3	3.3	76 - 91	87	83.2 ± 0.3	2.6 ± 0.2	3.1	74 - 89
R.	59	81.4 ± 0.3	2.3 ± 0.2	2.8	77 - 87	87	81.9 ± 0.3	2.4 ± 0.2	2.9	75 - 87
Total L.	70	83.0	--	--	76 - 91	120	83.2 ± 0.2	2.7 ± 0.2	3.3	74 - 89
R.	85	81.4 ± 0.2	2.3 ± 0.2	2.8	77 - 87	112	81.9 ± 0.2	2.3 ± 0.2	2.7	75 - 87
Midshaft index										
Paired L.	68	75.2 ± 0.7	5.3 ± 0.5	7.1	64 - 95	96	74.6 ± 0.5	5.0 ± 0.4	6.7	65 - 87
R.	68	75.6 ± 0.6	5.1 ± 0.4	6.8	63 - 90	96	73.2 ± 0.5	5.1 ± 0.4	7.0	63 - 88
Total L.	80	75.0	--	--	64 - 95	125	74.6 ± 0.5	5.1 ± 0.3	6.8	63 - 87
R.	86	75.3	--	--	62 - 92	121	73.2 ± 0.5	5.0 ± 0.3	6.9	63 - 88

Measurement		Males					Females				
	No.	Mean ± S.E.	S.D. ± S.E.	V.	Range	No.	Mean ± S.E.	S.D. ± S.E.	V.	Range
Robustness index											
Paired L.	47	20.2 ± 0.2	1.3 ± 0.1	6.3	17 - 22	82	18.0 ± 0.1	1.2 ± 0.1	6.5	16 - 20
R.	47	20.6 ± 0.2	1.3 ± 0.1	6.3	18 - 24	82	18.3 ± 0.1	1.2 ± 0.1	6.7	16 - 21
Total L.	64	19.9	--	-	17 - 22	115	18.0 ± 0.1	1.2 ± 0.1	6.8	15 - 21
R.	70	20.6 ± 0.2	1.3 ± 0.1	6.5	18 - 24	109	19.6 ± 0.1	1.2 ± 0.1	6.4	16 - 23
Ulna											
Maximum length											
Paired L.	40	265.4 ± 1.6	10.2 ± 1.2	3.9	242 - 285	64	240.2 ± 1.3	10.5 ± 0.9	4.4	216 - 270
R.	40	266.6 ± 1.7	10.9 ± 1.2	4.1	243 - 284	64	242.7 ± 1.3	10.6 ± 0.9	4.4	218 - 275
Total L.	62	266.1 ± 1.5	12.0 ± 1.1	4.5	242 - 294	77	240.0 ± 1.2	10.9 ± 0.9	4.5	216 - 270
R.	75	266.9 ± 1.4	11.7 ± 1.0	4.4	236 - 290	98	241.9 ± 1.0	10.1 ± 0.7	4.2	216 - 275
Midshaft circumference											
Paired L.	41	45.5 ± 0.4	2.6 ± 0.3	5.6	39 - 52	62	38.3 ± 0.4	2.8 ± 0.2	7.3	33 - 47
R.	41	46.3 ± 0.5	3.0 ± 0.3	6.4	40 - 54	62	38.8 ± 0.4	3.1 ± 0.3	8.0	33 - 50
Total L.	63	45.6 ± 0.4	3.1 ± 0.3	6.8	37 - 56	94	38.4 ± 0.3	2.7 ± 0.2	7.2	33 - 47
R.	75	46.2 ± 0.4	3.4 ± 0.3	7.3	38 - 55	98	39.2 ± 0.3	3.3 ± 0.2	8.5	33 - 50
Robustness index											
Paired L.	39	17.1 ± 0.2	1.0 ± 0.1	6.0	15 - 20	64	16.0 ± 0.1	1.1 ± 0.1	7.1	14 - 18
R.	39	17.4 ± 0.2	1.0 ± 0.1	5.5	15 - 20	64	16.1 ± 0.2	1.2 ± 0.1	7.2	13 - 18
Total L.	62	17.2 ± 0.2	1.2 ± 0.1	6.8	15 - 20	95	16.1 ± 0.1	1.1 ± 0.1	6.9	14 - 19
R.	74	17.4 ± 0.1	1.2 ± 0.1	6.8	15 - 20	98	16.2 ± 0.1	1.3 ± 0.1	8.2	13 - 20
Radius											
Maximum length											
Paired L.	42	248.0 ± 1.6	9.9 ± 1.1	4.0	226 - 267	71	221.7 ± 1.3	10.7 ± 0.9	4.8	196 - 249
R.	42	248.8 ± 1.5	9.8 ± 1.1	3.9	227 - 265	71	223.2 ± 1.3	10.9 ± 0.9	4.9	196 - 254
Total L.	67	248.0 ± 1.5	11.1 ± 1.0	4.5	226 - 267	94	222.2 ± 1.1	10.5 ± 0.8	4.7	196 - 249
R.	66	248.5 ± 1.1	8.6 ± 0.8	3.4	227 - 268	109	223.3 ± 1.0	10.1 ± 0.7	4.5	196 - 255
Midshaft circumference											
Paired L.	42	42.0 ± 0.5	3.1 ± 0.4	7.4	36 - 49	71	34.4 ± 0.3	2.7 ± 0.2	7.7	30 - 42
R.	42	43.0 ± 0.4	2.7 ± 0.3	6.4	37 - 48	71	35.6 ± 0.3	2.7 ± 0.2	7.6	31 - 42
Total L.	58	42.1	--	-	36 - 49	95	34.2 ± 0.3	2.8 ± 0.2	8.3	30 - 43
R.	66	42.9 ± 0.4	2.9 ± 0.2	6.7	36 - 50	99	35.5 ± 0.3	2.7 ± 0.2	7.7	30 - 43
Robustness index											
Paired L.	42	17.0 ± 0.2	1.2 ± 0.1	7.1	15 - 21	71	15.7 ± 0.1	1.1 ± 0.1	6.9	13 - 18
R.	42	17.2 ± 0.2	1.2 ± 0.1	6.7	15 - 20	71	15.9 ± 0.1	1.2 ± 0.1	7.4*	13 - 19
Total L.	58	17.0	--	-	15 - 21	94	15.7 ± 0.1	1.2 ± 0.1	7.5	13 - 19
R.	65	17.3 ± 0.2	1.2 ± 0.1	6.9	15 - 21	99	15.9 ± 0.1	1.2 ± 0.1	7.3	13 - 19
Humero-radial index											
Paired L.	26	77.7 ± 0.4	2.2 ± 0.3	2.9	74 - 83	51	76.0 ± 0.2	1.7 ± 0.2	2.2	70 - 80
R.	26	77.6 ± 0.5	2.4 ± 0.4	3.2	72 - 82	51	76.0 ± 0.3	1.9 ± 0.2	2.5	71 - 81
Total L.	37	77.5	--	-	74 - 83	63	75.9	--	--	70 - 80
R.	37	77.6	--	-	72 - 83	69	76.2	--	--	71 - 81
Clavicle											
Maximum length											
Paired L.	51	148.7 ± 1.2	8.3 ± 0.8	5.6	125 - 171	76	133.5 ± 0.5	4.2 ± 0.3	3.1	106 - 156
R.	51	147.6 ± 1.3	9.0 ± 0.9	6.1	123 - 171	76	132.0 ± 0.5	4.1 ± 0.3	3.1	107 - 156
Total L.	65	149.1 ± 1.0	8.3 ± 0.7	5.5	125 - 171	98	132.6 ± 0.8	8.0 ± 0.6	6.0	106 - 156
R.	67	147.9 ± 1.1	9.3 ± 0.8	6.3	123 - 171	105	133.3 ± 0.8	7.8 ± 0.5	5.8	107 - 156

Table 19 (continued)

Measurement	Males No.	Mean ± S.E.	S.D. ± S.E.	V.	Range	Females No.	Mean ± S.E.	S.D. ± S.E.	V.	Range
Midshaft circumference										
Paired L.	59	35.9 + 0.4	3.3 + 0.3	9.3	28 - 42	86	29.3 + 0.3	2.4 + 0.2	8.2	25 - 36
R.	59	37.2 + 0.4	3.4 + 0.4	4.5	31 - 43	86	29.6 + 0.3	2.5 + 0.2	8.6	25 - 36
Total L.	72	36.2 + 0.4	3.3 + 0.3	9.0	28 - 44	104	29.4 + 0.3	3.3 + 0.2	11.2	25 - 36
R.	70	36.4 + 0.4	3.4 + 0.3	9.4	30 - 43	107	29.7 + 0.3	2.7 + 0.2	9.0	25 - 39
Robustness index										
Paired L.	51	24.1 + 0.3	2.4 + 0.2	9.9	20 - 29	76	22.0 + 0.2	1.8 + 0.2	8.2	18 - 26
R.	51	25.3 + 0.4	2.6 + 0.3	10.4	21 - 32	76	22.4 + 0.2	2.0 + 0.2	8.8	19 - 28
Total L.	66	24.2 + 0.3	2.3 + 0.2	9.3	20 - 29	99	21.9 ± 0.2	1.9 ± 0.1	8.8	18 - 28
R.	67	25.0 + 0.3	2.5 + 0.2	9.9	21 - 32	105	22.6 + 0.2	2.2 + 0.2	9.6	19 - 29
Claviculo-humeral index										
Paired L.	25	46.9 + 0.6	3.0 + 0.4	6.0	40 - 54	51	45.9 + 0.3	2.1 + 0.2	4.6	41 - 50
R.	25	46.5 + 0.6	2.8 + 0.4	6.0	42 - 52	51	45.4 + 0.3	2.2 + 0.2	4.8	41 - 50
Total L.	34	46.5 + 0.5	2.8 + 0.4	6.1	40 - 54	64	45.8 + 0.3	2.1 + 0.2	4.5	41 - 50
R.	41	46.2 + 0.4	2.6 + 0.3	5.6	42 - 52	64	45.4 + 0.3	2.1 + 0.2	4.6	41 - 50
Scapula										
Total length										
Paired L.	16	151.3 + 2.2	8.5 + 1.6	5.6	140 - 167	40	132.4 + 1.3	8.0 + 0.9	6.0	112 - 146
R.	16	152.6 + 2.1	8.1 + 1.5	5.3	137 - 167	40	132.7 + 1.2	7.4 + 0.8	5.6	116 - 146
Total L.	32	152.4 + 1.5	8.6 + 1.1	5.6	136 - 167	47	132.3 + 1.1	7.2 + 0.7	5.4	112 - 146
R.	24	152.1 + 1.7	8.1 + 1.2	5.3	136 - 168	52	133.2 + 1.0	7.0 + 0.7	5.2	116 - 146
Inferior length										
Paired L.	17	118.1 + 2.1	8.4 + 1.5	7.1	102 - 133	39	101.3 + 1.0	6.2 + 0.7	6.2	85 - 112
R.	17	116.8 + 2.3	9.2 + 1.6	7.9	100 - 133	39	100.9 + 0.9	5.8 + 0.7	5.8	90 - 112
Total L.	36	119.0 + 1.5	8.8 + 1.0	7.4	99 - 134	47	100.4 + 0.9	5.9 + 0.6	5.9	85 - 112
R.	27	116.0 + 1.8	9.4 + 1.3	8.1	100 - 133	52	101.2 + 0.7	5.1 + 0.5	5.0	89 - 112
Breadth										
Paired L.	24	103.2 + 1.0	4.6 + 0.7	4.4	97 - 114	46	91.6 + 0.8	5.4 + 0.6	5.9	79 - 105
R.	24	101.9 + 1.0	4.6 + 0.7	4.6	95 - 112	46	91.0 + 0.8	5.4 + 0.6	5.9	77 - 104
Total L.	34	102.3 + 0.9	5.1 + 0.6	5.0	90 - 114	57	91.2 + 0.7	5.2 + 0.5	5.7	79 - 105
R.	34	101.2 + 0.9	5.3 + 0.6	5.2	92 - 112	59	91.0 + 0.7	5.0 + 0.5	5.5	77 - 104
Total index										
Paired L.	15	67.6 + 0.8	3.0 + 0.6	4.4	60 - 71	38	68.5 + 0.6	3.8 + 0.4	5.6	61 - 77
R.	15	65.8 + 0.8	3.2 + 0.6	4.8	61 - 73	38	68.0 + 0.6	3.9 + 0.5	5.8	58 - 76
Total L.	31	66.8 + 0.6	3.6 + 0.5	5.3	60 - 73	48	68.7 + 0.6	3.9 + 0.4	5.6	61 - 77
R.	23	66.4 + 0.7	3.1 + 0.5	4.6	61 - 73	50	68.1 + 0.5	3.5 + 0.4	5.1	58 - 76
Inferior index										
Paired L.	17	87.4 + 1.2	6.4 + 0.8	7.4	73 - 103	38	90.4 + 1.0	6.3 + 0.7	6.9	78 - 106
R.	17	87.5 + 1.9	7.6 + 1.3	8.7	73 - 106	38	90.0 + 1.1	6.7 + 0.8	7.4	73 - 106
Total L.	35	86.3 + 1.0	6.1 + 0.7	7.0	73 - 103	47	90.4 + 1.0	6.4 + 0.7	7.1	76 - 106
R.	26	87.3 + 1.3	6.6 + 0.9	7.6	73 - 106	51	90.1 + 0.9	6.3 + 0.6	7.0	72 - 106
Femur										
Maximum length										
Paired L.	49	441.0 + 2.7	18.6 + 1.9	4.2	408 - 485	87	410.8 + 2.0	18.8 + 1.4	4.6	369 - 454
R.	49	440.3 + 2.7	18.6 + 1.9	4.2	407 - 484	87	410.3 + 2.0	18.5 + 1.4	4.5	367 - 453
Total L.	63	443.3	--	--	408 - 485	106	411.0	--	--	369 - 454
R.	63	441.9	--	--	407 - 501	105	411.4	--	--	367 - 453

| | Males | | | | | Females | | | | |
Measurement	No.	Mean ± S.E.	S.D. ± S.E.	V.	Range	No.	Mean ± S.E.	S.D. ± S.E.	V.	Range
Physiological length										
Paired L.	50	438.1 + 2.6	18.5 + 1.9	4.2	404 - 481	89	406.2 + 1.9	17.9 + 1.4	4.4	364 - 448
Paired R.	50	436.8 + 2.7	18.6 + 1.9	4.3	403 - 473	89	405.2 + 2.0	18.5 + 1.4	4.6	361 - 449
Total L.	60	437.4	--	--	404 - 481	104	406.2	--	--	364 - 448
Total R.	63	438.3	--	--	403 - 499	105	405.9	--	--	361 - 449
Diameter of head										
Paired L.	68	46.0 + 0.2	1.9 + 0.2	4.2	42 - 52	105	40.7 + 0.2	1.9 + 0.1	4.6	35 - 45
Paired R.	68	46.4 + 0.2	2.0 + 0.2	4.3	42 - 52	105	41.0 + 0.2	2.0 + 0.1	5.0	35 - 47
Total L.	76	46.0	--	--	42 - 52	117	40.8	--	--	35 - 45
Total R.	78	46.4	--	--	42 - 52	124	41.1	--	--	35 - 47
Subtrochanteric minimum diameter										
Paired L.	65	23.9 + 0.2	1.8 + 0.2	7.6	19 - 29	109	21.2 + 0.2	1.6 + 0.1	7.6	17 - 26
Paired R.	65	23.8 + 0.2	1.6 + 0.1	6.8	20 - 28	109	21.1 + 0.2	1.6 + 0.1	7.5	17 - 26
Total L.	68	23.8	--	--	19 - 29	119	21.1	--	--	17 - 26
Total R.	72	23.9	--	--	20 - 28	123	21.1	--	--	17 - 26
Subtrochanteric maximum diameter										
Paired L.	65	33.4 + 0.3	2.4 + 0.2	7.3	28 - 41	109	30.3 + 0.2	1.9 + 0.1	6.3	26 - 35
Paired R.	65	33.4 + 0.3	2.4 + 0.2	7.2	28 - 38	109	30.2 + 0.2	1.9 + 0.1	6.2	26 - 37
Total L.	68	34.0	--	--	28 - 41	119	30.3	--	--	24 - 35
Total R.	72	33.4	--	--	28 - 38	123	30.3	--	--	26 - 37
Midshaft lateral diameter										
Paired L.	64	25.4 + 0.2	1.8 + 0.2	7.2	22 - 30	106	22.4 + 0.2	1.6 + 0.1	7.1	18 - 27
Paired R.	64	25.0 + 0.2	1.7 + 0.2	6.9	21 - 29	106	22.2 + 0.1	1.3 + 0.9	5.8	19 - 25
Total L.	75	25.5	--	--	22 - 30	117	22.3	--	--	18 - 27
Total R.	71	25.0	--	--	21 - 29	122	22.1	--	--	19 - 25
Midshaft anteroposterior diameter										
Paired L.	64	29.9 + 0.3	2.4 + 0.2	7.9	25 - 36	106	25.8 + 0.2	1.9 + 0.1	7.5	21 - 31
Paired R.	64	29.7 + 0.3	2.1 + 0.2	7.0	25 - 35	106	25.9 + 0.2	1.8 + 0.1	7.1	22 - 31
Total L.	75	29.9	--	--	25 - 36	117	25.8	--	--	21 - 31
Total R.	71	29.8	--	--	25 - 35	122	25.9	--	--	22 - 31
Midshaft circumference										
Paired L.	59	86.5 + 0.7	5.5 + 0.5	6.3	75 - 100	97	74.9 + 0.5	4.5 + 0.3	6.0	65 - 87
Paired R.	59	85.9 + 0.7	5.5 + 0.5	6.4	73 - 100	97	74.0 + 0.4	4.2 + 0.3	5.6	66 - 87
Total L.	72	86.9	--	--	75 - 100	110	74.4	--	--	61 - 87
Total R.	67	86.0	--	--	73 - 100	114	74.6	--	--	66 - 87
Subtrochanteric index (platymeric)										
Paired L.	65	71.7 + 0.6	4.6 + 0.4	6.4	60 - 81	108	70.0 + 0.5	4.9 + 0.3	7.0	55 - 89
Paired R.	65	71.6 + 0.5	4.1 + 0.4	5.7	58 - 79	108	70.2 + 0.5	4.8 + 0.3	6.8	58 - 85
Total L.	77	71.6	--	--	60 - 81	118	69.9	--	--	55 - 89
Total R.	72	71.6	--	--	58 - 79	123	70.0	--	--	58 - 85
Midshaft index (pilasteric)										
Paired L.	64	85.4 + 1.0	7.8 + 0.7	9.1	69 - 104	106	87.4 + 0.6	6.7 + 0.5	7.7	70 - 104
Paired R.	64	84.4 + 0.8	6.3 + 0.6	7.5	71 - 104	106	86.0 + 0.6	6.2 + 0.4	7.2	67 - 100
Total L.	75	85.6	--	--	69 - 104	117	87.5	--	--	70 - 104
Total R.	71	84.3	--	--	69 - 104	122	85.8	--	--	69 - 100

Table 19 (continued)

Measurement	Males					Females				
	No.	Mean ± S.E.	S.D. ± S.E.	V.	Range	No.	Mean ± S.E.	S.D. ± S.E.	V.	Range
Robustness index										
Paired L.	49	19.5 + 0.1	0.9 + 0.1	4.9	18 - 22	88	18.2 + 0.1	0.9 + 0.1	5.2	16 - 21
R.	49	19.2 + 0.1	0.9 + 0.1	4.7	17 - 22	88	18.2 + 0.1	0.9 + 0.1	5.1	16 - 20
Total L.	63	19.5	--	--	18 - 22	105	18.2	--	--	16 - 21
R.	63	19.3	--	--	17 - 22	104	18.1	--	--	16 - 20
Humero-femoral index										
Paired L.	25	72.0 + 0.4	1.9 + 0.3	2.6	68 - 75	58	71.0 + 0.3	2.1 + 0.2	2.9	64 - 76
R.	25	72.4 + 0.3	1.6 + 0.2	2.3	70 - 76	58	71.8 + 0.3	1.9 + 0.2	2.6	68 - 77
Total L.	31	71.8	--	--	64 - 75	69	70.8	--	--	64 - 76
R.	39	72.5	--	--	68 - 80	68	71.6	--	--	68 - 77
Tibia										
Maximum length										
Paired L.	46	363.4 + 0.3	18.0 + 0.2	5.0	314 - 401	84	335.5 + 1.8	16.2 + 1.3	4.8	294 - 376
R.	46	362.3 + 0.3	17.5 + 0.2	4.8	317 - 400	84	334.6 + 1.8	16.3 + 1.3	4.9	295 - 374
Total L.	61	363.8	--	--	314 - 406	115	335.8 + 1.5	16.0 + 1.1	4.7	294 - 376
R.	69	363.5 + 2.2	18.4 + 1.6	5.0	317 - 408	111	334.9 + 1.5	15.8 + 1.1	4.7	295 - 374
Physiological length										
Paired L.	50	350.5 + 2.6	18.4 + 1.9	5.3	306 - 393	87	322.8 + 1.7	16.1 + 1.2	5.0	280 - 360
R.	50	349.6 + 2.6	18.3 + 1.9	5.2	307 - 389	87	322.2 + 1.7	15.8 + 1.2	4.9	280 - 360
Total L.	65	350.6	--	--	306 - 393	118	323.3 + 1.5	15.9 + 1.0	4.9	280 - 360
R.	68	352.6	--	--	307 - 394	114	323.0 + 1.5	16.0 + 1.1	5.0	280 - 364
Nutrient foramen A. P. diameter										
Paired L.	61	36.6 + 0.4	3.0 + 0.3	8.1	27 - 43	96	30.6 + 1.8	1.8 + 1.3	5.9	26 - 34
R.	61	36.5 + 0.4	2.7 + 0.2	7.4	27 - 43	96	30.4 + 2.0	1.9 + 1.4	6.3	26 - 34
Total L.	77	36.4	--	--	27 - 43	127	30.6 + 0.2	1.9 + 0.1	6.3	24 - 35
R.	78	36.3	--	--	27 - 43	122	30.3 + 0.2	1.2 + 0.1	6.2	25 - 35
Nutrient foramen lateral diameter										
Paired L.	61	23.8 + 0.2	2.0 + 0.2	8.3	21 - 29	95	20.7 + 1.8	1.7 + 1.3	8.4	17 - 27
R.	61	24.3 + 0.3	2.1 + 0.2	8.7	20 - 29	95	21.2 + 1.9	1.8 + 1.4	8.7	17 - 28
Total L.	76	23.8	--	--	20 - 29	127	20.8 + 0.2	1.8 + 0.2	8.7	17 - 27
R.	77	24.1	--	--	20 - 29	121	20.7 + 0.2	1.7 + 0.1	8.2	17 - 28
Midshaft A. P. diameter										
Paired L.	61	32.1 + 0.4	3.1 + 0.3	9.7	23 - 38	96	26.5 + 1.8	1.8 + 1.3	6.7	21 - 33
R.	61	32.4 + 0.4	2.8 + 0.3	8.6	24 - 37	96	26.4 + 1.8	1.8 + 1.3	6.8	21 - 30
Total L.	76	32.4	--	--	23 - 38	130	26.6 + 0.2	1.8 + 0.1	6.7	21 - 33
R.	78	32.3	--	--	24 - 38	123	26.5 + 0.2	1.8 + 0.1	6.9	21 - 31
Midshaft lateral diameter										
Paired L.	61	21.0 + 0.2	1.8 + 0.2	8.6	17 - 26	95	18.2 + 1.6	1.5 + 1.1	8.3	14 - 23
R.	61	21.3 + 0.2	1.9 + 0.2	9.1	17 - 26	95	18.4 + 1.5	1.4 + 1.0	7.7	15 - 22
Total L.	76	21.0	--	--	17 - 26	129	18.3 + 1.3	1.5 + 0.9	8.2	14 - 23
R.	77	21.1	--	--	17 - 26	122	18.2 + 0.1	1.2 + 0.1	6.8	14 - 23
Midshaft circumference										
Paired L.	57	84.8 + 0.8	6.3 + 0.6	7.4	64 - 96	89	70.6 + 0.5	4.4 + 0.4	6.3	59 - 87
R.	57	85.3 + 0.9	6.6 + 0.6	7.7	64 - 97	89	70.6 + 0.4	4.0 + 0.3	5.7	61 - 82

	Males					Females				
Measurement	No.	Mean ± S.E.	S.D. ± S.E.	V.	Range	No.	Mean ± S.E.	S.D. ± S.E.	V.	Range
Total L.	74	84.7 --	--	--	64 - 96	124	71.0 + 0.4	4.5 + 0.3	6.4	59 - 87
R.	75	84.9 --	--	--	64 - 97	116	70.6 + 0.4	4.1 + 0.3	5.8	61 - 82
Nutrient foramen index (cnemic)										
Paired L.	61	65.2 + 0.8	6.1 + 0.6	9.3	55 - 81	95	67.6 + 0.5	4.8 + 0.4	7.0	56 - 82
R.	61	66.9 + 0.8	5.9 ± 0.5	8.8	54 - 79	95	69.7 + 0.6	5.5 + 0.4	7.9	59 - 85
Total L.	76	65.3 --	--	--	55 - 81	129	69.4 + 0.5	5.6 + 0.4	8.0	56 - 85
R.	76	66.8 --	--	--	54 - 87	127	72.3 + 0.5	5.3 + 0.3	7.4	59 - 85
Midshaft index										
Paired L.	61	65.2 + 0.7	5.2 + 0.5	8.0	56 - 78	95	68.7 + 0.5	4.7 + 0.3	6.8	57 - 80
R.	61	65.6 + 0.6	4.8 + 0.4	7.3	57 - 77	95	69.6 + 0.6	5.5 ± 0.4	7.9	57 - 85
Total L.	77	65.1 --	--	--	56 - 78	131	66.8 + 0.4	4.8 + 0.3	7.0	55 - 80
R.	76	65.4 --	--	--	56 - 81	124	69.3 + 0.5	5.3 + 0.3	7.7	57 - 85
Robustness index										
Paired L.	46	23.0 + 0.2	1.2 + 0.1	5.2	20 - 25	83	21.0 + 1.2	1.2 + 0.8	5.2	18 - 24
R.	46	23.2 + 0.2	1.2 + 0.1	5.2	20 - 25	83	21.1 + 1.2	1.1 + 0.8	5.2	19 - 24
Total L.	60	23.1 --	--	--	20 - 27	115	21.1 + 0.1	1.3 + 0.1	6.0	18 - 26
R.	66	23.2 + 0.2	1.5 + 0.1	6.6	20 - 28	111	21.1 + 0.1	1.1 + 0.1	5.3	19 - 24
Tibio-femoral index										
Paired L.	27	82.3 + 0.4	2.2 + 0.3	2.7	78 - 86	63	82.2 + 0.2	1.9 + 0.2	2.3	79 - 86
R.	27	82.3 + 0.5	2.5 + 0.4	3.0	78 - 86	63	82.1 + 0.2	1.9 + 0.2	2.3	78 - 87
Total L.	33	82.5 --	--	--	78 - 86	72	82.1 --	--	--	77 - 86
R.	38	82.1 --	--	--	74 - 86	74	82.0 --	--	--	76 - 87
Fibula										
Maximum length										
Paired L.	22	351.8 + 2.8	12.9 + 2.0	3.7	326 - 373	50	329.2 + 2.2	15.5 + 1.6	4.7	294 - 365
R.	22	350.4 + 2.8	13.0 + 2.0	3.7	323 - 370	50	328.6 + 2.2	15.6 + 1.6	4.7	295 - 366
Total L.	38	356.4 --	--	--	326 - 408	68	332.5 --	--	--	294 - 377
R.	36	356.4 --	--	--	323 - 404	67	329.9 --	--	--	295 - 366
Midshaft circumference										
Paired L.	25	46.1 + 1.0	5.0 + 0.7	10.8	36 - 57	52	40.1 + 0.5	3.5 + 0.4	8.7	32 - 47
R.	25	46.8 + 1.0	5.1 + 0.7	11.0	34 - 55	52	40.8 + 0.5	3.3 + 0.3	8.2	33 - 47
Total L.	41	47.1 --	--	--	36 - 57	69	40.3 --	--	--	32 - 48
R.	41	46.9 --	--	--	34 - 55	67	40.9 --	--	--	33 - 49
Robustness index										
Paired L.	22	13.0 + 0.3	1.3 + 0.2	10.0	10 - 16	50	12.3 + 0.2	1.0 + 0.1	8.3	10 - 15
R.	22	13.2 + 0.3	1.5 + 0.2	11.1	9 - 15	50	12.5 + 0.2	1.1 + 0.1	8.6	10 - 14
Total L.	38	13.1 --	--	--	10 - 16	68	12.2 --	--	--	10 - 15
R.	37	13.1 --	--	--	9 - 15	66	12.4 --	--	--	10 - 14
Lumbar vertebrae										
Segment 1										
Ant. ht.	43	24.0 ± 0.3	2.0 ± 0.2	8.3	18 - 28	60	24.4 ± 0.2	1.2 ± 0.11	4.8	21 - 27
Post. ht.	44	28.3 – 0.2	1.4 – 0.2	5.0	25 - 33	60	27.4 – 0.2	1.4 – 0.13	5.2	24 - 31
Segment 2										
Ant. ht.	46	25.0 – 0.3	1.9 – 0.2	7.7	19 - 28	60	25.5 – 0.2	1.9 – 0.18	7.5	16 - 29
Post. ht.	46	28.8 – 0.2	1.3 – 0.1	4.4	25 - 33	61	28.0 – 0.2	1.4 – 0.13	5.1	25 - 31
Segment 3										
Ant. ht.	44	26.3 – 0.2	1.5 – 0.2	5.8	23 - 29	60	26.1 – 0.2	1.6 – 0.14	6.0	24 - 30
Post. ht.	47	28.4 – 0.2	1.7 – 0.2	5.9	25 - 32	51	27.7 – 0.2	1.5 – 0.15	5.4	25 - 30

Table 19 (continued)

Measurement	Males					Females				
	No.	Mean ± S.E.	S.D. ± S.E.	V.	Range	No.	Mean ± S.E.	S.D. ± S.E.	V.	Range
Segment 4										
Ant. ht.	46	27.0 - 0.2	1.6 - 0.2	5.9	23 - 30	59	26.2 - 0.2	1.5 - 0.14	5.8	24 - 29
Post. ht.	47	26.9 - 0.3	1.9 - 0.2	6.9	22 - 31	59	25.9 - 0.2	1.5 - 0.14	5.7	23 - 30
Segment 5										
Ant. ht.	46	28.0 - 0.3	1.8 - 0.2	6.3	24 - 31	58	26.8 - 0.2	1.7 - 0.16	6.5	21 - 31
Post. ht.	46	24.1 - 0.3	1.9 - 0.2	8.0	19 - 28	58	23.0 - 0.2	1.8 - 0.16	7.6	19 - 26
Lumbar index	37	104.3 - 0.8	4.8 - 0.6	4.6	96 - 117	55	102.3 - 0.2	4.2 - 0.14	5.7	92 - 115
Average anterior hts.		130.3	–	–	–		129.0	–	–	–
Average posterior		136.5	–	–	–		132.0	–	–	–
Sacrum										
Length	58	109.4 - 1.4	10.4 - 1.0	9.5	91 - 131	79	106.7 - 1.2	11.0 - 0.9	9.7	85 - 135
Breadth	65	111.9 - 0.6	5.1 - 0.4	4.6	102 - 124	94	113.7 - 0.7	6.4 - 0.5	5.6	95 - 128
Index	57	102.9 - 1.2	8.7 - 0.8	8.4	82 - 121	79	106.8 - 1.3	11.4 - 0.9	10.6	84 - 141
Innominate										
Height										
Paired L.	56	208.4 + 1.2	8.6 + 0.8	4.1	190 - 225	78	195.6 + 1.0	8.8 + 0.7	4.5	181 - 214
R.	56	208.4 + 1.2	9.0 + 0.9	4.3	188 - 227	78	195.3 + 1.0	8.4 + 0.7	4.3	177 - 214
Total L.	75	209.0	–	–	190 - 225	92	195.3	–	–	178 - 214
R.	62	208.9	–	–	188 - 231	86	196.2	–	–	177 - 214
Breadth										
Paired L.	40	151.6 + 1.4	8.8 + 1.0	17.0	133 - 170	73	148.6 + 0.9	7.4 + 0.6	5.0	131 - 169
R.	40	152.4 + 1.3	8.1 + 0.9	15.5	135 - 168	73	148.5 + 0.9	7.3 + 0.6	4.9	132 - 169
Total L.	57	151.9	–	–	133 - 170	86	148.4	–	–	131 - 169
R.	54	152.5	–	–	135 - 168	86	148.6	–	–	132 - 169
Index										
Paired L.	37	72.4 + 0.4	2.5 + 0.3	3.4	68 - 76	67	76.1 + 0.4	2.8 + 0.2	3.7	68 - 85
R.	37	72.9 + 0.4	2.4 + 0.3	3.4	69 - 78	67	76.1 + 0.4	3.0 + 0.3	4.0	69 - 84
Total L.	53	72.6	–	–	68 - 76	82	77.0	–	–	68 - 85
R.	48	73.0	–	–	69 - 78	78	76.0	–	–	69 - 84
Pubic length										
Paired L.	51	79.1 + 0.7	5.2 + 0.5	6.5	70 - 89	70	80.7 + 0.5	4.0 + 0.3	5.0	71 - 93
R.	51	77.8 + 0.7	4.8 + 0.5	6.2	66 - 88	70	80.0 + 0.6	4.6 + 0.4	5.8	70 - 90
Total L.	64	79.0	–	–	70 - 89	85	80.3	–	–	70 - 93
R.	58	77.6	–	–	66 - 88	79	80.2	–	–	70 - 90
Ischial length										
Paired L.	65	88.4 + 0.5	3.7 + 0.3	4.2	81 - 97	88	80.8 + 0.4	3.6 + 0.3	4.5	72 - 89
R.	65	88.4 + 0.5	3.8 + 0.3	4.3	79 - 97	88	81.1 + 0.4	3.7 + 0.3	4.6	71 - 88
Total L.	79	88.8	–	–	70 - 100	95	80.9	–	–	72 - 89
R.	69	88.6	–	–	79 - 97	94	81.3	–	–	71 - 88
Ischio-pubic index										
Paired L.	48	89.4 + 0.5	3.7 + 0.4	4.1	82 - 98	66	99.8 + 0.5	3.8 + 0.3	3.8	92 - 108
R.	48	88.6 + 0.5	3.6 + 0.4	4.2	80 - 98	66	98.6 + 0.6	4.5 + 0.4	4.6	89 - 108
Total L.	59	89.0	–	–	76 - 98	81	101.3	–	–	91 - 108
R.	53	87.9	–	–	78 - 98	76	98.7	–	–	89 - 108
Acetabulum										
Depth of left	84	28.3 ± 0.2	2.0 ± 0.2	7.1	23 - 33	112	25.4 ± 0.2	2.2 ± 0.2	8.5	16 - 31
Diameter of left	84	53.3 ± 0.3	2.5 ± 0.2	4.7	48 - 59	112	49.3 ± 0.2	2.3 ± 0.2	11.9	42 - 54

Measurement	Males					Females				
	No.	Mean ± S.E.	S.D. ± S.E.	V.	Range	No.	Mean ± S.E.	S.D. ± S.E.	V.	Range
Pelvis										
Maximum breadth (bi-iliac)	52	253.3 ± 1.8	12.8 ± 1.3	5.1	225 - 282	86	248.7 ± 1.5	13.7 ± 1.1	5.5	215 - 286
A-P diam. of brim	52	99.8 ± 1.0	7.2 ± 0.7	7.2	84 - 114	83	112.5 ± 0.9	8.3 ± 0.6	7.4	88 - 132
Lat. diam. of brim	52	112.6 ± 1.0	7.0 ± 0.7	6.3	96 - 130	89	122.9 ± 0.8	7.6 ± 0.6	6.2	94 - 149
Brim index	48	89.4 ± 1.0	6.9 ± 0.7	7.8	77 - 108	82	92.4 ± 0.9	8.7 ± 0.7	9.4	75 - 124
Bi-ischiatic diam.	49	145.8 ± 1.1	7.7 ± 0.8	5.3	130 - 165	88	158.1 ± 1.1	10.4 ± 0.8	7.1	130 - 179
Interspine diam.	44	86.6 ± 0.8	5.2 ± 0.6	6.0	75 - 98	74	105.8 ± 1.0	8.5 ± 0.7	8.0	84 - 130
Total pelvic index	50	82.5 ± 0.5	3.6 ± 0.4	4.4	75 - 91	82	79.2 ± 0.3	3.0 ± 0.2	3.8	72 - 88
Biisch. ÷ max. br. index	51	57.5 ± 0.5	3.2 ± 0.3	5.6	52 - 65	85	63.9 ± 0.4	3.8 ± 0.3	5.9	56 - 73
Calcaneus										
Length										
Paired L.	40	74.8 + 0.7	4.3 + 0.5	5.7	66 - 84	53	67.9 + 0.4	3.1 + 0.3	4.6	61 - 75
R.	40	74.6 + 0.7	4.3 + 0.5	5.8	65 - 83	53	68.0 + 0.4	3.2 + 0.3	4.6	61 - 75
Total L.	52	74.8	–	–	66 - 84	68	68.1	–	–	61 - 76
R.	50	75.1	–	–	65 - 83	66	68.2	–	–	60 - 76
Breadth										
Paired L.	42	43.8 + 0.4	2.7 + 0.3	6.2	38 - 48	58	39.0 + 0.3	2.0 + 0.2	5.0	35 - 44
R.	42	43.8 + 0.4	2.8 + 0.3	6.4	37 - 50	58	38.8 + 0.3	2.1 + 0.2	5.4	35 - 42
Total L.	55	43.8	–	–	38 - 48	70	38.9	–	–	35 - 44
R.	51	43.7	–	–	37 - 50	70	38.7	–	–	35 - 42
Height										
Paired L.	34	45.0 + 0.5	2.7 + 0.4	6.0	39 - 52	50	40.1 + 0.3	2.2 + 0.2	5.4	33 - 44
R.	34	45.3 + 0.4	2.2 + 0.3	4.8	40 - 50	50	40.2 + 0.3	2.1 + 0.2	5.3	33 - 44
Total L.	50	44.9	–	–	28 - 52	67	39.9	–	–	33 - 46
R.	43	45.4	–	–	40 - 50	63	40.1	–	–	33 - 44
Length/breadth index										
Paired L.	39	58.5 + 0.6	3.6 + 0.4	6.1	51 - 65	54	57.4 + 0.4	2.5 + 0.2	4.4	53 - 64
R.	39	58.3 + 0.6	3.4 + 0.4	5.8	51 - 64	54	57.0 + 0.4	2.7 + 0.3	4.7	52 - 63
Total L.	50	58.0	–	–	51 - 65	68	57.2	–	–	53 - 64
R.	50	57.1	–	–	51 - 64	66	57.2	–	–	52 - 63
Length/height index										
Paired L.	34	60.9 + 0.5	3.0 + 0.4	4.9	55 - 67	51	59.1 + 0.4	3.0 + 0.3	5.2	52 - 64
R.	34	60.4 + 0.6	3.2 + 0.4	5.3	54 - 70	51	59.0 + 0.4	3.0 + 0.3	5.1	52 - 65
Total L.	50	60.0	–	–	54 - 67	67	58.8	–	–	52 - 64
R.	43	60.1	–	–	51 - 70	63	59.0	–	–	52 - 65
Breadth/height index										
Paired L.	34	103.6 + 0.9	5.4 + 0.7	5.2	93 - 112	51	103.6 + 0.8	5.9 + 0.6	5.7	92 - 123
R.	34	104.1 + 0.9	4.9 + 0.6	4.7	96 - 114	51	102.5 + 0.9	6.1 + 0.6	6.0	88 - 117
Total L.	50	103.4	–	–	93 - 115	67	103.5	–	–	92 - 123
R.	43	104.0	–	–	95 - 114	63	103.0	–	–	88 - 117
Talus										
Length										
Paired L.	49	54.2 + 0.4	2.6 + 0.3	4.9	50 - 61	68	48.4 + 0.3	2.2 + 0.2	4.6	43 - 54
R.	49	54.1 + 0.4	2.8 + 0.3	5.1	49 - 60	68	48.5 + 0.3	2.1 + 0.2	4.4	43 - 54
Total L.	62	54.0	–	–	49 - 61	79	48.4	–	–	43 - 54
R.	57	53.9	–	–	46 - 60	76	48.6	–	–	43 - 54
Breadth										
Paired L.	50	47.2 + 0.4	2.8 + 0.3	6.0	39 - 52	69	41.9 + 0.3	2.4 + 0.2	5.7	36 - 48
R.	50	47.2 + 0.4	2.6 + 0.3	5.6	40 - 52	69	42.1 + 0.3	2.1 + 0.2	5.0	36 - 48

Table 19 (continued)

Measurement	Males					Females				
	No.	Mean ± S.E.	S.D. ± S.E.	V.	Range	No.	Mean ± S.E.	S.D. ± S.E.	V.	Range
Breadth (*continued*)										
Total L.	62	47.1 --	--	--	39 - 52	79	41.9 --	--	--	36 - 48
R.	58	47.0 --	--	--	40 - 52	77	42.1 --	--	--	36 - 48
Height										
Paired L.	48	31.2 + 0.3	1.8 + 0.2	5.9	25 - 35	69	28.0 ± 0.2	1.4 + 0.1	5.9	25 - 32
R.	48	31.1 + 0.2	1.7 + 0.2	5.5	25 - 34	69	27.9 + 0.2	1.3 + 0.1	4.6	25 - 32
Total L.	62	31.2 --	--	--	25 - 35	79	28.0 --	--	--	25 - 32
R.	56	31.0 --	--	--	25 - 34	77	27.9 --	--	--	25 - 32
Length/breadth index										
Paired L.	49	86.9 + 0.6	4.5 + 0.5	5.2	77 - 93	68	86.6 + 0.5	4.4 + 0.4	5.1	77 - 98
R.	49	87.2 + 0.6	4.4 + 0.4	5.0	77 - 96	68	86.9 + 0.5	4.0 + 0.3	4.6	76 - 96
Total L.	62	87.0 --	--	--	77 - 94	79	86.5 --	--	--	77 - 98
R.	57	87.3 --	--	--	77 - 96	76	86.8 --	--	--	76 - 96
Length/height index										
Paired L.	48	57.7 + 0.4	2.9 + 0.3	5.1	50 - 67	68	57.7 + 0.3	2.3 + 0.2	4.0	49 - 63
R.	48	57.3 + 0.4	2.5 + 0.2	4.3	50 - 62	68	57.3 + 0.3	2.2 + 0.2	3.8	50 - 62
Total L.	62	57.7 --	--	--	50 - 67	79	57.7 --	--	--	49 - 63
R.	56	57.2 --	--	--	50 - 63	79	57.6 --	--	--	50 - 62
Breadth/height index										
Paired L.	48	66.1 + 0.5	3.3 + 0.3	4.9	62 - 75	69	67.0 + 0.4	3.5 + 0.3	5.2	59 - 75
R.	48	65.9 + 0.5	3.5 + 0.4	5.2	60 - 73	69	67.3 + 0.4	3.0 + 0.3	4.4	60 - 75
Total L.	50	66.0 --	--	--	61 - 75	79	67.0 --	--	--	59 - 75
R.	56	65.8 --	--	--	55 - 73	77	66.4 --	--	--	60 - 75
Left intermembral index										
Arm/leg	20	70.0 + 0.3	1.2 + 0.2	1.7	67 - 73	49	68.7 + 0.2	1.7 + 0.1	2.5	64 - 72

Table 20

Comparative Values of the Ischio-pubic Index and the Lengths of the Pubis and Ischium in Various Racial Groups

Series	I-P Index				Pubic Length				Ischial Length			
	No.	Range	Mean	S.D.	No.	Range	Mean	S.D.	No.	Range	Mean	S.D.
Mokapu												
Male	48	80 - 98	88.9	3.6	51	66 - 89	78.4	5.0	65	79 - 97	88.4	3.7
Female	66	89 - 108	99.2	4.2	70	70 - 93	80.4	4.0	88	71 - 89	81.0	4.6
American white*												
Male	100	73 - 94	83.6	4.0	100	65 - 83	73.8	4.1	100	75 - 98	88.4	4.3
Female	100	91 - 115	99.5	5.1	100	69 - 95	77.9	4.4	100	69 - 93	78.3	3.8
American Negro*												
Male	50	71 - 88	79.9	4.0	50	60 - 88	69.2	4.7	50	79 - 96	86.6	3.6
Female	50	84 - 106	95.0	4.6	50	63 - 86	73.5	4.4	50	67 - 86	77.5	4.4
Bantu†												
Male	82	70 - 91	82.5	4.6	82	57 - 78	66.2	4.5	82	71 - 92	80.3	4.5
Female	70	87 - 107	98.1	4.1	70	66 - 84	73.2	4.1	70	68 - 84	74.8	3.5
Bushman†												
Male	26	76 - 91	83.7	3.3	26	53 - 67	60.4	3.5	26	66 - 78	72.2	3.4
Female	29	93 - 108	100.0	3.9	29	60 - 76	66.8	4.0	29	61 - 76	66.9	3.9
Indian Knoll‡												
Male	96	84 - 99	91.2	3.7	96	68 - 85	74.7	4.1	96	74 - 90	81.1	3.7
Female	55	96 - 116	104.3	4.3	55	68 - 88	78.8	4.6	55	66 - 84	75.6	3.9
Eskimo@												
Male	129	73 - 92	83.9	3.7	129	68 - 85	74.1	4.0	129	79 - 98	88.4	4.0
Female	95	91 - 109	98.8	3.8	95	73 - 90	80.1	5.1	95	72 - 89	81.0	5.0

*Washburn, 1948.
†Idem, 1949.
‡Snow and Stille, 1951, pp. 251-52, and unpublished manuscript.
@Hanna and Washburn, 1953, pp. 21-27.

Table 21
Mokapu Paired Bone Asymmetries

Bone	Males No.	%	Females No.	%	Bone	Males No.	%	Females No.	%
Humerus					Left broader	9	28.1	20	38.5
Left longer	18	41.9	16	21.6	Equal	5	15.6	6	11.5
Equal	6	13.9	6	8.1	Right broader	18	56.3	26	50.0
Right longer	19	44.2	52	70.3	Total	32	100.0	52	100.0
Total	43	100.0	74	100.0	**Femur**				
Radius					Left longer	24	54.5	42	54.5
Left longer	18	45.0	10	15.9	Equal	5	11.4	11	14.3
Equal	7	17.5	8	12.7	Right longer	15	34.1	24	31.2
Right longer	15	37.5	45	71.4	Total	44	100.0	77	100.0
Total	40	100.0	63	100.0	**Fibula**				
Scapula					Left longer	13	65.0	28	60.8
Left longer	6	35.3	18	45.0	Equal	1	5.0	5	10.9
Equal	2	11.8	3	7.5	Right longer	6	30.0	13	28.3
Right longer	9	52.9	19	47.5	Total	20	100.0	46	100.0
Total	17	100.0	40	100.0	**Talus**				
Left broader	13	65.0	25	53.2	Left longer	14	29.2	10	15.2
Equal	5	25.0	14	29.8	Equal	25	52.0	38	57.5
Right broader	2	10.0	8	17.0	Right longer	9	18.8	18	27.3
Total	20	100.0	47	100.0	Total	48	100.0	66	100.0
Ulna					**Tibia**				
Left longer	14	35.0	12	20.7	Left longer	19	47.5	38	52.0
Equal	2	5.0	5	8.6	Equal	10	25.0	15	20.6
Right longer	24	60.0	41	70.7	Right longer	11	27.5	20	27.4
Total	40	100.0	58	100.0	Total	40	100.0	73	100.0
Clavicle					**Calcaneus**				
Left longer	30	58.8	41	54.0	Left longer	8	20.5	10	18.5
Equal	4	7.9	8	10.5	Equal	13	33.3	32	59.3
Right longer	17	33.3	27	35.5	Right longer	18	46.2	12	22.2
Total	51	100.0	76	100.0	Total	39	100.0	54	100.0
Innominate									
Left higher	24	49.0	29	45.3					
Equal	7	14.3	17	26.6					
Right higher	18	36.7	18	28.1					
Total	49	100.0	64	100.0					

Table 22
Mokapu Postcranial Features, Paired Bones

	Males				Females			
	Left		Right		Left		Right	
Feature	No.	%	No.	%	No.	%	No.	%
Humerus								
Mid-shaft shape	75*				101*			
Triangular	19	25.3	18	24.0	21	20.8	22	21.8
Prismatic (oblong)	31	41.4	31	41.3	42	41.6	44	43.6
Planoconvex	25	33.3	26	34.7	38	37.6	35	34.6
Muscularity	76*				101*			
Weak	13	17.1	13	17.1	35	34.7	37	36.6
Average	17	22.4	16	21.0	42	41.6	36	35.6
Strong	28	36.8	30	39.5	16	15.8	23	22.8
Very strong	18	23.7	17	22.4	8	7.9	5	5.0
Olecranon foramen (septal apertures)	75*				100*			
Absent	67	89.4	69	92.0	50	50.0	55	55.0
Small	7	9.3	4	5.3	27	27.0	26	26.0
Large	1	1.3	2	2.7	23	23.0	19	19.0
Lateral flare (supracondylar)								
(coracobrachialis)	73*				97*			
Small	8	11.0	7	9.6	39	40.2	37	38.2
Average	29	39.7	30	41.1	40	41.3	39	40.2
Large	28	38.3	28	38.3	17	17.5	20	20.6
Very large	8	11.0	8	11.0	1	1.0	1	1.0
Ulna								
Bowing	61*				75*			
Absent	6	9.9	6	9.9	2	2.7	2	2.7
Small	31	50.8	31	50.8	38	50.6	37	49.3
Average	23	37.7	24	39.3	32	42.7	33	44.0
Large	1	1.6	0	0	3	4.0	3	4.0
Notch	61*				71*			
Small	0	0	0	0	3	4.2	3	4.2
Average	10	16.4	10	16.4	35	49.3	34	47.9
Large	51	83.6	51	83.6	33	46.5	34	47.9
Muscular ridge	32*				33*			
Small	15	46.9	15	46.9	12	36.4	12	36.4
Average	1	3.1	1	3.1	4	12.1	4	12.1
Large	16	50.0	16	50.0	14	42.4	14	42.4
With groove	0	0	0	0	3	9.1	3	9.1
Radius								
Bowing	57*				83*			
Absent	0	0	0	0	1	1.2	1	1.2
Small	17	29.8	18	31.6	33	39.8	33	39.8
Average	37	64.9	36	63.1	48	57.8	48	57.8
Large	3	5.3	3	5.3	1	1.2	1	1.2
Interosseous crest	55*				81*			
Small	5	9.1	5	9.1	21	25.9	18	22.2
Average	30	54.5	29	52.7	44	54.3	44	54.3
Large	20	36.4	21	38.2	16	19.8	19	23.5
Pronator teres ridge (tuberositas								
pronatoria), lat. muscle scar length	65*				69*			
Less than 1 cm.	11	16.9	11	16.9	12	17.4	12	17.4
1 - 2 cm.	26	40.0	26	40.0	42	60.9	42	60.9
3 - 4 cm.	24	36.9	24	36.9	14	20.3	14	20.3
5 - 6 cm.	4	6.2	4	6.2	1	1.4	1	1.4
Clavicle								
Curvature	62*				91*			
Small	0	0	0	0	9	9.9	9	9.9
Average	47	75.8	47	75.8	76	83.5	76	83.5
Large	15	24.2	15	24.2	6	6.6	6	6.6

*Individuals observed.

Table 22 *(continued)*

Feature	Males				Females			
	Left		Right		Left		Right	
	No.	%	No.	%	No.	%	No.	%
Comparison of curvature, left with right	56*				89*			
Right greater than left	15	26.8	15	26.8	21	23.6	21	23.6
Right and left equal	40	71.4	40	71.4	59	66.3	59	66.3
Left greater than right	1	1.8	1	1.8	9	10.1	9	10.1
Closure of sternal epiphysis	59*				88*			
Open	4	6.8	4	6.8	9	10.2	11	12.5
Uniting (about 25-26 yrs.)	3	5.1	3	5.1	5	5.7	3	3.4
United	52	88.1	52	88.1	74	84.1	74	84.1
Scapula								
Shape	24*				45*			
Triangular	18	75.0	18	75.0	40	88.9	39	86.7
Triangular with extension of m. teres	6	25.0	6	25.0	5	11.1	6	13.3
Vertebral profile	23*				42*			
Concave	1	4.4	1	4.4	1	2.4	1	2.4
Convex	22	95.6	22	95.6	33	78.6	34	81.0
Straight	0	0	0	0	8	19.0	7	16.7
Lipping of glenoid cavity	27*				47*			
Absent	11	40.8	10	37.0	22	46.8	21	44.7
Beginning	4	14.8	6	22.2	13	27.7	15	31.9
Medium	7	25.9	5	18.6	10	21.3	8	17.0
Advanced	5	18.5	6	22.2	2	4.2	3	6.4
Femur								
Bowing	68*				113*			
Small	8	11.8	8	11.8	22	19.5	22	19.5
Average	48	70.6	48	70.6	84	74.3	84	74.3
Large	12	17.6	12	17.6	7	6.2	7	6.2
Midshaft shape	67*				113*			
Triangular	34	50.8	34	50.8	40	35.4	39	34.5
Planoconvex	22	32.8	22	32.8	66	58.4	68	60.2
Oval or round	11	16.4	11	16.4	7	6.2	6	5.3
Angle of neck	65*				110*			
Small	5	7.7	6	9.2	10	9.1	10	9.0
Average	54	83.1	54	83.1	74	67.3	74	67.3
Large	6	9.2	5	7.7	26	23.6	26	23.6
Muscularity	68*				112*			
Slight	6	8.8	6	8.8	22	19.7	22	19.7
Average	25	36.8	25	36.8	78	69.6	78	69.6
Great	37	54.4	37	54.4	12	10.7	12	10.7
Pilaster	68*				113*			
None	2	2.9	2	2.9	1	0.9	1	0.9
Small	16	23.5	14	20.6	47	41.6	48	42.5
Average	31	45.6	30	44.1	54	47.8	52	46.0
Large	19	28.0	22	32.4	11	9.7	12	10.6
Relief of trochanteric region	69*				103*			
Smooth (small)	9	13.1	8	11.6	4	3.9	4	3.9
Grooves	2	2.9	2	2.9	7	6.8	7	6.8
Crests	55	79.7	56	81.2	81	78.6	81	78.6
3rd trochanters	3	4.3	3	4.3	11	10.7	11	10.7
Squatting facets	64*				107*			
Absent	0	0	0	0	4	3.7	4	3.7
Neck only	3	4.7	2	3.1	2	1.9	2	1.9
Neck and condyle	35	54.7	36	56.3	42	39.3	42	39.3
Condyle only	26	40.6	26	40.6	59	55.1	59	55.1
Torsion	49*				93*			
Slight	17	34.7	14	28.6	14	15.1	19	20.4
Average	30	61.2	33	67.3	67	72.0	61	65.6
Great	2	4.1	2	4.1	12	12.9	13	14.0
Comparison of torsion	47*				91*			
Equal	12	25.5	--	--	20	22.0	--	--

	Males				Females			
	Left		Right		Left		Right	
Feature	No.	%	No.	%	No.	%	No.	%
Left greater	16	34.1	--	--	30	33.0	--	--
Right greater	19	40.4	--	--	41	45.0	--	--
Tibia								
Bowing	65*				110*			
Absent	0	0	0	0	11	10.0	11	10.0
Slight	19	29.2	19	29.2	43	39.1	43	39.1
Average	40	61.6	40	61.6	56	50.9	56	50.9
Great	6	9.2	6	9.2	0	0	0	0
Slope of plateau (head)	60*				108*			
None to slight	29	48.3	29	48.3	65	60.2	61	56.5
Average	27	45.0	27	45.0	35	32.4	36	33.3
Great	4	6.7	4	6.7	8	7.4	11	10.2
Midshaft shape (Hrdlička)	65*				110*			
I Prism	3	4.6	3	4.6	10	9.0	10	9.1
II Lateral prism	12	18.5	12	18.5	36	32.7	35	31.8
III Lateral concavity	33	50.7	31	47.7	49	44.6	49	44.5
IV Diamond	12	18.5	14	21.5	8	7.3	9	8.2
V Oval	5	7.7	5	7.7	7	6.4	7	6.4
Squatting facets on head or								
plateau (lateral condyle)	34*				78*			
Absent	6	17.6	6	17.6	10	12.8	10	12.8
Present	28	82.4	28	82.4	68	87.2	68	87.2
Squatting facets on malleolus (anterior)								
malleolus (anterior)	65*				105*			
Absent	2	3.1	2	3.1	3	2.9	3	2.9
Present	63	96.9	63	96.9	102	97.1	102	97.1
Muscularity	60*				110*			
Small	5	8.3	5	8.3	22	20.0	22	20.0
Average	21	35.0	21	35.0	65	59.1	65	59.1
Great	34	56.7	34	56.7	23	20.9	23	20.9
Extended anterior-muscle crest, S shaped	55*				87*			
None or small	5	9.1	5	9.1	5	5.7	5	5.7
Average	24	43.6	24	43.6	30	34.5	30	34.5
Large	26	47.3	26	47.3	52	59.8	52	59.8
Fibula								
Shaft shape	25*				68*			
Fluted triangle	18	72.0	18	72.0	43	63.2	43	63.2
Polygon	3	12.0	3	12.0	7	10.3	7	10.3
Prism (oblong)	4	16.0	4	16.0	17	25.0	17	25.0
Oval	0	0	0	0	1	1.5	1	1.5
Comparison of muscularity, arms to legs	55*				97*			
Arms greater	10	18.2	0	0	10	10.3	0	0
Arms equal	30	54.5	0	0	59	60.8	0	0
Arms less	15	27.3	0	0	28	28.9	0	0
Innominate								
Width of sciatic notch	76*				105*			
Narrow (ca. 37 mm.)	62	81.6	62	81.6	1	1.0	1	1.0
Medium (ca. 47 mm.)	14	18.4	14	18.4	35	33.3	35	33.3
Wide (ca. 59 mm.)	0	0	0	0	69	65.7	69	65.7
Preauricular sulcus	76*				105*			
Absent	31	40.8	31	40.8	1	1.0	0	0
Small	42	55.3	41	54.0	21	20.0	23	21.9
Medium	3	3.9	4	5.2	38	36.2	38	36.2
Deep	0	0	0	0	45	42.8	44	41.9
Unfused elements in acetabulum	76*				105*			
Absent	61	80.3	65	85.5	86	81.9	88	83.8
Present	15	19.7	11	14.5	19	18.1	17	16.2

Table 23
Mokapu Postcranial Features, Single Bones

Feature	Males No.	%	Females No.	%	Feature	Males No.	%	Females No.	%
Sternum					5th lumbar, both wings	3	4.2	6	5.2
Relative Length	31*		49*		5th lumbar, one wing	1	1.4	5	4.3
Short	1	3.2	14	28.6	Sacroiliac (wings of sacrum)	20	28.2	31	27.0
Medium	6	19.4	13	26.5	Sacroiliac, upper	13	18.3	33	28.7
Long	24	77.4	22	44.9	Sacroiliac, lower	2	2.8	3	2.6
Foramen	31*		48*		Reverse fossae	1	1.4	3	2.6
Absent	30	96.8	46	95.8	Curve	63*		90*	
Present	1	3.2	2	4.2	Small	13	20.6	35	38.9
Sternomanubrial joint	46*		61*		Average	40	63.5	52	57.8
Open	41	89.1	54	88.5	Large	10	15.9	3	3.3
Closed	5	10.9	7	11.5	V-cleft on body (AP groove				
Sternal angle	42*		56*		in promontory)	71*		112*	
Small	11	26.2	13	23.2	Absent	29	40.8	55	49.1
Medium	23	54.8	36	64.3	Present	42	59.2	57	50.9
Large	8	19.0	7	12.5	**Pelvis**				
No. of rib facets on body	28*		39*		Brim shape	64*		97*	
Five	0	0	2	5.1	Heart (polygon)	30	47.0	5	5.2
Six	15	53.6	29	74.4	Narrow oval	23	35.9	5	5.2
Seven	13	46.4	8	20.5	Round	4	6.2	15	15.4
Slope of sternomanubrial joint	14*		20*		Broad oval	4	6.2	58	59.8
Down to left side	13	92.9	14	70.0	Anterior pointed oval	3	4.7	14	14.4
Down to right side	1	7.1	6	30.0	Subpubic angle	62*		94*	
Sacrum					Angle less than 90°	51	82.3	3	3.2
Type†	67*		96*		Approx. 90°	10	16.1	9	9.6
Hypobasal	53	79.1	68	70.8	Greater than 90°	1	1.6	82	87.2
Hyperbasal	2	3.0	9	9.4	Anterior profile	69*		97*	
Homobasal	12	17.9	19	19.8	Wedge (rhomboid)	67	97.1	22	22.7
No. of segments	61*		86*		Rectangular	2	2.9	75	77.3
Five	43	70.5	69	80.2	**Talus**				
Six	18	29.5	14	16.3	Divergent head	52*		73*	
Seven	0	0	3	3.5	Much	47	90.4	62	84.9
Accessory articulations	71*		115*		Little	5	9.6	11	15.1
Absent	31	43.7	34	29.6	**Calcaneus**				
					Position at rest	42*		58*	
					Upright with tubercle	7	16.7	17	29.3
					On side (no tubercle)	35	83.3	41	70.7

*Individuals observed.

†See Martin, 1928, p. 1068, for illustrations.

Table 24
Lateral Elbow Articulations of Paired Humeri

	37 Males				52 Females					
	Left & Right		Right Only		Left & Right		Left Only		Right Only	
	No.	%	No.	%	No.	%	No.	%	No.	%
Small	7	18.9	1	2.7	15	28.8			1	1.9
Medium	19	51.4	1	2.7	15	28.8	1	1.9	1	1.9
Large	2	5.4			16	30.9			1	1.9
Absent	7	18.9			2	3.9				

Table 25
Tibial Torsion, Mokapu

	40 Males		57 Females	
	No.	%	No.	%
None	14	35.0	10	17.5
Small (± 10°)	9	22.5	17	29.8
Medium (± 20°)	12	30.0	18	31.6
Large (± 30°)	5	12.5	12	21.2

Table 26
Stature of Hawaiians

Group	Males			Females		
	No.	Average	Range	No.	Average	Range
Mokapu	75*	169.9 cm.† (66.7 in.)	158 - 183 cm. (62.2 - 72.1 in.)	115*	158.1 cm.† (62.7 in.)	145 - 175 cm. (57.2 - 69.0 in.)
Living Hawaiians‡ (20 - 59 years)	205	169.5 cm.	156 - 186 cm.	173	159.0 cm.	147 - 173 cm.
Living Hawaiians‡ (60 + years)	85	166.4 cm.	156 - 182 cm.	44	158.0 cm.	145 - 172 cm.
Pure Hawaiians@ (Adults)	70	171.3 cm.	160 - 186 cm.	34	162.6 cm.	150 - 176 cm.

*Total number of individuals compiled; actual count of limb bones: males, 385; females, 612; total, 997 separate bones.
†Trotter and Gleser, 1952, p. 463.
‡Sullivan, 1927, p. 281.
@Dunn and Tozzer, 1928, p. 102.

Table 27

Body Proportions from Bones, Various Populations

Index	Mokapu		Japanese*		Ky. Indians†		Europeans*		Ancient Greeks‡	Irish Monks‡	Australians*		Modern American and English‡
	Male	Female	Male	Female	Male	Female	Male	Female	Male	Male	Male	Female	Male
Bi-iliac ÷ femur	57.4	60.7	65.7	70.4	59.5	61.4	62.1	65.2	63.0	59.8	--	--	58.7
Bi-iliac ÷ femur + tibia	15.3	15.7	16.7	17.3	15.6	16.2	16.3	16.9	16.0	16.0	15.4	15.4	15.9
Bi-iliac ÷ stature	31.5	33.3	36.2	37.8	32.4	33.7	33.9	35.4	34.9	33.1	32.1	32.2	32.9
2 X clavicle ÷ bi-iliac	85.5	93.7	91.6	96.2	89.2	95.9	93.0	95.1	91.0	90.9	--	--	90.2
2 X clavicle + bi-iliac ÷ femur + tibia	10.6	12.5	12.3	14.4	11.1	12.8	11.3	12.7	11.6	11.0	--	--	10.9

*Schultz, 1937, pp. 293-302.
†Snow, 1948a, pp. 455-91.
‡Angel, 1946, p. 85.

Table 28
Interbone Comparisons of Various Series, Sexes Combined

Index	Mokapu	Ancient Greeks*	Whites†	Negroes†	Ky. Indians‡	Eskimos†	Australians†
Humero-radial	76.8	75.3	73.8	77.8	76.2	73.7	78.3
Claviculo-humeral	46.2	46.8	47.2	46.7	45.2	48.8	43.0
Tibio-femoral	82.2	81.8	83.4	86.2	82.9	85.5	88.8
Intermembral	71.8	69.1	69.8	70.1	70.5	71.4	70.2

*Angel, 1946, p. 71.
†Schultz, 1937, pp. 293-302.
‡Snow, 1948a, pp. 459-91.

Table 29
Porosities of the Skull, Mokapu

Affected Area	Males No.	Males %	Females No.	Females %
Skull vault	126	95.4	149	84.6
Skull base	63	47.7	136	77.2
Orbits	24	18.2	42	23.9
Palate	118	89.4	154	87.4
Total*	132		176	

*The porosity often appeared on more than one portion of the skull, as totals and percentages indicate.

Table 30
Arthritic Joints, Mokapu

Joint	Males Left	Males Right	Females Left	Females Right
Shoulder	--	1	--	--
Elbow	4	9	3	3
Wrist	--	1	--	--
Hip	2	2	1	1
Knee	12	14	7	6
Ankle	3	5	3	1

Table 31
Eburnation of Joints, Mokapu

Joint	Males Left	Males Right	Females Left	Females Right
Hip	1	--	--	1
Knee	2	3	3	3
Ankle	--	--	--	1

Literature Cited

Ackerknecht, Erwin H.
1953 Paleopathology. In *Anthropology today*, ed. A. L. Kroeber, p. 124. Chicago: Univ. of Chicago Press.

Angel, J. Lawrence
1944 A racial analysis of the ancient Greeks. *Am. J. Phys. Anthropol.* 2(4):329–76.
1946 Skeletal change in ancient Greece. *Am. J. Phys. Anthropol.* 4(1):69–97.

Barnett, C. H.
1954 Squatting facets on the European talus. *J. Anat.* 88(4):509–13.

Birdsell, Joseph D.
1951 The problem of the early peopling of the Americas as viewed from Asia. In *Physical anthropology of the American Indian*, ed. William S. Laughlin, pp. 1–69. New York: Viking Fund.

Black, G. V.
1902 *Descriptive anatomy of the human teeth.* 5th ed. Philadelphia: S. S. White Dental Manufacturing Co.

Boileau, Grant J. C.
1947 *An atlas of anatomy.* Baltimore: Williams and Wilkins.

Boucher, Barbara J.
1957 Sex differences in the foetal pelvis. *Am. J. Phys. Anthropol.* 15(4):581–600

Bowers, Warner F.
1959 *Skeletal material from the Morris site.* Bull. Oklahoma Anthropol. Soc., vol. 7. Norman.
1966 Pathological and functional changes found in 864 pre-Captain Cook contact Polynesian burials from the sand dunes at Mokapu, Oahu, Hawaii. *International Surgery* 45(2):206–17.

Briggs, Lloyd Cabot
1955 *The stone age races of northwest Africa.* Bulletin 18. Cambridge, Mass.: American School of Prehistoric Research, Peabody Museum, Harvard University.

Brues, Alice M.
1958 *Skeletal material from the Horton site.* Bull. Oklahoma Anthropol. Soc., vol. 6. Norman.

Buck, Peter H. (Te Rangi Hiroa)
1938 *Vikings of the sunrise.* Philadelphia: Lippincott.
1945 *An introduction to Polynesian anthropology.* Bernice P. Bishop Mus. Bull. 187. Honolulu.
1957 *Arts and crafts of Hawaii.* Bishop Museum Special Publication 45. Honolulu.

Charlot, Jean
1958 *Choris and Kamehameha.* Honolulu: Bishop Museum Press.

Coon, Carleton S.
1939 *The races of Europe.* New York: Macmillan.

Dahlberg, Albert A.
1945 The changing dentition of man. *J. Am. Dental Assoc.* 32(June):676–90.
1951 The dentition of the American Indian. In *Physical anthropology of the American Indian*, ed. William S. Laughlin, p. 142. New York: Viking Fund.

Dahlberg, Albert A., and Mikkelsen, Oscar
1947 The shovel-shaped character in the teeth of the Pima Indians. Abstract. *Am. J. Phys. Anthropol.* 5(2):234–35.

De Young, John Edward
1941 Preliminary measurements of the Hawaiian cranium with an emphasis upon the frontal region. Master's thesis, University of Hawaii.
1953 An analysis of the Hawaiian cranium in light of racial affinities and relation to migration routes of original proto-Polynesians. Abstract of paper, Eighth Pacific Science Congress, Manila, November 1953.

Dobzhansky, Theodosius
1957 The concept of heredity as it applies to man. *Columbia University Forum* 1(1):24–27. Reprinted in *Readings in anthropology.* New York: Crowell, 1959.
1958 *Evolution, genetics and man.* 3d printing. New York: Wiley.

DuBrul, E. Lloyd, and Sicher, Harry
1954 *The adaptive chin.* Springfield, Ill.: Thomas.

Dunn, Leslie C., and Tozzer, Alfred M.
1928 *An anthropometric study of Hawaiians of pure and mixed blood.* Papers of the Peabody Museum, vol. 11, no. 3. Cambridge, Mass.

Ellis, William
1832 Polynesian researchers. 2d ed. Vol. 1. London.

Ewing, J. Franklin
1950 *Hyperbrachycephaly as influenced by cultural conditioning.* Papers of the Peabody Museum, vol. 23, no. 2. Cambridge, Mass.

Fiddler, Frank
1956 Mokapu, a study of the land. (Mimeographed) Kaneohe, Hawaii: U. S. Marine Corps Air Station.

Genoves, Santiago T.
1958 *E studio de los restos oseos de Coixthalhuaca.* Estado de Oxaca, Mexico.

Halford, Francis John
1954 *Nine doctors and God.* Honolulu: Univ. of Hawaii Press.

Hambley, W. D.
1946 Craniometry of Ambryne Islanders. *Fieldiana Studies in Anthropol.* 37, no. 1.

Hanna, R. E., and Washburn, S. L.
1953 The determination of the sex of skeletons as illustrated by a study of the Eskimo pelvis. *Human Biol.* 25(1):21-29.

Harrison, R. J.
1958 *Man the peculiar animal.* Pelican Book A 412. London: Penguin Books, Whitefriars Press.

Hooton, Earnest A.
1918 On certain Eskimoid characters in Icelandic skulls. *Am. J. Phys. Anthropol.* 1 (1):53-76.
1930 *The Indians of Pecos Pueblo.* New Haven, Conn.: Yale Univ. Press.

Howells, William W.
1936 Some uses of the standard deviation in anthropometry. *Human Biol.* 8(4):592-600.
1941 The early Christian Irish: the skeletons at Gallen Priory. *Proceedings of the Royal Irish Academy* 46(3):144-46.
1959 *Mankind in the making.* Garden City, N. Y.: Doubleday.

Hrdlička, Aleš
1922 *Anthropology of Florida.* Publication of the Florida State Historical Soc., no. 1. Deland.
1927 *Catalog of human crania in the U. S. National Museum collection.* Proceedings of the U. S. National Museum, vol. 69, art. 5, no. 2631. Washington, D.C.
1937 The gluteal ridge and gluteal tuberosities (third trochanters). *Am. J. Phys. Anthropol.* 23(2):127-98.
1940 Lower jaw: I. The gonial angle. II. Bigonial breadth. *Am. J. Phys. Anthropol.* 27(2): 281-308.
1947 *Practical anthropometry.* 3d ed. Philadelphia: Wistar Institute.

Hughes, Byron O.
1944 Heredity and variation in the dento-facial complex. *Am. J. Orthodontic Oral Surgeons* 30(10):543-48.

Hulse, Frederick S.
1943 Physical types among the Japanese. *Studies in the anthropology of Oceania and Asia,* ed. Carleton S. Coon and James M. Andrews. Papers of the Peabody Museum, 20:122-33. Cambridge, Mass.
1957 Some factors influencing the relative proportions of human racial stocks. *Cold Spring Harbor Symposia on Quantitative Biology* 22:33-45.

Hunt, Edward E., Jr.
1959 Anthropometry, genetics and racial history. *Am. Anthropol.* 61(1):64-87.

Johnson, Lent C.
1954 Preface to *The structure, composition and growth of bone, 1930-1953,* by Marjory C. Spencer and Katherine Unler. Armed Services Medical Library. Washington, D.C.

Keith, Sir Arthur
1930 *New discoveries relating to the antiquity of man.* New York: Norton.

Krogman, Wilton M.
1939 A guide to the identification of human skeletal material. *FBI Law Enforcement Bull.* 8:1-29.
1940 Racial types from Tepe Hissar, Iran, from the late fifth to the early second millennium, B. C. In *The protohistory of Asia Minor and the Middle East.* Verhand, k. Nederland Ak. Wetensch., Afd. Natuurkunde, vol. 39, no. 2. Amsterdam.

1958   Changing man. *J. Am. Geriatrics Soc.* 6(3):242–60.

Krogman, Wilton M., and Sassouni, Viken
1957   *A syllabus in roentgenographic cephalometry.* Philadelphia: Center for Research in Child Growth.

Lasker, Gabriel W.
1946   Migration and physical differentiation: a comparison of immigrants with American-born Chinese. *Am. J. Phys. Anthropol.* 4(3):273–300.

Life Magazine
1955   Issue of January 24. Chicago.

McKern, Thomas W., and Stewart, T. Dale
1957   *Skeletal age changes in young American males.* Technical Report EPA 5. Natick, Mass.: Quartermaster Research and Development Center.

Marshall, Donald S.
1955   Precondylar tubercle incidence rates. *Am. J. Phys. Anthropol.* 13(1):147–51.

Marshall, Donald S., and Snow, Charles E.
1956   An evaluation of Polynesian craniology. *Am. J. Phys. Anthropol.* 14(3):405–27.

Martin, Rudolf
1928   *Lehrbuch der anthropologie.* 2d ed. Jena: Fischer.

Martin, Rudolf, and Saller, Karl
1957   *Lehrbuch der anthropologie.* Rev. ed. Jena: Fischer.

Meredith, Howard V.
1957   Change in the profile of the osseous chin during childhood. *Am. J. Phys. Anthropol.* 15(2):247–52.

Montagu, M. F. Ashley
1951   *An introduction to physical anthropology.* 2d ed. Springfield, Ill.: Thomas.

Moorrees, Coenraad F. A.
1957   *The Aleut dentition.* Cambridge, Mass.: Harvard Univ. Press.
1959   *The dentition of the growing child.* Cambridge, Mass.: Harvard Univ. Press.

Morris, Sir Henry
1944   *Morris' human anatomy.* 10th ed. Ed. J. P. Schaeffer. Philadelphia: Blakiston.

Nelson, Carl T.
1938   The teeth of the Indians of Pecos Pueblo. *Am. J. Phys. Anthropol.* 23(3):261–93.

Neumann, Georg K.
1946   The question of classification of the American Indian. Abstract. *Am. J. Phys. Anthropol.* 4(2):258–59.
1952   Archeology and race in the American Indian. *Yearbook of Physical Anthropology.* New York: Wenner-Gren Foundation.

Pedersen, Paul O.
1949   *The East Greenland Eskimo dentition.* Medelelsen om Gronland. Copenhagen: Bianco Lunos Bogtrykkeri.

Pratt, Helen Gay
1941   *The Hawaiians—an island people.* New York: Scribner's.

Riesenfeld, Alphonse
1956   Shovel-shaped incisors and a few other dental features among the native peoples of the Pacific. *Am. J. Phys. Anthropol.* 14(3):505–21.

Roberts, D. F.
1953   Body weight, race and climate. *Am. J. Phys. Anthropol.* 11(4):533–58.

Schaeffer, Bobb
1950   The functional evaluation of adaptive morphological characters. *Am. J. Phys. Anthropol.* 8(3):281–94.

Schultz, Adolph H.
1937   Proportions, variability and asymmetries of the long bones of the limbs and the clavicles in man and apes. *Human Biol.* 9:281–328.

Scott, J. H.
1957   Muscle growth and function in relation to skeletal morphology. *Am. J. Phys. Anthropol.* 15(2):197–234.

Seipel, C. M.
1948   Trajectories of the jaws. *Acta Odontologica Scandinavica* 8:81–191.

Shapiro, Harry L.
1939   (Field assistance by Frederick S. Hulse) *Migration and environment.* London: Oxford Univ. Press.
1943   *Physical differentiation in Polynesia.* Papers of the Peabody Museum of Harvard University. Cambridge, Mass.

Simpson, George G.
1947   *Tempo and mode in evolution.* 2d ed. Columbia Biological Series. New York: Columbia Univ. Press.

Snow, Charles E.
1940   *Condylo-diaphysial angles of Indian humeri from north Alabama.* Museum Pa-

per 16, Alabama Museum of Natural History, Alabama Geological Survey. University, Ala.

1943 The skeletal remains. In *The Riley mound and the Landing mound*, by William S. Webb. Publication of the Department of Anthropology and Archaeology, Univ. of Kentucky, 5, no. 7, pp. 608–09. Lexington.

1945 Physical anthropology of Adena. In *The Adena people*, by William S. Webb and Charles E. Snow. Reports in Anthropology and Archaeology, vol. 6. Lexington: Department of Anthropology and Archaeology, Univ. of Kentucky.

1946 Anthropometric instruments. Abstract. *Am. J. Phys. Anthropol.* 4(2):258.

1948a Indian Knoll skeletons. Reports in Anthropology, vol. 4, no. 3, pt. 2. Lexington: Department of Anthropology, Univ. of Kentucky.

1948b The identification of the unknown war dead. *Am. J. Phys. Anthropol.* 6(3):323–28.

1957 Adena portraiture. In *The Adena people*, No. 2, by William S. Webb and Raymond S. Baby. Columbus: Ohio State Historical Society and Ohio State Univ. Press.

Snow, Charles E., and Stille, Glenn G.
1951 The ischio-pubic index of the people of Indian Knoll. Abstract. *Am. J. Phys. Anthropol.* 9(2):251.

Snyder, Laurence H.
1949 The genetic approach to human individuality. *Scientific Monthly* 68(3):165–71.

Spoehr, Alexander
1957 Reflections on oceanic prehistory: Marianas prehistory. *Fieldiana Studies in Anthropol.* 48:175–82.

Stewart, T. Dale
1931 Incidence of separate neural arch in the lumbar vertebrae of Eskimos. *Am. J. Phys. Anthropol.* 16(1):51–62.

1938 Accessory sacro-iliac articulations in the higher primates and their significance. *Am. J. Phys. Anthropol.* 24(1):43–55.

1943 Relative variability of Indian and white cranial series. *Am. J. Phys. Anthropol.* 1(3):264–70.

1947 Racial patterns in vertebral osteoarthritis. Abstract. *Am. J. Phys. Anthropol.* 5(2):230–31.

1957 Evaluation of evidence from the skeleton. In *Legal medicine*, ed. R. B. H. Gradwohl, p. 446. St. Louis: C. V. Mosby.

1958 The rate of development of vertebral osteoarthritis in American whites and its significance in skeletal age identification. *Leech* 28(3,4,5):144–51.

Stokes, John G.
1920 Artificial deformations in Hawaii. *Am. J. Phys. Anthropol.* 3(4):489–91.

Sullivan, Louis R.
1924 Race types in Polynesia. *Am. Anthropol.* 26(1):22–26.

1927 Observations on Hawaiian somatology. Prepared by Clark Wissler. *Bernice P. Bishop Museum Memoir* 9(4):269–342. Honolulu.

Summerson, Hank Oser
1954 *Practical physiological chemistry.* New York: Blakiston.

Suzuki, Hisashi
1948 On the thickness of the soft parts of the face of the Japanese. *J. Anthropol. Soc. Nippon* 60:7–11.

Taber, Clarence W., et al.
1944 *Taber's cyclopedic medical dictionary.* Philadelphia: F. A. Davis.

Tappen, Neil C.
1954 A comparative functional analysis of primate skulls by the split line technique. *Human Biol.* 26(3):220–38.

Thieme, Frederick P.
1950 *Lumbar breakdown caused by erect posture in man.* Anthropological papers, no. 4. Ann Arbor: Museum of Anthropology, Univ. of Michigan.

Theime, Frederick P., and Schull, William J.
1957 Sex determination from the skeleton. *Human Biol.* 29(3):242–73.

Trotter, Mildred
1937 Accessory sacro-iliac articulations. *Am. J. Phys. Anthropol.* 22(2):247–61.

Trotter, Mildred, and Gleser, Goldine C.
1952 Estimations of stature from long bones of American whites and Negroes. *Am. J. Phys. Anthropol.* 10(4):463–514.

Turner, W.
1884 Report on human crania and other bones of the skeletons. *Zoology of the Challenger expedition*, pt. 29, pp. 63–67. Edinburgh: H. M. Stationery Office.

Wagner, Konrad Adolf
1937 The craniology of the oceanic races. *Skrif-fer Utgitt av Det Norske Videnskaps Akademi, i Oslo l. Mat.-Naturv. Klasse*, no. 2:7–193.

Washburn, S. L.
1946 The effect of facial paralysis on the growth of the skull of rat and rabbit. *Anatomical Record* 94, no. 2. Philadelphia: Wistar Institute.

1947 The effect of the temporal muscle on the form of the mandible. *J. Dental Research* 26:174.

1948 Sex differences in the pubic bone. *Am. J. Phys. Anthropol.* 6(2):199–207.

1949 Sex differences in the pubic bone of Bantu and Bushman. *Am. J. Phys. Anthropol.* 7(3):425–32.

1951 The new physical anthropology. *Trans. N. Y. Acad. of Sciences*, ser. 2, vol. 8:298–304.

Whitney, Caroline
1926 Asymmetry of vertebral articular processes and facets. *Am. J. Phys. Anthropol.* 9(4):451–55.

Wilder, Harris H.
1912 The physiognomy of the Indians of southern New England. *Am. Anthropol.* 14(3):415–36.

Williams, Herbert U.
1929 Human paleopathology. *Archives of Pathology* 7:839–902. Buffalo, N. Y.

Yule, George Udny, and Kendall, M. G.
1953 *An introduction to the theory of statistics.* 14th ed., rev. 2d impression. London: Griffin.

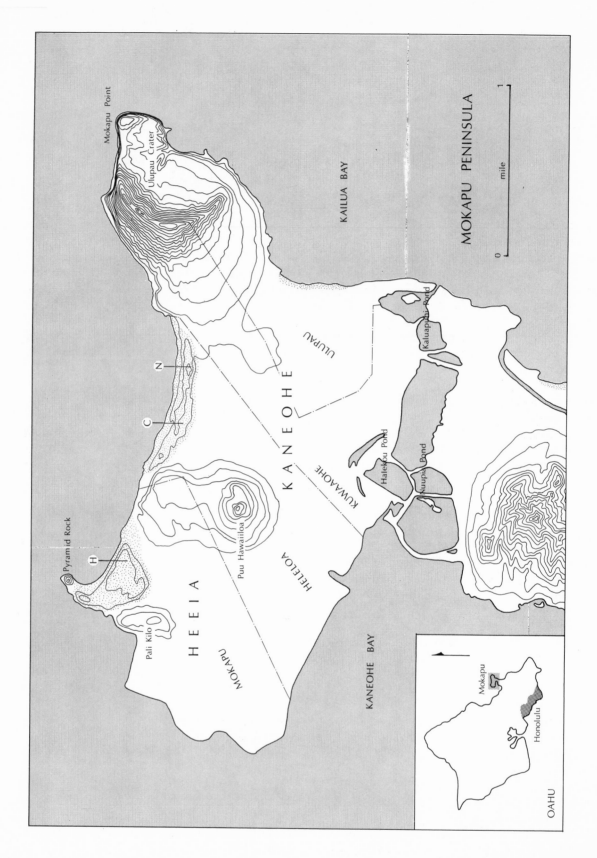

MOKAPU PENINSULA

Mokapu Point

Ulupau Crater

KAILUA BAY

0   mile   1

Z

C

ULUPAU

KANEOHE

Kaluapuhi Pond

Halekou Pond

KUWAAHE

Nuupia Pond

Pyramid Rock

H

HEEIA

Puu Hawailloa

HELEIOA

MOKAPU

KANEOHE BAY

Pali Kilo

Mokapu

Honolulu

OAHU

Mokapu: Its Historical and Archaeological Past

Robert N. Bowen

In the formative years of Polynesian anthropology, archaeology played a relatively minor role. Emphasis was placed on the rich and voluminous body of native oral literature and on personal observations of Europeans viewing changing native cultures. Anthropologists saw little use for archaeological excavations in the 1920s and 1930s, although descriptive surveys were made of the many stone surface structures dotting the islands. Polynesian settlement was thought to have occurred in relatively recent times, with little opportunity for extensive accumulation of nonperishable materials so necessary in cultural reconstructions.

Limited surveys of some disposal sites for the dead were made during this period, although descendants naturally resented such intrusions by archaeologists. As emphasized by Suggs (1960, p. 33), those collections which were made "were largely obtained by rather dubious means without location and association data, thus making it impossible to date the collections in any way at all, or often, even to know where they were made."

Historic observations of Hawaiian dead and their resting places began in 1778, three days after European discovery of the Hawaiian Islands. Captain James Cook, his surgeon, Anderson, and his artist, Webber, walked from the beach at Waimea, Kauai, into the valley to examine a war temple (*luakini heiau*). In describing the structure, Cook mentions the graves of fifteen people located within its walls.

Archaeological investigations began when the German naturalist Otto Finsch spent four days at Waimanalo, Oahu, in 1879, observing sand burials and their associations. Since Finsch's time, archaeological information has continued to accumulate, although prior to 1955 much data was vague and incomplete. Within the past fifteen years, however, careful excavations have been conducted by Bernice P. Bishop Museum and the University of Hawaii.

HAWAIIAN DISPOSAL OF THE DEAD

Before discussing the Mokapu burial site it is perhaps important to describe Hawaiian sepulcher in general, since burial was only one of at least ten distinct methods of disposing of the dead. This relatively complex pattern, when compared with contemporary American culture, can be attributed to various factors. These include a relatively dense horticultural population (approximately 300,000 people at the time of contact), an intricate and rather rigid class structure, an elaborate land tenure system, a broad spectrum of supernatural beliefs including the deification of certain kings upon their deaths, and an extensive number of physiographic features. The latter include such diverse environments as 2,000 miles of nearly open ocean in all directions, volcanic peaks (two exceeding 13,000 feet in elevation), deserts, rain forests, miles of meandering lava-tube caves, active and inactive volcanoes, freshwater lakes and streams, coral flats, and coastal sand ridges.

Of the ten basic disposal methods, exposure of human remains on the surface of the ground and their placement in freshwater environments are currently known only from historic documents. Cremation and the use of active volcanic pits, inactive pits, temples, and houses are known primarily from written records, although a limited amount of archaeological data also exists in each case. Relatively large amounts of historical and archaeological information exist for cave disposal, the use of monuments, and burial. The only documentation for underground chambers, or cists, is archaeological. The social, religious, and physiographic character of each of these methods, prehistoric and historic temporal changes which occurred, and the ways in which the dead and their associations serve as a mirror for Hawaiian life—all these have been discussed in a previous report (Bowen, 1961).

Archaeological reports of burial sites come from Kauai, Oahu, Molokai, Lanai, Kahoolawe, Maui, and Hawaii. From site distributional patterns, it is clear that Hawaiians buried their dead in sandy coastal areas as well as in inland areas having sufficient soil cover. This picture coincides closely with Hawaiian settlement patterns which were basically coastal, with some scattered inland occupation. The high concentrations of burials in sand environments, particularly where dunes exist, indicate that these areas were set aside for the dead and may have been used for long periods of time. Dunes were waste areas incapable of food production and were usually some distance from residences. Digging was easy and preservation of bone material was generally excellent.

The lack of concentrated inland burials, as exemplified by the scattered pattern of burial throughout the Honolulu area, supports the statement by Ellis (1963, pp. 258–59) that the dead were sometimes buried in secluded places near habitations, including nearby gardens. Thus, for the most part, coastal sand burial represented communal burial grounds, whereas earth burial assumed a more dispersed, familial residence pattern.

As exemplified by the Mokapu site, more information on the Hawaiian population as a biological entity can be gleaned from burials than from any other type of archaeological site. Sand burials in particular, when they occur in upper levels, are generally in excellent condition. Burials exposed by shifting winds may be bleached, cracked, and scattered, but those below the surface retain their original positions. Occasionally, when burials lie at considerable depths or in relatively impervious pockets where they are subjected to increased moisture, considerable decomposition may occur.

On the island of Oahu, coastal sand burials have been found at a number of sites, including Waikiki, Ewa Beach, Maili, Kahuku, Kaawa, Kapapa Islet, Mokapu, Kailua, Waimanalo, Makapuu, and Waialae-Kahala. Of these locations, the greatest number of skeletons have come from Mokapu. To date, it is the most extensive burial area known for the Hawaiian Islands, and one of the largest in the Pacific.

MOKAPU: THE LAND

Mokapu Peninsula extends into the North Pacific about four miles beyond the general windward coastline of Oahu, and divides Kaneohe Bay on the west from Kailua Bay on the east. A series of shallow marine fishponds, with fingers extending into adjacent low-lying swampy areas, separates the peninsula into two parts: an expanded windward mass 3.5 miles broad at its widest point, and a constricted leeward neck little more than a mile across. The ponds are separated from the ocean on the east by a beach ridge about 300 feet wide and 10 feet above sea level. On the western side, Hawaiian walls (*kuapa*) of unknown antiquity separate the ponds from Kaneohe Bay.

The windward part of the peninsula is a large flat limestone plain formed by the emergence of a coral reef. This plain is broken by five prominent features: the Heeia and Heleloa sand dunes (93 feet), which contain most Mokapu burials; Puu Hawaiiloa (300 feet), a steep cinder and lava cone; Pyramid Rock (90 feet), the peaked remnant of a lava ridge, extending from Hawaiiloa; Pali Kilo (100 feet), another remnant of the ridge; and Ulupau Crater (680 feet), a large secondary tuff cone. Aside from these salient features, the plain does not exceed 15 feet above sea level.

Mokapu dunes are the highest on Oahu, with an average height of about 50 feet and a maximum height of 93 feet at their eastern terminus. They extend for nearly two miles between Ulupau Crater and Pyramid Rock. The only place along the crescent-shaped coast where sand has not accumulated is on the lava ridge protruding from Puu Hawaiiloa to the ocean. The ridge divides the dunes into two distinct physiographic units, one in the political district of Heeia and the other in Kaneohe.

The dunes are geologically recent. Dune formation began well after the peninsula was formed and entered a period of stability; it is the result of strong northeasterly trade winds, which blow eroded calcareous fragments of marine organisms upward from the beach and out of normal wave reach. These particles include fragments of mollusk shells, coral, coralline algae, foraminifera, echinoderm spines, and occasional bits of olivine and lava. At most points along the Oahu coast this wind action does not continue long before large storm waves return fragments to the ocean. However, at Mokapu the winds are sufficiently strong to counteract wave action and dunes are formed through the continuous accumulation of particles (Stearns and Vaksvik, 1935, pp. 39–43, 56–57).

The dunes are cream-colored and permeable and contain brackish or salt water in their deeper portions. Traces of crossbedding are evident at many eroded points and are the result of shifting winds and the accumulation of sand in pockets. Although most deposits are unconsolidated, commercial and archaeological excavations have revealed the beginning of cementation at the eastern end of the dunes where they reach their greatest height. The only well-defined stratification is located in this area.

ARCHAEOLOGICAL HISTORY

The observations of Otto Finsch (1879, pp. 326–31), although not specifically concerned with Mokapu

Peninsula, are important in the archaeological history of windward Oahu and have an important bearing on the Mokapu site. They are not only detailed but, to my knowledge, also the earliest.

Finsch spent four days at Waimanalo, just eight miles southeast of Mokapu, taking notes on exposed sand burials in wind-blown pockets edging Waimanalo Bay. He estimated that at the time of his visit the coast was inhabited by barely fifty people, but that it had evidently supported a much larger population in the past, as evidenced by the many stone walls surrounding once cultivated fields and irrigation ditches. Depopulation, he concluded, was the result of smallpox and measles epidemics which struck the area in the 1830s and 1840s. He also concluded, and rightly so, that the skeletons were "by no means the signs of an old battlefield, as they [the contemporary inhabitants] are so apt to suppose here."

Skeletons were found in extended positions on their backs and sides and in flexed positions on their sides. Finsch gives no information or orientation, sex, or age, except that "The children's skulls all fall to pieces."

No European artifacts were associated with the dead. Finsch explains this by saying, "It is only a few years since Europeans set foot here, and this part of the coast has remained untouched by them. Thus far, no ships, except very small boats, have landed at this very shallow and dangerous bay." Bird bones and broken crab claws were found near the burials, and two bird bones were sent to Europe for identification. One was "probably" the breastbone of a fowl and the other belonged to a goose, possibly the Hawaiian *nene, Anser sandvicensis.* Several tortoise shells were recovered as well as fish teeth. There were no associated domestic animal bones, except cow and horse crania on the surface.

The collection of specific archaeological information about Mokapu and its population began more than 30 years after Finsch's study when, in 1912, artifacts from the peninsula were first accessioned by John F. G. Stokes, curator of collections at Bishop Museum. He was actively engaged in expanding the museum's archaeological and ethnological holdings by encouraging local collectors to hunt for surface artifacts with the understanding that significant items would be purchased. An adz from Mokapu was sold to the museum on April 19, 1912, by a Chinese resident, Lam Zi Sun. During the next two years this collector brought in more Mokapu artifacts, which were also purchased. Included were poi pounders, polishing stones, game stones, grindstones, adzes, slingstones, a coral fishhook file, a stone mirror, a stone gouge, and a sinker. In 1914 another Mokapu resident, Nam Chay Sing, brought more slingstones, polishing stones, and adzes, another sinker, and a shell ornament (#11748) to the museum.

Three years later, MacCaughey and Austin (1917, pp. 180–96), professors of biology and astronomy at the College of Hawaii, visited the peninsula. While crossing land divisions they found "no traces of their boundaries, no vestiges of former industry. Long ago their native occupants, like those of Nu'u-anu, had dwindled and vanished." MacCaughey and Austin described the fishponds as being large arms of Kaneohe Bay cut off from the sea by heavy stone walls. The wall of Nuupia Pond was from 4 to 6 feet wide with an average height of about 5 feet and at high tide stood about 18 inches above the water. It was constructed of two laid stone walls, and the central part between the walls was filled with earth and loose rubble.

From Puu Hawaiiloa, they surveyed the plain, which then was a treeless pasture marked by cattle trails, with grazing herds of horses, mules, and cattle. Between Puu Hawaiiloa and Pyramid Rock they saw "a scattering meshwork of low stone walls, irregularly spread over the plain, and in ruins. The longer we looked, the more extensive we found these ruins to be. Later in the morning we transversed this tract, and satisfied ourselves that in the days of ancient Hawaii, Mo-kapu had been the site of several villages."

On the summit of Pali Kilo they found a maze of ruins—walls forming enclosures and irregular patterns. Among the ruins were traces of a temple, which, according to Thrum, was of the husbandry class. Near Pyramid Rock they saw fish gods represented by two lava rocks, about two feet high and mounted on a low platform. Adjacent to Kaluapuhi Pond they observed the remnants of Hawaiian salt pans.

Although MacCaughey and Austin described the dunes in detail, they were evidently unaware of the burials they contained. "These dunes are sufficiently grassed on the leeward slopes," they said, "to exclude them from the typical 'white' class, although their seaward faces are glaring white. So far as we could observe, their movement with the wind is not great, and they did not appear to be encroaching further upon the plain." Hibiscus thickets grew along the lee side of the ridge.

Few people inhabited the peninsula in 1917. According to MacCaughey and Austin it was a remote and little-known region of Oahu. A dilapidated wooden cabin, made partly of driftwood, occupied the former village site of Keaalau on leeward Mokapu. Terraced taro patches were overgrown, and a grove of coconut palms, which six years before had contained a dozen palms, had been reduced to two. At Nuupia Pond they saw the "hovel" of a Chinese keeper. In 1917 the fishponds were largely operated by Asians, including perhaps the two Chinese residents who had sold artifacts to the museum a few years before.

The only other habitation observed on the two-day trip was the home of Wally Davis, "a well-known part-Hawaiian who has long held sway over Mo-kapu." The habitation consisted of several unpainted wooden structures on the barren windswept flats. The houses were surrounded with "several patched outrigger canoes, a broken-down 'brake,' wandering disheveled fowls, noisy pigs and dogs, nondescript odds and ends."

Human skeletal material was first accessioned in 1921 when, on December 14, Edward S. C. Handy brought a "human skeleton" to Bishop Museum that had been "buried close to the sea near Mokapu Peninsula." Evidently the remains were not from the Mokapu dunes but from a coastal point on or near leeward Mokapu. The skeleton was in poor condition and was subsequently discarded.

During his archaeological survey of Oahu in 1930, J. Gilbert McAllister (1933, pp. 184–95) recorded a number of sites, including several mentioned by MacCaughey and Austin. One of his photographs (BM 15392 M163) is labeled "Exposed sand dune burial at Mokapu Peninsula." It shows a sun-bleached cranium on the surface of a dune with a large nonhuman bone beside it. The photograph was evidently taken in the Heeia dunes, as McAllister says elsewhere that Site 367, Heeia, Mokapu, is a burial site, although he gives no additional information.

While conducting his survey, McAllister investigated three structures mentioned by MacCaughey and Austin: Halekou, Kaluapuhi, and Nuupia fishponds (Site 364); the temple atop Pali Kilo (Site 365); and the fishing shrine near Pyramid Rock (Site 367). In addition, he measured an "old brackish well" (Site 366) called *Lu o wai o Kanaloa* (the dripping water of Kanaloa, great Hawaiian god of healing) in the Heeia section and mentions a legendary spring (Site 368) once located near the top of Puu Hawaiiloa.

Two years after McAllister's survey, Harold Kainalu Castle, a resident of Mokapu, found burials in the Heleloa dunes near his house. The report was investigated by Edwin H. Bryan, Jr., curator of collections at Bishop Museum, and David F. Thrum, who brought "two skulls, two mandibles, miscellaneous material, and root casts" to the museum. These were accessioned on November 7, 1932.

More finds were reported in the following two years. In 1933, John F. G. Stokes received a skull from Fred E. Harvey of Honolulu which had been found in a sand hummock near Heleloa, and more skeletal material was accessioned by Gordon MacGregor of the museum staff in 1934. In 1938, Kenneth P. Emory, museum ethnologist, was notified by a friend that a young man, Keith K. Jones, Jr., had come across human bones and ornaments in the Heeia dunes. Upon investigation Emory discovered the boy had found a unique bone and shell bracelet (c. 8939). The bracelet and eight skulls were accessioned January 27, 1938.

Emory decided to make an exploratory excavation at the site of Jones's discovery. With volunteer assistants William Lessa, Jack Porteus, and various museum staff members, he began probing the Heeia dunes on Sunday, March 6, 1938. Investigation continued on March 13 and May 8. During this initial three-day excavation the remains of approximately forty individuals were recovered. Dog teeth (c. 8940), eighty-seven land shells, a necklace, and a cone shell were found with the burials.

The survey group realized that the Heeia dunes held many burials and required large-scale excavation. Emory called Gordon T. Bowles, University of Hawaii physical anthropologist, suggesting that students participate. A nuclear group of investigators was assembled, composed of anthropology students and other interested individuals.

Bowles laid out a grid system and excavation began on October 8, 1938, with the removal of one skeleton. Excavation continued, principally on Sundays, for nearly 15 months. Altogether 41 days were spent in the field, with over thirty-six people participating in the work. With the exception of Bowles, the group's composition varied nearly every weekend. Fieldwork was voluntary and people participated when they could find time. Digging ended on January 6, 1940.

At the time excavations began, a housing development was planned for Mokapu and there was free access to the burial site. However, when World War II became imminent and land negotiations began for a naval air station on the peninsula, restrictions were imposed.

Although excavations began in the Heeia dunes, other burials were soon discovered at two points in the Heleloa dunes and a lettered site designation was established. The Heeia site was assigned the letter H, for either Heeia or Hawaiian. The Heleloa site, located in the central portion of the ridge, was called C for Castle, and the one at the eastern end, N for Navy. The N site was discovered as a result of commercial sand removal. According to field records, the following numbers of burials were removed from each location: H, 297; C, 40; N, 64; total, 401.

Due to the outbreak of war, excavation notes were not published. Peter H. Buck, director of Bishop Museum at the time the project was under way, briefly summarized the results in his book *Arts and Crafts of Hawaii* (1957, pp. 570–71), saying the excavations "revealed skeletons of women and children, among those of men, and burials in both the extended and flexed positions. Ornaments were found, chiefly the *lei palaoa* hook in bone, stone, and shell, indicating early stages in the development of the ornament. Bones of pigs, dogs, and birds were also found with the skeletons. More than 300 perfect skeletons and numbers of individual bones which had been scattered were rescued, and are now preserved in a safe mausoleum chamber provided by Bishop Museum."

During the war undocumented skeletons from various Oahu locations entered the museum, including some from Mokapu. Between 1945 and 1957 more Mokapu remains were brought to the museum by visitors to the peninsula as well as residents. On January 15, 1952, the naval station, which embraced the three sites, was commissioned as a Marine Corps air station. Technical Sergeant Frank Fiddler wrote a detailed account of Mokapu's military history in 1956, including comments on important land transactions and a summary of archaeological research up to that time.

A second major excavation, at the two Heleloa sites, was conducted by myself in 1957. At that time I was a graduate student in anthropology at the University of Hawaii, working in close cooperation with Kenneth P. Emory of Bishop Museum on a study of Hawaiian disposal of the dead as part of a master's degree program. Burials were uncovered in the central Heleloa dunes (C site) in March by Marine Corps bulldozers enlarging the existing military golf course. Responding to suggestions from museum staff members that I attempt to recover what information could be salvaged, incorporating it into my study, I began excavating on March 15. While the project was under way, additional burials were uncovered at the Ulupau end of the ridge (N site) by a commercial firm and some of these were recovered. Seventeen days were spent in the field within one month's time. Excavation began and was largely carried out under salvage conditions with little assistance. The remains of at least 116 individuals were removed; a minimum of 88 from site C and 28 from site N. In each case only about half could be recorded properly, the others having been partially or completely disturbed by bulldozers.

In the absence of complete 1938–1940 field notes, data gleaned during the 1957 excavations provide the bulk of archaeological documentation for Mokapu burials. In the following brief summary of this 1957 data, specific burial numbers and detailed statistics have been omitted for the most part. Readers who wish this information should consult the original report (Bowen, 1961, pp. 191–253).

From the close of the 1957 project through February 1969, ten more museum accessions of skeletal material came from Mokapu.

LAND DIVISIONS

In reconstructing Mokapu life, the land itself, with its political subdivisions as recorded in early documents, is an important consideration. Present divisions, shown on the map (p. 128) may or may not have existed when the Mokapu people lived. One burial site, H, lies in the Heeia land division (*ahupua'a*) and, more specifically, in the Mokapu section ('*ili*) of that division. The other two lie in the Kaneohe division and the Heleloa section. The name Mokapu may be an abbreviation of the two words, *moku kapu*, meaning a section of land which is forbidden or taboo. Heleloa, or *hele loa*, means "to go with no hope of returning" (Pukui and Elbert, 1957, p. 61). Considering recent attitudes toward death and the dead as reflected in writings by Hawaiians, it is possible that one or perhaps both of these land names were related to the dunes and the burials they contained.

The division of Heleloa burials into two distinct

units, when suitable burial areas exist in between, is of interest. Lacking a physiographic reason for separation, as between the Heeia and Heleloa sites, the division may correspond to extended family residential patterns which have left no archaeological evidence.

The land divisions, with their generations of inhabitants, may be of considerable antiquity. Writers of the last century, such as Malo (1951, p. 61) and Kamakau (1961, p. 376) say that such divisions frequently remained unchanged for long periods of time, and that while kings and chiefs fought for political control and therefore could be somewhat transient, the common people remained "fixed residents of the land" generation after generation.

CLASS

Who were the Mokapu people? To which class of Hawaiian society did they belong? One can legitimately list few or many Hawaiian classes depending on one's purpose, from two or three divisions to dozens. In examining disposal patterns, a five-class division seems useful: kings (ali'i 'ai aupuni), chiefs (ali'i), attendants (kanaka), commoners (maka'aina-na), and slaves (kauwa). The bulk of present evidence indicates that most Mokapu residents were commoners.

The body preparation of kings was highly ritualized, involving either underground heat decomposition or direct application of dissected body parts over fires, with disposal in highly inaccessible caves and niches or in guarded houses (hale poki). The bodies of lesser chiefs and officials, including shamans (kahuna), were not prepared in this manner but were sometimes distinguished by placement in religious structures or marked enclosures.

There is no evidence that Mokapu graves were marked in any way. In fact there is some evidence that extra effort was expended to conceal locations. The entire setting corresponds closely to comments made in 1804 by Urey Lisiansky (1814, p. 122), who says: "The poor are buried anywhere along the beach."

Also, as pointed out in 1879 by Finsch, repeated by Bennett (1931, p. 26), and confirmed during the 1938–1940 and 1957 excavations, coastal sand burials, including those at Mokapu, do not represent war dead, as even now popularly believed, but rather the cumulative dead of coastal Hawaiian communities. Samuel Whitney (1827, p. 184), a missionary, was told this in 1826 by Hawaiian guides as he

looked upon exposed burials at Koloa, Kauai. He says: "We passed over a mound of sand, white with human bones. I asked whether they were slain in battle; and was informed that this was the place for burying the dead, and that the wind had blown the sand away from the bones."

There remains the question of the three curved neck pendants (niho palaoa) found with Mokapu burials during the 1938–1940 excavation, and which in historic times have been thought of as representing royalty. It is my belief that too little is known about the developmental history of this ornament and its social implications to draw conclusions at this time. Buck (1957, pp. 570–71) feels the Mokapu ornaments may indicate royalty and represent early developmental stages. It is important to remember that the three Mokapu ornaments and other miniature neck pendants of this type found in archaological sites on Hawaii, Oahu, Kahoolawe, and Kauai, are not only smaller than historic royalty-associated whale and walrus pendants, but are also made of common materials, such as coral, rock oyster shell, pig upper molars and canines, whale bone, and other animal bones (Sinoto). Perhaps, rather than marking the bodies of kings and chiefs, the Mokapu ornaments may identify persons given some local authority by chiefs of the local land division, region, or island.

It is also important to note that there is a total lack of tooth evulsion in the Mokapu series. Numerous historic references, including the noted missionary and ethnohistorian William Ellis (1963, p. 122), authenticate the practice among attendants and dedicated followers of kings residing close to them of knocking out upper and lower incisors when such high-ranking people died as a sign of extreme grief. Skeletons showing this tooth pattern have been found in the Waikiki area of Oahu, a historically-documented royal residence, but no examples have come from Mokapu.

CHRONOLOGY

Of critical importance to the study of the more than 1,000 individuals recovered is the time range represented. Unfortunately, the only dates obtained so far have been relative. Mokapu burials are intrusive elements into sterile dune deposits and are unstratified among themselves, except in those rare instances when burials intersect each other or lie in direct superposition. No temporal assumptions can be made by observing burial depths beneath present dune surfaces, since surfaces at the times burials occurred were uneven and Mokapu people buried bodies at different depths.

At the eastern end of the Heleloa dunes (N site), where the main ridge reaches a height of 93 feet, ages of some burials can be determined relative to the dune's geological history. Here grave pits occasionally penetrate clearly defined strata and in a few cases there is some evidence revealing the position of the dune's surface at the time of burial. Since the only stratification found at Mokapu so far is in this location, its character will be described in some detail.

The surface of Dune 93 is stable at present, due to a substantial floral covering which has established itself and prevents further shifting. Below the vegetation is a homogeneous sand layer varying in depth from about 2 to 10 feet. Aside from dark traces of organic matter sifting down from the surface, the layer consists of light-colored, unconsolidated, calcareous sand. It has undergone little change since its deposition and appears similar to shifting surface sand in other parts of the Mokapu dunes. Irregular cross-bedding, caused by wind shifts during deposition, is clearly shown at many points.

Under this layer is a thin, black, carbonaceous sand stratum averaging about 4 inches in thickness. This layer was evidently formed by a past floral covering, perhaps similar to the present one, when the dune surface was relatively stable.

Below this thin layer and extending to the base of the commercial excavation, is a continuous body of partially cemented sand. At its greatest depth in the center of the excavation, this base layer is approximately 24 feet thick. The sand, instead of being cream-colored like the upper layer, is pinkish-gray and has a chalky appearance. Portions of the deposit are loosely consolidated, while other parts are firmly consolidated into nodules. Cross-bedding is present, but less evident than in the upper layer.

In reconstructing the geological history of the dune, an understanding of the processes causing cementation in this lower layer is necessary. Branner says that cementation of calcareous sands occurs when carbonated rain water percolates down through the sand, dissolving out the lime carbonate in upper parts and depositing it in lower parts. Stearns and Vaksvik concur with Daly that vegetation on the surface of the sand may be necessary to initiate the process and may supply the necessary

organic acids to dissolve out the lime (Stearns and Vaksvik, 1935, pp. 41–43).

The following developmental reconstruction of Dune 93 is proposed. The height and stratification of the dune may indicate that it was one of the first Mokapu dunes to form. Formation may have begun through the accumulation of sand around an irregularity in the coast. As shown by the height, arching, and cross-bedding of the lower layer, sand collection continued at a relatively constant rate accompanied by minor surface shifting as a result of changes in wind direction. A substantial dune was formed. Then, because of some environmental change, perhaps a basic shift in the direction or strength of the trade winds, or a change in climate, plants began to grow on the surface of the previously barren dune. Once established, the flora seems to have flourished for some time, holding the surface of the dune fast and preventing further movement. During this period, rain water percolated down through the vegetation carrying with it organic acids from the floral cover and dissolving out the lime; thus cementation began.

Later, because of other environmental changes, the vegetation was covered by fresh sand accumulations, with constantly shifting surfaces, although the general dome-shape of the original dune was preserved. Sand deposited during this latter period reaches a maximum height of about 10 feet in the exposed portion. Another environmental change, perhaps similar to the first, allowed the present flora to establish itself.

Burials were made during the last phase of accumulation and shifting. They began after the death of the first flora, when a considerable amount of sand had collected over it. The exact surface of the dune during the time it was being used for burial is difficult to determine, as dark traces of excavated grave fill are not evident. Sand continued to collect over the burials until the present flora established itself, stabilizing the surface of the dune.

Thus, burials at Dune 93 can be assigned a date relative to the geological history of sand accumulation at that spot.

ARTIFACT SERIATION

Lacking a ceramic tradition, Hawaiian prehistoric chronology rests primarily on changes in the style of fishhooks (Emory, Bonk, and Sinoto, 1968). Fishhooks varied widely in form, were constructed of long-lasting materials, and were abundant and breakable, thus fulfilling most prerequisites for effective time indicators.

Few artifacts have been found *in situ* with Mokapu burials. Those recovered include the three small neck pendants, two bracelets, a perforated shell pendant or stopper, a fragment of mineralized matting, an octopus fishhook point, and numerous simple basalt flake tools. Unfortunately, the one octopus point, found in 1957, is of a type of hook which ranges throughout Hawaiian occupation and is not unique to a given time period.

One important feature of the man-made evidence at Mokapu is the complete absence of European materials. While over 1,000 individuals have been recovered, no glass beads, buttons, nails, metal smoking pipe fittings, or pieces of European pottery have been found. All artifacts have been of native materials, fashioned in typically Hawaiian styles. This complete lack of European influence perhaps justifies the conclusion that the burial ground was founded, used, and abandoned prior to the time when European material culture spread to windward Oahu from leeward anchorages. The assumption that burials predate European influence is strengthened by the fact that foreign objects have been found with sand burials at other Oahu sites, showing that such items were placed with the dead when available. For example, a flexed female skeleton was found at Kailua in 1953, just four miles from the Mokapu dunes, with eighteen solid yellow glass beads, ten hollow red glass beads, and the metal parts of a smoking pipe. All came from outside the Hawaiian Islands.

RADIOCARBON DATING

While engaged in his Mokapu skeletal study, Dr. Snow found a considerable quantity of carbonaceous sand associated with an infant's skeleton (H–132). According to prewar field notes and photographs, the sample was collected on February 25, 1939, from an infant burial unearthed three feet below the surface in the Heeia dunes. The carbon completely enveloped the skeleton.

Dr. Snow sent some of this material for testing to the Groningen Radiocarbon Laboratory. The result was a dating of 75 years, ± 75 years, or 0–150 years old. According to Dr. Hessel de Vries (personal communication to Dr. Snow, March 24, 1959), who directed the sample's analysis: "It is 'impossible' that the age is more than 200. . . . Recent contamina-

tion cannot have affected the result by more than about 5 years."

Thus, in this single attempt to obtain an absolute date using radiocarbon methods, the result falls completely within the European period.

OTHER DATING METHODS

Dr. Snow also experimented with relative dating via fluorine analysis. On April 17, 1957, he sent bone samples from four burials to the Truesdail Laboratories of Honolulu to determine fluorine content. The specimens contained the following concentrations per gram of bone: H–146: 2.7 mg; H–270: 4.8 mg; C–6: 8.2 mg; and N–2: 6.5 mg.

The validity of using such data in establishing the relative chronology of bone material which does not lie in direct association has not been established. Caution should be used, since many variables are involved (Cook, 1959, pp. 276–90). Fluorine concentrations in environmental sands should be known, as content varies from site to site and may vary at the same site. Other factors may also influence fluorine concentrations and the rate of uptake at Mokapu, including the presence or absence of past and present floral cover, amount of water percolating through the sand, porosity of the sand, differences in environmental temperatures, depths of skeletons below the surface, and the amount of sodium chloride percolating through the sand from surface salt spray.

Fluorine data from Mokapu skeletons may be useful in determining relative ages in the future, when variables have been established, but the method cannot be used at present.

Dr. Snow also worked with hydroxyproline values at the University of Kentucky in 1961. Seven bone specimens were used, four from Mokapu and three from other Hawaiian sites. Values ranged from 15.7 mg per gram of bone to 32.0 mg. Since I did not participate in these efforts, I cannot comment further on results or interpretations.

BODY PREPARATION

There is little direct evidence as to the ways in which the bodies of Mokapu people were prepared. Most burials were primary, that is, individuals were buried soon after death and before decomposition, although several secondary burials were found, consisting of disarticulated bones which apparently had been collected by Hawaiians from their original disposal places and subsequently buried in the Mokapu dunes.

By reviewing historic references to Hawaiian body preparation by commoners in general, it is possible to gain some insights into what the Mokapu pattern may have been. For example, Handy and Pukui (1958, pp. 151–52) say that care of the body (*kupapaʻu*) was the responsibility of a devoted relative and was considered "a labour of love" and that a man's body was usually prepared by his wife, son, or grandson, a woman's by her daughter or granddaughter. The body was washed by the closest relative: the wife, mother, or eldest child.

There is no mention that external openings were closed, either naturally or artificially, or that the body was painted or decorated in any way. Two Mokapu burials, however, show that colored pigments may have been used occasionally, either in the house prior to burial or at the grave site. A fine wash of red clay was found covering parts of a heavily-muscled male. The entire surface of the skull, as well as adjacent sand, was stained with the red deposit. However, the left side, that is, the upper surfaces, of both the cranium and the mandible showed the most intense coloring, and stain also extended along the entire left side of the skeleton. The clay, as a powder or liquid, may have been applied directly to the body, or may have been sprinkled over it. As nearly all the long bones of this individual had been removed by Hawaiians subsequent to burial and decomposition, it is possible that these late intruders added the clay. However, a small concentration of red clay was also found over the upper part of the right femur of a semi-extended child and there had been no postmortem vandalism in this case. Special red water-soluble ocherous earth (*ʻalaea*) is even today considered by some Hawaiians to have medicinal properties and is mixed with salt and consumed. Formerly it was thought to have a fleshlike redness and was used in the purification ceremony (*hiʻuwai*), as a dye, and as a land marker (Pukui and Elbert, 1957, p. 16).

Several references describe the washing of bodies with salt water and the use of *tapa* and tree-fern fiber (*pulu*) padding between the legs to absorb polluting fluids (Green and Beckwith, 1926, p. 176; Handy and Pukui, 1958, p. 152). The same writers say clothing worn by the dead followed that worn in life. Apparently no special dress or decoration was used. Life-style clothing, of both pre-European

and European manufacture, has been found in many Hawaiian disposal caves.

Considering Hawaii's subtropical climate, one would think that burial would take place in a day or two, and apparently it did in most cases. However, Malo (1951, p. 97) says that if the person was much loved the body would be kept "a good many days" and Kaaie (ms) mentions "five days and even longer." Handy and Pukui (1958, p. 152) explain that banana stalks might be used as a bier and changed several times a day to keep the body cool, thus slowing decomposition.

Descriptions of attempts at more permanent preservation vary from effective efforts, where bodies were eviscerated and filled with salt or tree-fern fiber, to token efforts involving superficial exterior applications of salt and vegetable washes (Malo, 1951, p. 97; Handy and Pukui, 1958, pp. 152, 222; Thrum, 1928, p. 78; Green and Beckwith, 1926, pp. 176–77).

An interesting note on the persistence of exterior salt application in recent times, and therefore its possible employment at Mokapu, is given by Mr. C. S. Gray, owner of Williams Mortuary, Honolulu (personal communication). He recalls delivering coffins to Hawaiian families along the windward Oahu coast in the 1920s and 1930s. The body was usually placed on a table and services held in the home. He remembers that, while lifting bodies into coffins, sometimes Hawaiian salt would drop out of the clothing. He says: "They packed salt between the fingers, under the arms, and between the legs, believing that it preserved the body. Actually, it didn't preserve the body at all, but was just an old superstition." No clear evidence of attempts at body preservation has been found at Mokapu.

Buck (1957, p. 569) lists three methods for transporting the dead to disposal places: a carrying pole (*hoʻolewa*), a stretcher of two or more poles (*manele*), and substantial wooden supports or containers. In the first method, the body was flexed and suspended with bindings from the center of a single carrying pole. Strips of *tapa* or rope (*hau*) were used to secure the body and the pole was then lifted to the shoulders of two bearers, one at either end. The flexed position was most practical, since it offered a more compact bundle with weight concentrated in the center of the pole, providing greater maneuverability. The second method involved the use of two long poles with short cross pieces tied between them. The stretcher was carried by two men with the ends of the poles on their shoulders or by four men with one end of each pole on the inner shoulder of each bearer. Old canoe sections or boards were used in the third method.

There are numerous descriptions of the flexing process used in the *ho'olewa* method, and perhaps employed in the other two methods as well. Ellis (1827, p. 362) gives a detailed account, saying: "After death, they raised the upper part of the body, bent the face forwards to the knees, the hands were next put under the hams, and passed up between the knees, when the head, hands, and knees were bound together with cinet [sennit] or cord. The body was afterwards wrapped in a course mat." Kaaie's (ms) statement supports Ellis's description, indicating that the body was first manipulated into position and then tied. He also says the flexed position was achieved by bending the head over between the thighs and flexing the legs until the knees were level with the shoulders.

Malo (1951, p. 97) mentions that a rope was tied around the knees and then brought up and around the back of the neck. It was tightened until the knees touched the chest and "the body was then done up in a rounded shape and at once closely wrapped in *tapa*." Other writers (Green and Beckwith, 1926, p. 179) say the hands were doubled into fists and placed against the cheeks.

It is interesting that no two historical descriptions of the flexing process are identical. The variations may correspond to actual differences in practices. As revealed by *in situ* Mokapu skeletons, considerable variation existed within the community, as well as within extended families. Exact body positions were different in each case.

No identifiable traces of cordage or wrappings have been found at Mokapu except for a small deposit discovered over the left foot of a flexed adult skeleton at the N site in 1965. By some peculiarity in matrix conditions a small mineralized fibrous fragment of matting was preserved which showed a clear checkerboard pattern. It may represent the remnants of a fine mat, since the weavesize is nearly identical to some ethnographic specimens in Bishop Museum.

GRAVE PITS

Because Dune 93 is stratified with a light layer of unconsolidated sand overlying a darker, partially cemented layer, pits penetrating the lower layer were easily recorded since they were filled with light sand. All observed graves were basket-shaped and cramped, being just large enough to accommodate the body.

Despite the clear outlines of the lower parts of numerous graves, it was not possible to determine their exact depths from the surface at the time of burial. None of the pits interrupted the present surface humus layer. All burials, therefore, originated in the light sand just below it. Where graves continued down, penetrating the darker sand below, one would expect to find dark sand lenses above, within the light layer, marking the surfaces at the times of burial, since all these penetrating pits were filled with light sand. A few faint traces were found, but not in nearly the quantities one would expect when compared with the volumes of sand removed.

The absence of dark sand may be explained by Kaaie's (ms) comments on burial secrecy. He says: "In digging, the earth is carried away in a piece of matting, or a gourd, lest a trace be seen. . . . People believe that if a burial place is known, the bones will be taken for fish hook-making." This explanation seems adequate in explaining the absence of dark sand and gives considerable insight into the fears Mokapu people may have had that the bodies of their dead might be molested.

Although exact grave depths could not be ascertained, it was possible to acquire some information on relative depths. One male lay entirely within the upper light sand, the cranium resting approximately six feet below the present surface. The grave of another penetrated five feet into the underlying darker layer, the skeleton lying 11 feet 4 inches below the present surface. A considerable amount of light sand must have existed at the time both men were buried, since the first was completely enveloped in it and the grave of the second was filled with light sand. The depths of these two burials show that some bodies were buried relatively close to the surface while others were placed six or more feet deep, and that considerable latitude existed for individual or family preferences.

Historic reports on grave shapes support archaeological conclusions. Kaaie (ms) says, "In taking the corpse to be hidden, only two or three persons go and not a multitude. This work is done at night, not in the day time. In digging a hole, a round one is made, like that for bananas. The depth is as far as the waist (literally the part to which the loin cloth is attached). Such a hole is called a *pahe'e*."

In examining general body positions, it was clear that heads as well as trunks and legs were somewhat flexible at the time of interment and settled into positions conforming to grave contours. Throughout most of the Heleloa dunes, where no stratification is present, predominantly nonerect head positions show that graves were usually rounded at the bottom, being just large enough to accommodate bodies in desired positions. This conclusion is supported by direct evidence at Dune 93. Thus, if the body was placed on the back the head was generally tilted forward to the chest. If placed on the side it was canted to the opposite side, and if placed on the stomach, or ventral surface, it was tilted back. Eight burials did not conform to this general pattern. In these cases pits may have been larger with more expansive horizontal flooring dug to accommodate bodies in uncramped positions.

The mouths of about one-third of the burials with skulls *in situ* were open. Mouths may have been this way at the time of burial, for there has been little sand movement within the Heleloa dunes since interment. For the most part, bones have remained articulated in their natural positions. In some cultures objects are placed in the mouths of corpses, but there is no evidence of this with the Mokapu dead.

The body positions of burials excavated in 1957 were classified according to the system suggested by the Committee on Archaeological Terminology (Heizer, 1958, p. 62). Accordingly, of the forty-one burials in which positions were discernible, twenty-four were tightly flexed, thirteen were semiextended, two were fully extended, one was semiflexed, and one was sitting upright in a tightly flexed position.

Possible correlations between age, sex, and body positions were explored for tightly flexed and semiextended burials, where sufficient numbers were available to indicate tendencies. Only one possible relationship emerged within the limitations of the sample. There seemed to be an association between the semiextended position and adult females, since nearly half the Mokapu women were buried in this position, while only one semiextended male and two children were recovered. A relationship between this position for women and death during or after childbirth was considered. In some societies, the bodies of pregnant women are treated differently from those of other members of the community (Seligman, 1954, p. 126). Semiextended Mokapu women

Excavation and photos by R. N. Bowen.

BURIAL 34. A tightly flexed 40–45 year-old female. This individual exhibited the greatest degree of arthritis shown in the 1957 series and was the only burial found in a sitting position.

ranged in age from approximately 20 to 50 years and no fetal remains were found with them. Thus no definite conclusions could be reached. The relationship certainly should be investigated in the future.

The tightly flexed position was not restricted to either sex, as half of the burials in this position were males and half were females. There was no set position for children. One was fully extended, two were semiextended, and two were tightly flexed.

ARM AND HAND POSITIONS

Considering only the two most frequent burial positions, the arms and hands of nearly all tightly flexed burials were flexed, while there was considerable leeway in semiextended burials.

In the former position, the arms were flexed, with the hands placed in a variety of locations: over the shoulders, over the chest, together over the sternum, or, less commonly, in dissimilar positions. In only three cases was one or both arms extended along the sides of the body.

The arms of three tightly flexed burials were in uncommon positions. In one, they were flexed around and under the thighs between the upper and lower portions of the flexed legs, in a position similar to the one described by Ellis. In another, the arms lay crossed over the chest with each hand resting on the opposite shoulder, and in the third both arms were flexed across the abdomen, with their lower portions nearly parallel.

In most cases Hawaiians burying people in semiextended positions flexed both arms toward the upper part of the body or extended them down along the sides of the trunk. Arms were in dissimilar positions in only four semiextended burials.

RESTING POSITIONS

Of the forty burials whose body positions and resting positions were discernible, twenty-two lay on their backs, three on their stomachs, three on their right sides, and nine on their left. Two were twisted and one was sitting upright. The tendency seems to have been to place extended and semiextended bodies on their backs, while those which were tightly flexed were placed in a variety of resting positions, with most on their backs or left sides.

ORIENTATION

Some evidence supports the belief that Mokapu burials took place at night according to a Hawaiian tradition noted by many writers. This evidence is in the form of small bits of charcoal in the fill of some graves which may have come from lighting devices. Orientation at night could have been accomplished by star observation, knowledge of rising and setting sun positions, or by reference to the main dune ridge.

In this sample, there seems to have been some tendency to bury the dead with heads in a general westerly direction, since half of the burials recorded were oriented within or close to the transit of the setting sun, with bodies aligned to the main dune ridge. However, the fact that the remaining half was oriented in nearly every other direction, with seven toward the east, indicates a flexible cultural pattern. Thus a tradition of placing the head in a specific direction did not exist at Mokapu.

ASSOCIATED REMAINS

Historic writings of Hawaiians mention a wide range of artifacts, as well as plants and animals, which might accompany the dead. These associations can be conveniently grouped in the following categories: personal possessions, pets, food, offerings, keepsakes, contaminated objects, and intrusions.

It is difficult to assign with confidence a specific Mokapu association to one of these categories. However, the character of some associations makes reasons for their placement clear.

Perishable Material: Carbonaceous sand, probably resulting from the decomposition of perishable materials, was found with nearly all burials. Only four primary burials were surrounded by a relatively clean sand matrix. Some skeletons were almost completely enveloped in dark sand while others showed slight traces of it. Percolating rain water has generally altered these carbon deposits, preventing specific identifications. Only wavy lines and darkened areas adjacent to different parts of the skeletons remain, specifically, next to the head, neck, shoulders, chest, abdomen, pelvis, arms, and legs.

These organic traces may be remnants of body wrappings, such as lauhala mats, tapa, and cordage. They may also represent calabashes, gourds, vegetable foods, clothing, and other perishable items which accompanied the dead, or in some cases perhaps decomposed body tissues. The relatively large carbon deposits found under the heads of eight burials may have been pillows made of *pulu* fiber or some other material. Such pillows have been found under the heads of cave disposals.

Because some of this material may be decomposed food, historic sources are of value in revealing which foods might accompany the dead. Hawaiians cite a number of specific items, including bananas, sugar cane, coconut, taro and poi, fish, chicken and wild duck, and pork (Kamakau, ms; Kaaie, ms; Handy and Pukui, 1958, p. 147). Historic reasons for placement fall into three categories: because the person had been fond of the food in life, to entice the soul ('uhane) to stay near the grave, or as nourishment for the soul during its journey into darkness and obscurity.

Mammals: Remains of dogs, pigs, and fowl have been found with the dead at a number of Hawaiian sites, both in caves and with sand burials, including those at Mokapu. Such finds may represent pets, since they are specifically mentioned in this context by some Hawaiian writers, or they may have been placed there for other reasons, such as food items.

Two dog canine teeth were found under the right knee of a 2- to 3-year-old Mokapu child. The teeth were not worked, although the enamel tips of both were broken off. A bracelet, made entirely of dog canine teeth, was also found with this child. It is described on page 144. Several documents furnish insights into the reasons why dog teeth might accompany a child. Handy and Pukui (1958, p. 89) say that when a pet dog died "its fangs were removed and made into a charm for the child" and that if the child died first the dog was strangled and buried with the body. Elsewhere, Mrs. Pukui (ms) says, "It was a custom among Hawaiians to bring up a puppy as a playmate and guardian of a child. When the child was still suckling at the breast the puppy was allowed to suckle from the child's mother also. This act dedicated the dog to the child. If the dog died first, one of its teeth was strung on a chord [sic] and used as an ornament around the child's neck. It was supposed that the spirit of the dog still protected the child." The two dog canine teeth found with the Mokapu child fit the playmate description closely. It is possible that in this instance the teeth had been extracted from the pet when it died and were subsequently placed with the child upon the latter's death.

The practice of burying mementos of pets or the pets themselves with the dead persisted into the post-European period, but was regarded as heathen by Hawaiians practicing Christianity. This undated statement by Daniela (ms) describes such a burial:

On the 4th of January last, that is, last Saturday, we arrived at Kawaiaha'o Church and a grave being dug. I drew close and found Mo'o and Auwa'a there. The coffin was lowered and after it was tossed a live dog with legs bound. It was still barking and continued to do so until it was covered with earth.

Say! Harken, O companions of mine, look at this cruel practice of our ancient people. It is being practiced yet, as it was done in the long ago, this burying alive of a dog with its master. If the [pet was a] pig, the pig was buried with him. If a hen, the hen was buried and so on. Ha! Endless are the erroneous ideas! Friends shouldn't it be that when the light of God has come here that the practices of darkness and its folly be done away with.

An immature pig was buried with one Mokapu woman. The posterior portions of both skeletons had been damaged by earth-moving equipment, leaving only the cranium and mandible of the woman *in situ* and the undisturbed cranium, mandible, one scapula, and a few anterior ribs and vertebrae of the pig. The articulated bones of the pig remaining showed that the complete body had been included, rather than just a segment. The skulls of the pig and the woman lay on their left sides, with the woman facing the back, or posterior, part of the pig's skull. Both bodies were oriented in the same direction with heads adjacent.

This burial seems to represent the same sort of pattern as that of the child with accompanying dog teeth, except that in this case the pig was either killed prior to placement or, as in Daniela's reference, tied and buried. It is also possible that the pig might represent a food item, but the chance of this is lessened by the inclusion of the entire immature animal and by prehistoric food patterns—women were not allowed to eat pork (Malo, 1951, p. 29).

The only other mammal association was the fragmentary cranium of a rat located next to the right tibia of a tightly flexed man. The burial had been disturbed by earth-moving equipment and the remainder of the rat's skeleton may have been carried away with falling sand.

The rat may have been purposely placed with the individual or it may have been an intrusive element at the time of burial. However, the relatively great depth of this particular burial makes intrusion questionable. The body was interred at least 6 feet below the then existing dune surface and over 11 feet below the surface at the time of excavation.

It is difficult to interpret this association. The rat was a family guardian spirit ('aumakua) in some

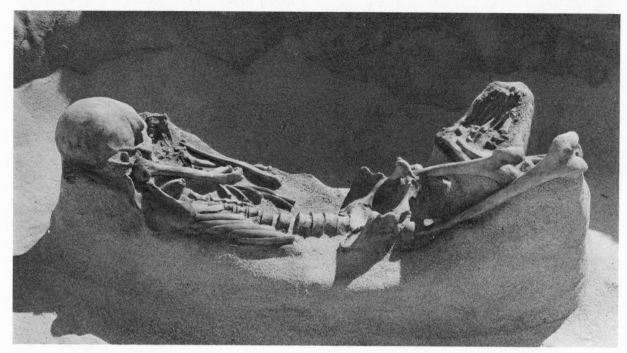

BURIAL 42. A semi-extended adult female, accompanied by several small fish, 3 to 4 inches long, and a young fowl. The fish lay under the flexed right arm, and the bird was cupped between the left hand and the face.

cases (as were also dogs, pigs, fowl, and a host of others) and the question arises whether such guardian animals might have been buried with the dead. Mary K. Pukui (personal communication) says they could not have, since the animals would have been killed in the process and patrons were not allowed to harm their guardians. An individual and his 'aumakua could be placed together, possibly, if death occurred simultaneously. However, such a disposal would be a matter of chance. The association might also be possible if the 'aumakua died first. Then portions of the animal's body might be retained and subsequently placed with the patron's. More evidence will have to be recovered before this question can be explored adequately.

Fowl: The skeletons of domestic or wild fowl were found with four women and the bones sent to Dr. Frank Richardson of the University of Washington for identification. According to Richardson (personal communication), it is not possible to differentiate between breeds of chickens and closely related jungle fowl or pheasant types from skeletons unless the bones are nearly perfect, are complete, and can be compared with extensive reference collections. Even then identification is difficult.

The Mokapu bird remains are possibly from *Gallus gallus*, the jungle fowl, which Polynesians are thought to have brought with them to the Hawaiian archipelago at the time of settlement, along with other fellow-travelers such as the Polynesian dog and rat.

The remains of six fowl were found with the four women. Two of the women were tightly flexed and two were semiflexed. One complete bird had been placed in the shoulder, neck, or facial region of each. The birds were young, three being smaller than bantams and one being baby-chick size. The two other fowl were represented by single bones, one in the form of a bone fishhook point and the other a bone fragment. Both bones were from large adult fowl, larger, for example, than white leghorns.

Certainly this interesting relationship between certain females and immature chickens should be investigated further. Were they placed by family members as favorite foods or pets, or should other interpretations be sought?

Fish: Fish skeletons accompanied four females, three males, and one salvaged burial whose sex could not be determined. Dr. William Gosline of the

University of Hawaii examined the fish bones to determine family, number of individuals, parts present and their condition, approximate size of individuals, and ecological niches occupied by the fish in their natural habitats.

A single fish had been placed with each of five burials, and three or more with three burials. They ranged in size from about 3 inches to 18 inches. In all cases except one, complete fish seem to have been placed. In one instance only the head seems to have been included.

The fish bones were found adjacent to the head, neck, chest, abdomen, and pelvis. Of these fish, bones of the Mullet family (*Mugilidae*), a pond or inshore fish, were found with five burials and those with three burials were reef varieties, including the families *Mullidae* (Goatfish), *Priacanthidae* (Big Eye), and *Pomacentridae* (Damsel Fish).

Since mullet were one of the favorite fishes Hawaiians raised in constructed ponds, it is tempting to conclude that these buried fish came from Nuupia pond, or one of the others, and therefore reveal that the Mokapu dead, or at least some of them, were contemporaneous with the ponds. It is difficult to prove this, however, since mullet also may be found in inshore areas.

The fish remains do show that Mokapu residents were taking reef fish, as well as inshore fish, and that they occasionally placed them with the dead, perhaps as food for the soul.

Shark: A single unworked shark's tooth was found adjacent to the neck of a semiextended female. The tooth, 1.2 cm. long, is of a generalized type which is difficult to identify, except to say that it came from a shark about five feet long. The tooth could represent any of the following families: *Galeorhinidae* (Gray Shark), *Isuridae* (Great White Shark), or *Sphyrnidae* (Hammerhead Shark).

The shark (*mano*) was a guardian spirit to some families and the tooth may indicate such a relationship.

Mollusks: Two mollusks were found, one with each of two burials. The right valve of a pelecypod, *Tellina rugosa*, was found next to the head of an extended male, imbedded in a carbonaceous layer of sand extending under the posterior part of the cranium. The valve shows no signs of external wear that would indicate it was obtained from beach wash, and thus it was probably caught alive, perhaps for food. However, the interior of the valve shows no obvious scratches such as might be made in cutting the soft parts from the shell.

Another mollusk, a gastropod, *Terebra crenulata*, lay on the chest of a salvaged burial. Such shells were used as stoppers, but because of its location this one may have been a neck pendant. It has a small hole in its side near the aperture, through which a neck cord could have passed. Its exterior surface is polished and worn, perhaps from use as an artifact.

Coral: The only other animal association was a large unworked piece of coral found next to the skull and left shoulder of a flexed female. Although no explanation for such an association has been found in Hawaiian literature, Ellis (1831, p. 403) mentions coral in connection with a Tahitian burial. The account is included as a possible explanation:

... all who had touched the body or the garments of the deceased, which were buried or destroyed, fled precipitately into the sea, to cleanse themselves from pollution ... which they contracted by touching the corpse; casting also into the sea, the clothes they had worn while employed in the work. Having finished their ablutions, they gathered a few pieces of coral from the bottom of the sea, and, returning with them to the house, addressed the dead body by saying, "With you may the ... pollution be," and threw down the pieces of coral on top of the hole that had been dug for the purpose of receiving every thing contaminating, connected with the deceased.

Although in this case the coral was not included with the body, there was a belief that contamination could be transferred to coral fragments. The piece found with the Mokapu female may signify a belief of this sort, since Hawaiians also believed that corpses could defile (*haumia*) the living, in the case of commoners for a day or two (Malo, 1951, pp. 96–99), and that salt water was a cleansing agent.

Artifacts: Most of the artifacts found in 1957 have already been discussed. The only other artifacts found were crude basalt flakes, and these will be discussed with vandalized burials because of their associations.

Certainly the most significant and elaborate artifact found (#Oa 19) was the small canine bracelet around the flexed child's right wrist. The bracelet contains thirty-three units. Each link is a thin, nearly crescent-shaped section of tooth 1.5 cm. long, 0.8

cm. wide, and 0.3 cm. thick, pierced transversely by two stringing holes. The lower edge, lying next to the wrist, is slightly convex, while the upper has a sharp concave groove. The flat side surfaces of the units are beveled toward the lower edge, so that when placed together they conformed to the shape of the child's small wrist. Because of the bracelet's shape when the links are held close together, there is little question that the bracelet was made specifically for the child either during life or at the time of death.

It is difficult to determine why such ornaments were not placed with the Mokapu dead more frequently. Perhaps not many were worn or, if plentiful, they may have been retained by the living as keepsakes. James Cook (1961, pp. 20–21) commented on the general lack of ornamentation among Hawaiians at Wailua, Kauai, in 1778, saying: "They had no ornaments about their persons." However, this may not have been true of the Mokapu people. Ethnohistorical research, coupled with archaeological data, may help to explain the paucity of burial ornaments.

VANDALIZED BURIALS

In citing fishhook materials, Malo (1951, p. 79) lists human bones first, then tortoise shell and the bones of dogs and pigs. Higher ranks of people seem to have been particularly fearful of having their bones used in making fishhooks, arrows, needles, and standard (*kahili*) handles (Kamakau, 1961, p. 215).

The use of human bone is confirmed by material from archaeological sites. For example, Emory, Bonk, and Sinoto (1968, p. 21) list human bone as a major source of fishhook material.

The probable fear of the Mokapu people of having their dead molested for workable bone material by other Hawaiians, revealed by the absence of dark sand at Dune 93 and supported by Kaaie's statement about the secrecy of burials, is also supported by at least two incomplete burials which had been pilfered for this purpose. Four other incomplete burials may also have been vandalized for artifact material.

Of the two burials in which vandalism seems most clear, one (C–43) is in such condition that the temporal sequence of long-bone removal can be reconstructed. Both burials reveal which fragments vandals sought.

In burial C–43 the distal and proximal ends of all arm and leg bones, accompanied by a large quantity of shaft fragments from the same bones, were found lying in an oblong pile directly under the upper back of the individual, that is, under the thoracic vertebrae. The articulated left and right foot and right hand lay over the abdomen and pelvis, and the articulated left hand lay on the chest. Their arrangement, however, was unnatural and, in addition, a basalt flake lay under the burial's right hand. Both patellae were present. Since long-bone fragments lay under the skeleton, the body had evidently been taken from the pit before the long bones were removed. In order to remove the body intact, decomposition could not have been complete. Decomposition had possibly progressed to a stage of desiccation, with some binding tissue remaining.

Apparently, the long bones were removed after the body was taken from the pit. As the hands and feet were found articulated, but in unnatural positions, they were evidently severed from the arms and legs, either before or after the latter were separated from the trunk. The narrow, knife-size basalt flake found in the abdomen may have been used for this purpose, as its size and shape indicate it would have made an effective cutting tool.

The vandals pounded the entire shafts of all twelve long bones into fragments, leaving only the distal and proximal ends intact. One or more large basalt tools, which were not left behind, may have been used to break the bones. An examination of the bone fragments present shows that larger flat pieces are missing and thus were the ones most desired by the grave-robbers. Unwanted small fragments, narrow slivers, pieces from curved areas, and distal and proximal ends were thrown into the empty grave.

Following fragmentation, the body, lacking appendages, was apparently returned to the grave, on top of the pile of fragments, the basalt cutting tool was thrown on top of the abdomen, and the hands and feet were placed on top of the trunk.

This burial then is particularly important because it shows that at least some vandalism probably occurred while the burial ground was in use.

A second male (N–6) was treated in a similar manner. In this case, the complete and articulated body, lacking appendages, lay on the back with the head turned sharply to the left. All long bones of both arms and legs had been removed and fragmented, and lay in a pile on the right side of the body. The pile contained the distal and proximal ends of both femora, the distal and proximal ends of the right

humerus, and the proximal ends of the radii. As with the first burial, most of the pile consisted of unworkable fragments. The patellae could not be identified; they either were missing or had been fragmented. The articulated hands and feet lay in what may have been natural positions on top of the body. One hand was next to the left side of the face and the other lay on the chest. Both feet were in the abdominal area.

Seven basalt tools were found with the latter male; three were fist-axe size and four were knife-size. Five tools lay over the body and two were found in the pile of bone fragments, along with eighteen small basalt chips.

As with the first male, the body may have been desiccated when uncovered by vandals, requiring dissection, or it may have been sufficiently decomposed so that no cutting was necessary. The long bones may have been broken up at some distance from the body, outside the pit. If this was the case, unwanted fragments were collected, including two basalt flakes and miscellaneous chips, and placed in the pit on the right side of the body. On the other hand, the presence of the chips and small fragments may mean that the vandals dug enough sand away from the body to be able to crush the bones in the pit.

All of the basalt tools recovered in 1957 have sharp edges and were evidently brought to the dunes by long-bone hunters to be used in dismembering desiccated burials and breaking bones into desired fragments. The smaller knifelike flakes were probably used for cutting and the larger fist-axe type for pounding.

No bone fragments were found with the four other incomplete burials, although three basalt flakes were found with one (C–41). These burials may also have been vandalized for artifact material, but direct evidence is missing. If they were, long bones were not pounded at the site, but were taken away and broken up elsewhere. It is also possible that bones may have been taken by relatives for keepsakes.

It is interesting to note that of the six incomplete burials, five were males. Perhaps this is only a sampling feature, since it is difficult to imagine how vandals would know the locations of male burials, which, of course, would supply slightly larger bone material, and which might have more supernatural power (*mana*) if from men who had been outstanding fishermen in life.

SECONDARY BURIALS

Three secondary burials were found, each consisting of disarticulated skeletal parts. In the first, the right femur and tibia of one individual had been placed with the left and right femora and left tibia of another. The five bones lay parallel to each other as if in a bundle, with four of the five having their proximal ends aligned. The placement seemed to be contemporary with surrounding primary burials, one of which was at the same level and only 3 feet away.

These secondary bones were not worked and show no signs of having been polished. They may have been parts of burials exposed by the wind, which were reburied; they may have been reburied by vandals; or they may have been keepsakes which were returned when affection waned.

Several writers describe the recovery of skeletal material by relatives. Malo (1951, pp. 98–99) says that sometimes a person would exhume the body of a loved wife or husband "and remove the four leg bones and the skull, washing them in water until they were clean." They were then enclosed in a pillow which the relative slept with each night. "The number of corpses treated in this way was considerable among those who were fond of each other."

Campbell (1816, pp. 206–7) saw an example of this tradition in May 1810 at Honolulu. He says: "My patroness, the Queen, preserved the bones of her father, wrapt in a piece of cloth. When she slept in her own house they were placed by her side; in her absence they were placed on a feather bed she had received from the captain of a ship, and which was only used for this purpose. When I asked her the reason of this singular custom, she replied, 'it was because she loved her father so dearly.'"

Mary K. Pukui (personal communication) also says that sometimes the living would keep mementos of the dead, which would then be buried with them upon their deaths or buried with other relatives, so that they could "sleep together" (moepu'u). A possible example of the latter relationship was found in the Heleloa dunes. The long bones of a 2- to 3-year-old child were associated with one female, 30 to 35 years old, and the complementary body bones, less the skull, of a child of about the same age were found with another female, also from 30 to 35 years old, about 60 feet away. Both sets of bones with the women had a texture which was different from surrounding burials, in that they were rather glossy, as if they had been polished or rubbed, and had a brownish-orange exterior coloration. If both sets are from the same child, the women may have been related. For example, when death occurred to a favorite child, the body might be buried and the bones later retrieved and placed in a container, rubbed with oils, and handled frequently by loved ones. Upon the death of one of the child's relatives, perhaps the mother, a sister, or an aunt, a portion of the child's remains may have been selected to accompany the deceased. Later, when another relative died, the remaining bones may have been included with that person. In the Mokapu case, the child's missing cranium and mandible may have been retained in the home or placed with another unexcavated or destroyed Mokapu burial.

MULTIPLE BURIALS

Two multiple burials were found. In the central Heleloa dunes, two females, both from 45 to 50 years of age, seem to have been placed in the same grave, one semiextended and the other semiflexed. Although no stratification was present, the two women were at exactly the same depth, were oriented in the same direction, and lay next to each other only about 14 inches apart. The legs of both skeletons were canted in directions conforming to the outline of a large oval pit.

The second example, from the eastern end of the Heleloa dunes, involved a male, 21 to 30 years old, and a child, 1 to 2 years old. The anterior part of the man's skeleton had been disturbed, but the child's was complete. Both skeletons were tightly flexed, the man lying on the left side and the child on the right, with the latter oriented in the opposite direction. The child's skeleton lay on top of the man's lower left leg and foot, which protruded from under his right leg.

In these two multiple burials, the individuals may have died simultaneously from the same ailment or accident. Or they may have died within a few days of each other from the same or different causes. In any case, some mutual relationship probably caused them to be placed in the same grave.

SUMMARY

From the foregoing account it is obvious that the Mokapu burial ground has had a relatively long and complex archaeological history, beginning in 1912 and continuing to the present time. The extensive skeletal series it has produced provides an invaluable and endless source of osteological information on a segment of the Hawaiian population, as well as insights into Hawaiian life on this peninsula before the penetration of European culture.

Cumulative evidence to date produces a picture of windward Oahu as a region of rather extensive prehistoric coastal settlement, both on Mokapu peninsula and on the mainland, which by 1879 had diminished to a few families.

Scattered surface artifacts and excavation data from the peninsula mirror basic Hawaiian coastal subsistence patterns, marine as well as horticultural, with perhaps intermittent periods of warfare.

Mokapu fishponds, predating Monsarrat's map of 1899, possibly were a major food focus, yielding a variety of fish for Mokapu residents, some of which may have been exchanged with inland extended families (*ohana*) for crops requiring large amounts of moisture.

Coastal evaporating pans may have furnished salt, while an inland well or wells provided fresh water. Religious activities perhaps centered at Pali Kilo and, when death came, the Heeia and Heleloa dunes served as burial grounds.

The specific character of human burials in the Heleloa dunes, as revealed by 1957 excavations and the rich Hawaiian ethnological literature, has been outlined in the preceding pages, answering many questions and posing a host of others. An unknown number of skeletons remain in the Mokapu dunes and some of these may be important in filling gaps in our understanding.

Future excavations should concentrate on Site N because of its unique stratification. And attempts should be made to obtain additional radiocarbon dates, linking them to interment sequences based on stratigraphy, to provide a basic chronological framework for the site.

The time left for such exploration is short. Northeast trade winds relentlessly expose burials to erosion, and human destruction, which began with Hawaiians themselves, continues. Hopefully, since the sites are located on federal land, the laws which exist to protect such important archaeological features may help to slow the latter process. Most Mokapu dead now rest at Bishop Museum in "a safe mausoleum chamber," so-called by Peter H. Buck, himself part-Polynesian and one who was deeply concerned about the care of these prehistoric people.

LITERATURE CITED

Bennett, Wendell C.
1931   *Archaeology of Kauai.* Bishop Museum Bulletin 80. Honolulu.

Bowen, Robert N.
1961   Hawaiian disposal of the dead. M.A. thesis, University of Hawaii.

Buck, Peter H.
1957   *Arts and crafts of Hawaii.* Bishop Museum Special Publication 45. Honolulu.

Campbell, Archibald
1816   *A voyage around the world, from 1806 to 1812. . . .* Edinburgh.

Cook, James
1961   The discovery of the Hawaiian Islands [1778]. In *A Hawaiian reader,* ed. by A. Grove Day and Carl Stroven, pp. 18–27. New York: Popular Library.

Cook, James, and King, James
1784   *A voyage to the Pacific Ocean . . . .* London: G. Nicol and T. Cadell.

Cook, S. F.
1959   An evaluation of the fluorine dating method. *Southwestern J. Anthropol.* 15(3): 276–90.

Daniela, W. P.
       Body buried with a live dog. Manuscript. Trans. by Mary K. Pukui. Hawaiian Ethnological Notes, 6:3144. Bishop Museum Library, Honolulu.

Ellis, William
1827   *Narrative of a tour through Hawaii . . . .* 2d ed. London.

1832–
1836   *Polynesian researches.* 2d ed. Vols. 1–4. London.

1963   *Journal of William Ellis.* Reprint of London 1827 ed. and Hawaii 1917 ed. Honolulu: Advertiser Publishing Co.

Emory, Kenneth P.; Bonk, William J.; and Sinoto, Yosihiko H.
1968   *Fishhooks.* Bishop Museum Special Publication 47. Honolulu.

Fiddler, Frank
1956   Mokapu: a study of the land. (Mimeographed.) Kaneohe, Hawaii: U. S. Marine Corps Air Station.

Finsch, Otto
1879   Bericht über die Insel Oahu. *Zeitschrift für Ethnologie* 11:326–31.

Green, Laura C., and Beckwith, Martha W.
1926 Hawaiian customs and beliefs relating to sickness and death. *Amer. Anthropol.* 28: 176–208.

Handy, E. S. Craighill, and Pukui, Mary K.
1958 *The Polynesian family system in Ka'u, Hawai'i.* Wellington, New Zealand: Polynesian Society.

Heizer, Robert F.
1958 *A guide to archaeological field methods.* Palo Alto, Calif.: National Press.

Kaaie, S. W. L.
Concerning the dead. Manuscript. Trans. by Mary K. Pukui. Hawaiian Ethnological Notes, 6:3147–49. Bishop Museum Library, Honolulu.

Kamakau, Samuel M.
Ka Moolelo Hawaii. Manuscript. [Written in mid-nineteenth century.] Bishop Museum Library, Honolulu.
1961 *Ruling chiefs of Hawaii.* Honolulu: Kamehameha Schools Press.

Lisiansky, Urey
1814 *A Voyage round the world in the years 1803, 4, 5, and 6 . . . in the ship Neva.* London.

McAllister, J. Gilbert
1933 *The archaeology of Oahu.* Bishop Museum Bulletin 104. Honolulu.

MacCaughey, Vaughn
1917 A footpath journey. *Mid-Pacific Mag.* 14: 180–96.

Malo, David
1951 *Hawaiian antiquities.* [c. 1840.] Bishop Museum Special Publication 2. Honolulu.

Pukui, Mary K.
Customs: burial, dog and child relationship. Manuscript. Hawaiian Ethnological Notes 1:1063. Bishop Museum Library, Honolulu.

Pukui, Mary K., and Elbert, Samuel H.
1957 *Hawaiian-English dictionary.* Honolulu: University of Hawaii Press.

Seligman, Brenda Z., ed.
1954 *Notes and queries on anthropology.* 6th ed. London: Routledge and Kegan Paul.

Sinoto, Yosihiko H.
Hawaiian archaeology: ornaments. Manuscript. Department of Anthropology, Bishop Museum, Honolulu.

Stearns, Harold T., and Vaksvik, K. N.
1935 *Geology and ground-water resources of the island of Oahu, Hawaii.* Bulletin 1. Honolulu: Territory of Hawaii, Division of Hydrography.

Suggs, Robert C.
1960 *The island civilizations of Polynesia.* New York: Mentor Books.

Thrum, Thomas G.
1928 Pulu, its rise and decline. *Thrum's Hawaiian annual, 1929,* pp. 77–82.

Whitney, Samuel
1827 Extracts from Mr. Whitney's journal. *Missionary Herald* 23 (6).

APPENDIX B

Report on Pathological Specimens from Mokapu

Lent C. Johnson and Ellis R. Kerley

These interpretations are not offered with any sense of certainty that they are necessarily final. They merely represent the best interpretations that the authors can make, in consultation with Dr. T. Dale Stewart of the Division of Anthropology, United States National Museum, Washington, D.C., and Dr. Walter G. J. Putschar of the Pathology Department, Massachusetts General Hospital, Boston.

SPECIMEN 1

A fairly rugged tibia (CXX-16) of moderate length, essentially rhomboid in shape with some thickening of the middle and lower shaft. It is adult in age. All epiphyses are closed. There is an exostosis around the medial condyle both anterior and posterior to the condyles. Mechanical eburnation has occurred on the posteromedial third of the medial articular surface. The upper fourth of the tibia exhibits considerable vascularization except around the fibular facet. The popliteal line near the midshaft and the lower third of the interosseus ridge are slightly roughened. The distal articular surface is essentially normal but the whole articular surface is sharply delineated, possibly reflecting hyperactivity to compensate for the injured knee.

The medial plateau is enlarged medially and posteriorly, compacted and smooth with lipping both posteriorly and medially. On the posterior medial half there is a shallow gouge which is very smooth and polished as rocks may be polished in glacial grinding. This lies beneath the site of the medial meniscus and could not occur if the meniscus were present. Therefore, it is clear that the medial meniscus had been destroyed and its protective action lost for some considerable period of time. The posterior lateral side of the medial plateau has an enlarged knot which projects posteriorly and a little bit upward from the plateau at the site of the posterior attachment of the meniscus. This represents ossification of the menisceal attachment. The anterior

lateral margin of the medial plateau contains a bony excrescence at the site of attachment of the anterior cruciate ligament. On the anterior surface of the tibia, between the plateau and the tibial prominence to which the quadriceps tendon attaches, there is an excessive degree of vascular pitting. On the medial surface of the tibia beneath the medial plateau there is likewise excessive vascular pitting in the area where the medial ligaments and the pes anserina attach. To a lesser degree similar pitting is seen laterally. Associated with these areas of pitting is old periosteal reactive bone proliferation.

A long thin wedge taken from the plateau extending deep into the bone and traversing both medial and lateral plateaus was taken for a dissecting microscope study. This revealed a normal structure of cancellous bone except beneath the polished eburnated area where the medial meniscus has been missing.

Putting this material together, it would appear that the anterior cruciate ligament was partially torn or perhaps totally torn and that the basal portion of it subsequently ossified; that the medial meniscus was sheared off and its posterior attachment ossified; that the medial posterior half of the tibial plateau was excessively ground down in the absence of the meniscus; that the extensive marginal lipping medially and posteriorly developed because of instability from partial loss of cruciate ligament; that the same instability through mechanical stress applied to the quadriceps led to excess vascularity on the anterior surface of the tibia; and that the excessive mechanical stress on the medial collateral ligaments and the pes anserina insertion led to excessive vascular pitting in this area. All of the anatomic findings put together point in the direction of torn cruciate ligament and macerated or extensively destroyed medial meniscus. This usually results from an injury with hyperextension and medial rotation of the leg on the thigh.

SPECIMEN 2

Three vertebrae (H-45)—T-12, L-1, L-2,—all articulating. (See Fig. B1, A, B.) T-12 has a constriction of the dorsal part of the centrum that results in an hourglass-shaped defect in the dorsal region of the centrum. There is a small crater in the right side of the inferior surface and another small lesion on the left inferior articular facet.

L-1 has a small lesion on the left superior articular surface articulating with that on T-12. The

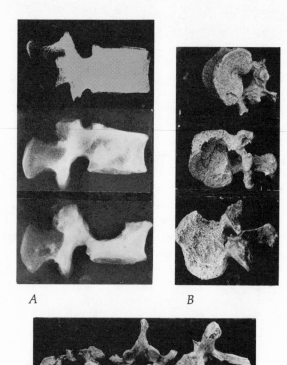

A

B

C

FIG. B1. *A* X-ray and *B* gross views of three lumbar vertebrae (H-45) with possible tuberculosis. *C* lower view of three thoracic vertebrae (H-282) with similar lesions.

A slab in the anteroposterior plane (in the midline) through the lower part of the vertebra was examined under the dissecting microscope and shows several scattered areas of sclerosis along the margin of the destruction. Several millimeters away from the main cavity are areas where trabeculae are missing, suggesting satellite lesions. On the raw surface of the main cavity are trabeculae with abruptly cut-off edges and others with flattened edges indicative of a feeble effort to develop a sclerotic margin. Everywhere proliferative sclerosis is minimal though definite.

A developmental anomaly or posttraumatic lesion can be eliminated from consideration. This leaves only neoplasm and inflammation to be considered. The reactive sclerosis about the margin of the main cavity, even though it is minimal, and the evidence of satellite lesions both weigh very heavily against a neoplasm and in favor of an inflammation. Because of the massive size of the lesion and the minimal amount of proliferative response, the inflammation was probably a granulomatous one of long standing. While several organisms can produce such long-standing granulomas, tuberculosis is much the most common cause. This is also the area of the vertebral column that is most often affected by tuberculosis.

SPECIMEN 3

Four vertebrae (H–272), two middle thoracics, which articulate, and one lower thoracic which appears to belong to the same individual. All three have some lipping and sharply defined margins around the articular surfaces. Therefore, they are interpreted as belonging to an adult, probably in the middle age range. All three have irregular "punched-out" cavities.

The fourth vertebra appears younger in age, though fully adult, and is from a different individual. This vertebra has several cavities in the centrum with well defined sclerotic margins.

The paired vertebrae have two independent lesions which do not face each other but are separated by what was probably an intact disc and an intact half vertebral body. Inflammation and metastatic neoplasm are the two possibilities. Independent scattered lesions of this type are much more likely to be metastatic than inflammatory, particularly in view of the absence of any periosteal reaction. In older individuals, one of the most common of the neoplasms to produce such lesions would be a multiple

centrum has a deep cavity which communicates with a larger cavity in L–2 to form a large, continuous lesion involving both vertebrae.

These vertebrae appear to be from an adult of middle age. There is some coarsening of the centrum on all three.

The uppermost vertebra shows no significant damage except for the hourglass deformity of the midportion of the posterior part of the body, which is usually normal, although in this case it may be related to the pathology. There is also a small depressed area on the intervertebral disc face which may well have been the site of a small angioma. The other two vertebrae participate together in a very large area of massive destruction posteriorly and laterally which must have involved the destruction of most if not all of the disc. Furthermore, there is excessive vascular pitting and pocking of the lateral and anterior surfaces of all the vertebrae.

myeloma. However, this is usually accompanied by some evidence of generalized porosis with a refining of caliber and a decrease in the number of cancellous trabeculae. These are not present. Therefore, a metastatic neoplasm rather than a primary neoplasm is more probable.

The single lower thoracic vertebra of about the same age, which may come from the same individual, shows a great deal of osteoarthritis and one single large hole without any sclerosis about the lesion and without any porosis of the remaining bone. If this belongs to the same individual as the above two vertebrae, then it probably represents another metastatic lesion. Inflammation seems unlikely.

The fourth vertebra in this group, which appears to come from a younger individual and has the stumps of pedicles without the lamina or spinous process, shows a very extensive lobulated lesion with the lobules emphasized by sclerosed trabeculae lining the defect. The periosteal surfaces away from the areas of destruction (particularly posterolaterally on either side) show some rather large holes resembling cloacae that represent areas of marked increased vascular porosity. The sclerotic trabeculation of the main cavity suggests that this lesion is probably inflammatory in nature. Because of the extensive destruction and the absence of sclerosis in the underlying cancellous bone (despite a single coarse trabeculum), granulomatous inflammation is more likely than a suppurative inflammation.

SPECIMEN 4

An adolescent skull (H–85A) with osteoporosis and postmortem erosion of the right parietal. There are bilateral areas of osteoporosis in the orbital roofs, on the parietal eminences, and along the parietal border of the lambdoid suture; a focal lesion of the right parietal on the border of the eroded areas; and a paracondylar process in the condylar fossa of the left occipital condyle.

All sutures are open, including the basal suture. The roots of the third molars are completely unformed, and these teeth have not begun to erupt. Since the third molars are on the verge of eruption, and in view of the basal suture, the age of the skull is within the adolescent range.

There is a rather extensive, partly artifactual defect of one parietal area. On the medial margin of this large defect is a focal area of abnormal surface bone which somewhat resembles the fine whorled structure of an eddy current. On the lateral margin is an area of extensive porosis. On the underside of the large defect most of the inner table is missing over a considerably wider region than the external table, due largely to postmortem erosion.

The paracondylar process is widely reported and seen in otherwise normal individuals. It may be bilateral but most commonly occurs unilaterally: it may fuse with the atlas, form a pseudoarthrosis, or not quite meet the atlas. It probably does not represent an old fracture.

In addition to these findings, there are symmetrical foci of coarse tubelike patterns on the outer table located posteriorly adjacent to each lambdoidal suture and over each of the parietal bosses, and on the orbital plate just around the corner from the supraorbital ridges. These areas will be spoken of as sieved areas. The special regions medial to the large defect which resembled an eddy current will be spoken of as the ribbed area.

The various sieved areas were studied in situ by a dissecting microscope; from several of them slices were taken through the entire thickness of the skull and these were also studied under the dissecting microscope. In all of these areas, the diploic canals and cancellous bone structure are entirely normal and the inner tables are entirely normal. The primary abnormality consists of an excessive porosity of the external tables. This excessive porosity can be clearly related to vascular channels. The three pairs of sieved areas are located at three special anatomical sites, in which there is a confluence of the main diploic canals (Toldt, 1919; Schaeffer, 1953). The larger diploic canals into which the smaller diploe empty meet in a confluence in these regions and in such areas there is normally a tendency for numerous tiny vascular collaterals to penetrate the outer table and communicate with the soft tissue and subcutaneous circulation. Paired sieves over the parietal bosses and the orbital plates are the site at which diploic canals first begin to develop within the skull, and such development is associated with excessively large communications with the soft-tissue veins and venules.

The interpretation of the sieved areas is in some doubt. Dr. Stewart feels that the generally accepted view of a nutritional background is most probable and believes that a continuous series can be established ranging from a few vascular pock marks in the orbital plate to extensive vascular pitting of the entire skull.

Dr. Johnson, while recognizing the continuous

series data, is reluctant to agree to the assignment of a single etiology for the entire series, suspecting rather that different portions of the spectral series may have different causes (Hamperl and Weiss, 1955). Because of the total lack of alteration in cancellous pattern, because of the lack of thickening or hyperosteosis, and because of the geographic distribution, he interprets this case as an exaggeration of the normal developmental vascular foci which in the adult may serve as secondary or tertiary communications between diploe and extracranial venous systems (that is, as additional drainage sites to the better known emissory veins).

The small, sharply localized nature of the foci in the skull would also speak against an inflammatory, traumatic, or general nutritional disturbance. In view of the lack of porosis of the cancellous bone it is unlikely that anemia, with its attendant marrow hyperplasia and vascular engorgement, would produce such small foci in a mid-adolescent (comparable to the extensive alteration of the skull of children with certain congenital types of anemia). Hence, Dr. Johnson favors a developmental explanation (but without implicating any congenital, familial, or genetic factors).

Dr. Kerley feels that the condition may well have a genetic basis, whether through a form of hemolytic anemia or through specific control. Two things favor this view. One is that the sites initially or most commonly affected are those involved in some of the cleidocranial and craniofacial dysostoses. The other is that there has been reported (Moodie, 1923) a variety of incidence rates in populations of the same general ethnic and geographic background, and that the condition occurs in populations with considerably different dietary and ecologic backgrounds.

The ribbed areas are a somewhat different matter. Here there is surface erosion of bone and proliferation of new bone as seen under the dissecting microscope that indicates a pathologic alteration of the outer table. The diploe are entirely normal. Therefore, it is probable that this represents an area of surface bone resorption followed by repair. Because of the sclerosing component of the repair, it appears probable that this is a reaction to an inflammatory process in the overlying soft tissues of the scalp.

In summary, then, there appear to be four types of lesions here: a probably artifactual gross hole in one parietal bone, a paracondylar exostosis, a developmental anomaly involving the areas of conflu-

ence of the large diploic canals with their secondary emissary venules, and a small focus of reactive osteitis and periosteitis, probably related to a focal area of scalp inflammation.

SPECIMEN 5

The frontal bone of a child (H–246) with bilateral osteoporosis of the orbital plates and elongated suture spicules. The bone is unusually thin, being translucent in spots, and has fairly definite digital impressions.

This frontal bone shows the same type of sieving as that seen in Specimen 4 and in the same portions of the two orbital plates just around the corner from the supraorbital area. In addition, the frontal bone, while rather large, is quite thin with prominent digital impressions in the regions of the frontal poles of the brain which make the bone almost transparent. There is also an exaggerated spiking of the suture line. Because of the thinning, the exaggerated digital impressions, and the spiked suture line, it is probable that this comes from a hydrocephalic child. The frontal bone is a single plate without the diploic canals except in the region where they are just beginning to develop in the orbital plate. Here, the relationship between the sieving and the vascular pattern on the outside of the skull can be clearly established by tracing these vascular canals into the diploe. The sieving occurs only in areas where the diploic canals are present, or in the area of the undeveloped supraorbital sinus. This frontal bone is abnormal for its lack of diploe, a condition also common in hydrocephaly.

In some small children diploic canals are very pronounced, as excessively rapid development of the skull occurs, particularly with some of the anemias, such as the Mediterranean and sickle cell anemias. It results from extreme bone marrow hyperplasia within the diploic canals. Other severe anemias might on occasion do this, and if occurring in childhood might lead to an exaggeration of the sieving areas and account for the occurrence of such sieved areas in a high percentage of certain populations. Usually such sieving due to marrow hyperplasia is associated with osteophytic overgrowth of the outer table and a change in the structure of the cancellous bone.[1] Thus, there are two different developmental possibilities: One is congenital and

1. An anemic explanation also requires changes in the rest of the skeleton (Blomberg and Kerley, 1966).

related to the speed of diploization of the skull and the extent to which the subsidiary emissary venules are retained at the diploic canal confluences. The other is the result of a disease which involves marked bone marrow hyperplasia and consequently interference with the venous drainage from the diploic canals.

As in the previous case, Dr. Stewart prefers the nutritional explanation of the sieving, while agreeing with the diagnosis of probable hydrocephalus.

SPECIMEN 6

The shafts of four long bones (H–188) which appear to be left and right ulnae and femora. These are the bones of a child. Their size and general proportions are in the range of a 7- or 8-year-old.

These bones are covered with a fine porous sheath of healthy periosteal new bone which has flaked off in several spots. The new bone is aligned in a very orderly lattice, as seen by microscope. The underlying cortex has been made porous by a fine, regular resorption of the bone.

The exaggerated porosity of the periosteal surface readily flakes off, leaving a much-pitted surface 1 mm. beneath. Only the outermost layer flakes off. When cross sections are prepared and studied under the dissecting microscope, it is apparent that in some areas the periosteal reaction is eccentric. For example, in the cross section of the ulna, half the ulna shows entirely smooth endosteal and periosteal surfaces and a completely compact cortex. The other half of the circumference shows a very rough endosteal surface due to beginning cancellization of the inner cortex, and a periosteal coat which flakes off easily. The periosteal coat is made up of typical osteophytic bone. The half circumference which shows simultaneous periosteal, endosteal, and cortical changes is part of the normal eccentric growth mechanism in long bone which comes with the prepubertal growth spurt. The endosteum is roughened and pitted due to growth in the diameter of the marrow cavity. The periosteum is lifted and new bone is laid down very rapidly in the form of delicate osteophytic bone while the spaces so created have not yet filled with pseudo-Haversian systems. The compact cortex is being cancellized and rendered porotic preparatory to reconstruction in association with this eccentric growth in circumference of the ulna.

The cross section of the femur shows a similar relationship with eccentric growth in the form of endosteal cancellization, cortical porosis, and periosteal lamination which is osteophytic in type.

The uniform and widespread distribution of this outer mantle over long distances along the length of the bone makes it clearly incapable of interpretation as a periosteal new bone resulting from inflammation. The rough, pitted character of the surface of the mantle of bone in contrast to the scattered areas of much smoother outer cortex where no mantle is present, and the uniform size and spacing of the short stubby pillars that attach this mantle of bone to the underlying cortex all bespeak a uniform mechanism spread over very great distances along the length (though sharply limited with respect to circumference). The only way in which the eccentricity and the very precisely coordinated endosteal, periosteal, and cortical changes can be accounted for is in terms of normal growth at this age, which is known to be eccentric in character. Accordingly, this material is all regarded as normal bones from a rapidly growing, prepubertal adolescent child.

The above interpretation is Dr. Johnson's based upon investigations now under way, of the mechanisms of growth.[2]

Dr. Stewart, however, does not agree. He feels that this generalized osteoporosis is not a part of normal growth, since various parts of the body, even parts of a single bone, do not grow at the same rate. Normal remodeling of the shaft may be taking place, as evidenced by the eccentric nature of the new bone; however, the osteoporosis in this and similar cases has been considered as pathologic for some time by people who work with large numbers of gross bones. The most probable cause is a low-grade infection, possibly associated with dental caries.

SPECIMEN 7

A left femur (C–5) that is very light and badly eroded on both sides. All epiphyses are fused, but both the head and the condyles are separated from

2. On reviewing the manuscript in 1972, the authors would alter this interpretation because the studies referred to have been completed (Johnson, 1966). The changes seen here are more likely to apply to an infant or teen-ager than to a 7- or 8-year-old child. Therefore, one would have to consider a general long-bone reaction such as occurs in some childhood leukemias. A low-grade inflammation is possible but it would have to be an unusual one that would involve the length of multiple long bones but only a part of their circumferences with medullary changes limited to beginning cancellization of the cortex in only a part of its circumference.

the shaft as a result of postmortem erosion. There is exostosis of the anterior surface in the area of the surgical neck and also on the border of the separate femoral head. The head of the femur is detached, with a sclerosed surface where it should attach to the femoral neck. This femur appears to be from a rather old individual.

The linea aspera is solid in the lower two-thirds but very delicate and easily fragmented in the upper third. Much of the neck of the femur is missing. When the separated head was studied under the dissecting microscope, the articular surface was found to be fairly regular. There are some small areas which suggest the possibility of mild subchondral sclerosis but the bulk of the surface is a normal subchondral plate. There are extensive areas where the subchondral plate is missing, revealing the underlying cancellous bone pattern, but this is believed to be artifactual.

The flat undersurface of the separated femoral head when studied under the dissecting microscope shows the result of antecedent disease. While there are many places where the underlying cancellous bone structure can be seen as clearly as on the artifactual areas on the articular surface, there is a very considerable portion where this is not true and where the normal cancellous bone pattern that should be present is covered by something that resembles a new subchondral bone plate. This is particularly apparent on the medial side. This plate is much thicker than any normal subchondral plate and represents the site where callus formation and repair have begun but, having failed, a pseudoarthrosis has undoubtedly developed. The periosteal surface immediately adjacent to this callus plate shows an osteophytic projection. The fact that the cancellous bone within the interior of the head of the femur is all entirely normal indicates that there was no circulation to produce the considerable resorption of cancellous bone that normally follows a fracture without damage to the circulation. Therefore, it may be presumed that there was avascular necrosis of the head of the femur and that the original disease represented a fracture that failed to unite, produced inadequate callus, and left only a thin plate of callus on the fractured surface where a pseudoarthrosis may have developed.

The neck of the femur is missing over a very wide area and we believe this may not be entirely a matter of artifactual loss due to archaeological conditions, for just such a loss of the neck occurs normally following a fracture because of the excessive circulation near the fracture site and its attendant resorption of bone. On the medial side of the femur, in the region where the lesser trochanter belongs, there is a sizable osteophyte or exostosis which corresponds to the small exostosis on the head of the femur. The site of this exostosis further suggests that the loss of much of the neck may be a resorptive phenomenon that occurred during life. Such paired osteophytes usually mark the opposite surface of a joint, whether pseudoarthrotic or normal.

Two cuts halfway through the thickness of the shaft of the femur were made on the posterior surface to study the bone structure in relationship to the linea aspera. One cut was in the mid-shaft, the other at the upper end of the linea aspera. The cut section of the mid-shaft demonstrates under the dissecting microscope that the cortex of the entire femur is somewhat thinner than one would normally expect and that the cortex of the linea aspera itself is no thicker than the rest of the cortex; yet the linea aspera is a very prominent line externally. Therefore, this thinning of the cortex indicates an old and slowly progressive osteoporosis which did not involve cancellization of the cortex and which probably existed prior to the fracture.

The section into the upper third of the femur across the linea aspera shows what is believed to be a recent and very extensive local resorption involving the entire thickness of the cortex of the linea aspera and leaving only a small shell of the linea aspera in many areas. The rest of the cortex is of the same thickness as in the lower cuts. Therefore, the extensive resorption of the linea aspera represents a focal area of osteoporosis, and this localized osteoporosis could only have developed if the muscles attached to the linea aspera had all ceased to function. Such a cessation of function is of course to be expected with fracture. Therefore, we presume that this individual had been in an inactive state for a period of time due to a fractured femoral neck, resulting in avascular necrosis of the femoral head, extensive resorption of the femoral neck, and marked focal resorption along the sites of muscle attachment following a traumatic pseudoparalysis and extensive local muscle atrophy.

SPECIMEN 8

Right talus and calcaneus and left calcaneus, adult (HX). (See Fig. B2.)

Talus: When the talus is oriented so that the superior articular surface is in the plane of articulation with the tibia and fibula, the navicular articular surface appears rotated sharply toward the medial side and twisted upward medially. The superior articular surface is flattened and pulled forward laterally and backward medially, giving it a rough diamond shape. The posterior portion of the surface has an area of increased density and smoothness, which is a suprafacet resulting from a relatively "fixed" articulation with the tibia. The same sort of facet may be seen on the fibular surface. On the inferior aspect, the posterior calcaneal surface has been distorted rearward on the medial side, rotating the calcaneus medially.

Calcaneus: Both calcanei are distorted in essentially the same manner, forming a "mirror image" of each other. The posterior articular surface is elongated forward and medially, tending to rotate the whole calcaneus medially. The cuboid surface is rotated sharply downward and medially, and the rear of the calcaneus at the attachment of the Achilles tendon is rotated so that the superior border is lateral and the inferior border is medial.

Interpretation: With the right calcaneus and talus articulated and oriented with respect to the tibia and fibula in terms of the suprafacets, the posterior of the calcaneus is rotated laterally about 30 degrees and twisted laterally about 60 degrees. The cuboid articular surface is pulled medially and downward directly under the navicular surface of the talus. Both are rotated medially. From this it becomes clear then that the whole foot was rotated inward and downward and was supinated, with the toes being aligned vertically rather than horizontally. This is the typical picture of talipes equinovarus, or clubfoot.

The etiology of clubfoot is by no means straightforward or clear-cut. Causative factors include trauma, paralysis, and developmental defects. Several forms of clubfoot are known to be hereditary, though not exclusively so. Hereditary clubfoot is usually transmitted as an irregular dominant trait with poor penetrance and varied expressivity. The incidence of congenital clubfoot has been estimated in the general European and American population as 1:1,000–1,500. It is often associated with *spina bifida*, and in such cases seems to be the result of paralysis of some of the lower leg and foot muscles during a period of rapid intrauterine growth. The

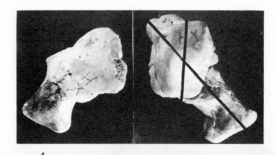

A

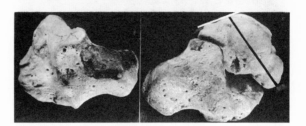

B

FIG. B2 (Specimen 8). *A*, top views of paired calcanei and the articulating right talus oriented as they may have been in life. *B* lateral aspects of these same specimens with the lines of support and weight-bearing surfaces indicated. These bones are probably from a young adult female. Photos courtesy Armed Forces Institute of Pathology.

postnatal or acquired type may be associated with trauma, poliomyelitis, Friedereich's ataxia, and peroneal atrophy. In this particular case, however, the clubfoot seems to be of the congenital variety, since the bones appear to have been malformed rather than deformed. Quite possibly it was hereditary.

In congenital clubfoot, the actual mechanism of malformation is not entirely clear. The anatomic structure of the tarsals in this case provides some interesting clues, however. The concavity of the plantar surface of the calcaneus in conjunction with the twisting of the medial side of the foot upward and inward suggest strongly that there was a rather inelastic tension of the long plantar ligament and the anterior and posterior tibialis tendons. The posterior part of the calcaneus is twisted in a manner that would suggest tension of the Achilles tendon along the inferior attachment, pulling the inferior part upward and twisting and swinging the superior part laterally. The picture that emerges, then, is of several tendons and ligaments in the foot and ankle being tense and shortened, probably as a result of arrested or unequal fetal development, with the

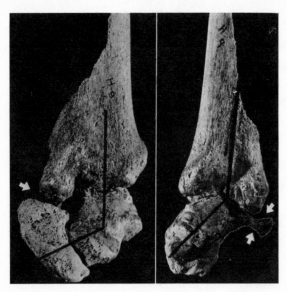

A B

FIG. B3 (Specimen 10). *A* front and *B* back views of the left ankle of a 33-year-old male showing the lower end of the tibia with articulating talus and navicular bones in proper relationship. The weight-bearing lines and their transmission are indicated. Note the absence of a squatting facet in view *A*.

bones being ossified from mechanically distorted cartilage.[3]

Diagnosis: Bilateral talipes equinovarus.

SPECIMEN 9

Right talus and calcaneus, adult (HX).

Talus: The superior articular surface is considerably flattened, suggesting some restriction of movement. The navicular facet is sharply rotated medially and eburnated. The fibular facet lies farther forward than normal, and there is arthritic lipping around all articular surfaces.

Calcaneus: The posterior part is twisted laterally and the cuboid facet is rotated directly under the navicular facet of the talus. There is arthritic lipping around all articular surfaces.

Interpretation: When both bones are articulated and oriented with respect to the tibia and fibula,

3. More recent investigations suggest that a localized abnormality of development, involving the soft tissues, ligaments, and capsules that connect the calcaneus and talus may account for the development of congenital idiopathic clubfoot (Reimann, 1967).

they present a picture very similar to those of Specimen 8, with the posterior calcaneus twisted and projecting laterally. The rotated articular facets on the anterior aspect strongly suggest that the whole foot was twisted sharply inward and downward and was supinated. The lipping and eburnation are the result of osteoarthritis with destruction of the articular cartilage between the talus and navicular, probably due to the repeated compression of that cartilage resulting from walking, and possibly initiated by local injury. When the foot is twisted as this one was and the weight is supported on the lower outer aspect of it, the talonavicular cartilage is in a position of both torsion and compression.

Diagnosis: 1) Talipes equinovarus. 2) Osteoarthritis with destruction of the talonavicular cartilage and subsequent eburnation due to mechanical friction.

SPECIMEN 10

Left talus, navicular, and lower condyle of a badly eroded left tibia, all articulating. All are adult (H–9). (See Fig. B3.)

Talus: The talus is flattened and quite thin posteriorly, where it narrows considerably. The posterior articular surface is wedge-shaped and "pinched off" laterally where the calcaneus appears to have articulated directly with the tibia. There is an accessory facet on the posterior margin of the talus where it articulated with the calcaneus. The navicular surface is rotated sharply downward and medially. To articulate with this talus the calcaneus would have had to be sharply elevated posteriorly and rotated laterally.

Tibia: The lower end of the tibia is essentially normal, except for a lengthening and thickening of the medial malleolus, which has a large pseudofacet on its inferior surface. There is some suggestion of an accessory facet on the posterolateral border, but there is too much postmortem erosion to reconstruct the complete outline of this facet.

Navicular: When articulated with the talus, the navicular is nearly medial to it. There is a broad pseudoarticular facet on its posteromedial surface that matches the one on the medial malleolus. These appear to have been separated by a fairly thick cartilage plate.

Interpretation: The whole foot was rotated sharply downward and inward. The medial malleolus and navicular formed a buttress-shaped pseudoarticulation, which gave some degree of stability to the severely distorted ankle. The calcaneus was elevated posteriorly and rotated so that the posterior part was lateral to its normal position. The ankle appears to have been fairly rigid, and it seems evident that this individual walked on the outer anterior edge of his foot.

Diagnosis: Severe talipes equinovarus.

SPECIMEN 11

Left and right talus, adult (H–118).

Talus: Both tali are somewhat flattened and the calcaneal surface is pulled slightly forward and laterally. The navicular surface is slightly rotated medially but not appreciably depressed. This surface is also roughened or billowed, as though the range of movement in this joint was restricted after a period of normal use. The superior surface has some suggestion of suprafacets on the rear of the articular area, suggesting that the talotibial joint had been in a more or less "fixed" position of extension for some time.

Interpretation: The malformation of these tali is rather minimal, although there is some evidence to suggest that they may represent clubfoot, or at least a marked degree of inward pointing of the feet. Combined with other of the foot bones, these tali might give a more definite picture of clubfoot, but by themselves they can only suggest that there was a considerable degree of talipes equinus with a mild degree of varus probable.

Diagnosis: Talipes equinovarus, probably moderate. Marked equinus with mild varus, bilateral.

SPECIMEN 12

A badly eroded right talus, navicular, and portion of calcaneus (N–24).

Talus: The talus appears to be essentially normal. There is no flattening nor are the inferior articular facets distorted. The navicular facet is twisted slightly clockwise, but may well be in the range of normal variation.

Calcaneus: The part of the calcaneus that is present appears normal except for an accessory pseudoarticular facet just above the cuboid facet.

Navicular: The navicular appears normal except for an accessory pseudoarticular facet on the lateral border which matches the one on the calcaneus. Most of the anterior articular surface is missing due to erosion.

Interpretation: When articulated and oriented in the tibiofibular plane, these bones appear to be in normal alignment. The navicular is buttressed laterally by pseudoarticulation with the calcaneus and is elevated medially. However, the uniform smoothness of the talonavicular surfaces suggests that there was mobility in that joint. Possibly the inner aspect of the foot was elevated except when weight was put on the foot, rotating the navicular slightly. There is no evidence of equinus, varus or valgus.

Diagnosis: Essentially normal, with possible moderate pes cavus.

This group of tarsals raises some interesting considerations. In the only two cases containing bones from both feet of the same individual, the talipes is bilateral. Were additional foot bones available in the other cases but not submitted for examination because they were normal? Is it possible that we are seeing in this population a single variety of talipes equinus which was uniformly bilateral? If so, it would strongly favor a common etiologic factor for this population.

It would also be interesting to know if there were any other malformed or pathologic tarsals in this population that might represent patterns of clubfoot other than the talipes equinovarus of these bones. If not, that fact would suggest a single variety of clubfoot in this population with a fairly uniform expression but with some variation in degree and of a hereditary type.

Since genetics may be involved, the archaeologic temporal and spatial relationships of these burials are important. It would be interesting to know whether they were buried in the same general area or scattered, and whether they were in the same general stratum or buried at various depths. Such information might provide some clue as to whether these individuals represented two or three generations of one family or were sporadic cases.

LITERATURE CITED

Blomberg, J. M., and Kerley, E. R.
1966 *Human paleopathology,* ed. Saul Jarcho, pp. 154–57. New Haven: Yale University Press.

Hamperl, H., and Weiss, P.

1955 Uber die spongiöse hyperostose an schäd-
eln aus AH-Peru. *Arch. path. Anat.* 327:
629–42.

Johnson, Lent C.

1966 Kinetics of skeletal remodelling. Birth
Defects: Original Article Series 2:66–144.

Moodie, R. L.

1923 *Paleopathology: an introduction to the
study of ancient evidences of diseases.* Ur-
bana: University of Illinois Press.

Reimann, Inge

1967 *Congenital idiopathic clubfoot.* Copenhagen: Munksgaard.

Schaeffer, J. Parsons, ed.

1953 *Morris' human anatomy.* 11th ed. New
York: Blakiston.

Toldt, Karl, assisted by Rosa, Alois

1919 *An atlas of human anatomy for students
and physicians.* Adapted by M. Eden Paul.
Rev. ed. New York: Rebman.

APPENDIX C

An Oral Examination of the Early Hawaiians

Leonard J. L. Lai

The dental structures of 261 skulls of early Hawaiians from Mokapu were examined; 154, or 59 percent, were female, and 107, or 41 percent, were male. The palates of the majority of the skulls may be described as having broad and high vaults (Fig. C1) with gently curved, U-shaped arches. Those in the next largest group were also broad but had lower vaults. Finally, a few had narrow and high vaults. Some palatal surfaces not only were porous but had very sharp bony projections. These spines were usually located at the junction of the palatine process of the maxilla and the palatine process of the pterygoid bone. Accessory foramens for the incisal foramen and the posterior palatine foramen were also observed. In one skull there was a perforation through the palatine process of the maxilla (Fig. C3 C). Enlarged incisal foramens were also noted. The posterior teeth of the maxilla tended to be perpendicular to the alveolar process.

Fifty-six percent of the male and 64 percent of the female mandibles had the so-called rocker jaw effect (Marshall and Snow, 1956) (Fig. C2 A); that is, the mandibles will rock on a flat surface when the incisal teeth or the condylar head is depressed. The sites of muscle attachments on the mandibles were prominent in some cases in both sexes. In these cases, the size of the mandible was also larger. An exostosis on the buccal surface was noted on one female specimen (Fig. C4).

A comparison of the location of the mental foramen in these Hawaiians (see also Chappell, 1927) with a series of Americans that included 160 females and 425 males, studied by Sweet (1959), gives the following results:

Location of Mental Foramen	Number of Foramen	
	Mokapu	Sweet
Between 2nd bicuspid and 1st molar	154	20
Below 2nd bicuspid	116	148

Location of Mental Foramen	Number of Foramen	
	Mokapu	Sweet
Between 1st and 2nd bicuspid	15	409
Below 1st molar	11	2

The pre-European Hawaiians may be classified as having the following types of occlusion, according to Angle's Classification:

Occlusion	Class I	Class II
Overbite	55	24
Overjet	7	2
Edge to edge	32	5

The compensating curve and reverse curve were apparent in the plane of occlusion. The reverse curve occurs when the first and second bicuspids of the maxilla are on a higher level than the first and second molars and cuspids of the maxilla (Fig. C3 A). Spaces were noted between the first bicuspid and the cuspid. The upper central incisors of some were in mesiolingual relationship (Fig. C3 C). Malalignment of teeth was uncommon except for cases where teeth were lost through either decay or periodontal disease.

Although the Hawaiians pulverized the bones of fish with their teeth and ate them in order not to be wasteful,[1] attrition of the tooth surfaces was not severe. In many, however, the enamel was worn without any cusp obliteration or exposure of dentine; in others the cusp was worn down and dentine exposed, or an appreciable amount of the crown was worn away. The greater the wear of the occlusal surface, the broader was the contact area with the adjacent teeth (Fig. C3 B).

The temporomandibular joints of some skulls displayed signs of pathology such as: 1) facets or smooth areas on the condylar head of the mandible, the glenoid fossa, or the articular eminence; 2) pitting or porosity of the bone on the condylar head of the mandible, the glenoid fossa, or the articular eminence (Fig. C5); 3) lipping of the bone on the condylar head and the articular eminence; and 4) differences in the size of the right and left condylar heads on the same mandible. When these conditions existed, posterior teeth were usually missing, either unilaterally or bilaterally; in some, however, all teeth were present.

The existence of periodontal disease in both sexes was shown by horizontal loss at the crest of the

1. Mary Kawena Pukui, personal correspondence, 1958.

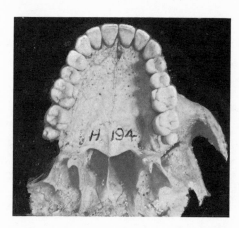

FIG. C1. Typical palate with large Carabelli's cusps on first molars and small, peg-shaped third molars (H-194, female).

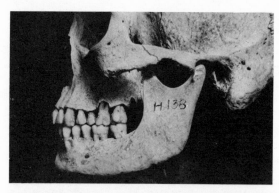

A

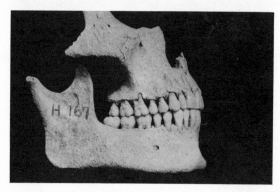

B

FIG. C2. Rocker jaw (H-138, female) and non-rocker jaw with alveoclasia (H-167, female).

alveolar bone, resorption of the alveolar bone in the labial and lingual areas of the alveolar crest, cupping of interseptal bone, increased bone deposition at the alveolar crest, and bone resorption resulting from periodontal abscesses. Calculus was present in varying amounts (Fig. C6). Carey D. Miller (Appendix E, below) writes: "It is difficult to understand how the ancient Hawaiians could have sufficient ascorbic acid for proper tooth formation and yet not enough to maintain the alveolar processes in adult life." The suggested treatment for periodontal disease, as related by Pukui,[2] was as follows: "The root of the puakala or beach poppy, washed free of soil, was bitten into and held between the teeth for about 15 minutes to half an hour. Then the biter waded into the sea, drooling all the while; it did not do to swallow the bitter juice. Then the mouth was thoroughly rinsed with sea water. This was repeated until the condition was healed."

Healed fractures of the zygomatic arch and mandible were noted.

The anatomy, size, shape, number, and variation of the teeth were similar to those of modern man. There were cusps of Carabelli (Fig. C1), shovel-shaped upper central and lateral incisors (Fig. C3 C), protostylids (Fig. C7), peg-shaped upper lateral incisors and third molars (Fig. C1), supernumerary teeth, lower molars with six cusps, growth rings (Fig. C8), impacted and congenitally missing third molars, and fused deciduous teeth. Enamel pearls were also seen (Fig. C9). Twenty-five percent of the upper and lower first and second molars had enamel extending into the bifurcation of the roots. Since these people used their teeth as a viselike tool, fractures of the cuspal and incisal surfaces were very common.

Dental caries were present in both children and adults. Where the maxilla and mandible of a specimen were both present, twenty-three, or 21 percent, of the males and thirty-nine, or 25 percent, of the females had no decay. Caries found in children were on the buccal and occlusal surfaces of the first and second deciduous molars or on the labial surfaces of the anterior teeth; there were no interproximal caries in the anterior or posterior teeth.

The order of frequency of the sites of caries in adults may be listed as follows, according to Dr. G. V. Black's classification of dental decay:

1) Class V. Buccal and labial surfaces of an-

2. Personal correspondence, 1958.

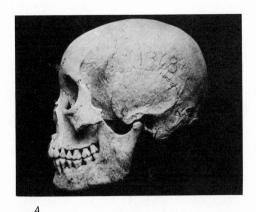
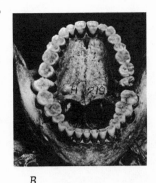
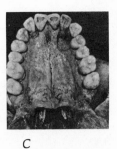

A   B   C

FIG. C3. *A*, reverse occlusal curve (1368, female). *B*, crowns of teeth worn down and dentine exposed; smooth contact areas (H-219, male). *C*, mesiopalatal (lingual) torsion of shovel-shaped central incisors, a large abscess opposite left canine and first premolars, and an unerupted upper right third molar (H-34).

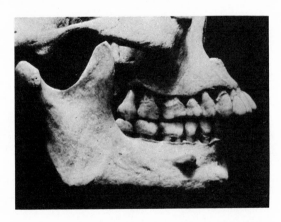

FIG. C4. Large overjet, exostosis, lipping of buccal plate of bone on mandible at alveolar crest, and advanced bone resorption surrounding teeth (273, female).

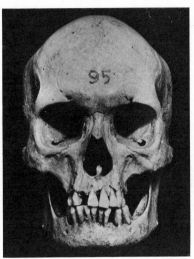

FIG. C6. Calculus formation on the labial root surfaces of the mandibular teeth and advanced resorption of bone in edentulous areas (H-95, female).

A   B

FIG. C5. *A*, pitting of the articular eminence on the right side (H-245, male). *B*, pitting of the glenoid fossa on the right side (1342, female).

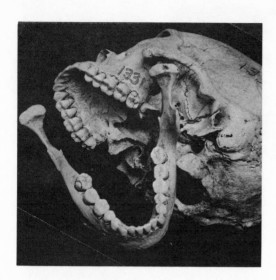

Fig. C7. Protostylids on the buccal surface of the third molars (H-1331).

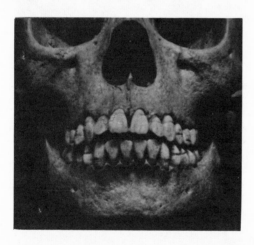

Fig. C8. Growth rings on a young teen-ager (transverse grooves) (H-200, female).

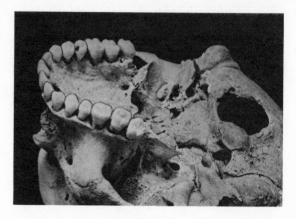

Fig. C9. Enamel pearl on the palatal root of the upper left third molar and dental decay on the upper left second premolar (H-106, female).

terior and posterior teeth; lingual surface of posterior teeth. (Gingival caries.)

2) Class I. Occlusal surface of posterior teeth; buccal pit of posterior teeth; lingual surface of anterior teeth.

3) Class III. Interproximal surface of anterior teeth.

4) Class II. Interproximal surface of posterior teeth.

Advanced stages of tooth destruction invariably led to the formation of abscesses.

The Hawaiians' principal food, poi, may have been a factor in the great number of gingival caries found. Miller (Appendix E, below) quotes Stewart, who wrote in 1823 that the Hawaiians preferred poi when it was four or five days old. She also states that at two to three days, fermentation has occurred and the mixture has attained a pH of 4.0 to 3.0. According to Jones (n.d.), the Hawaiians ate 5 to 15 pounds of poi daily per person. If these people had used the brackish water from the seashore, they would have been drinking water having 2.22 parts per million of fluoride. The spring water they drank showed only 0.10 to 0.35 parts per million of fluoride. There was no evidence of mottled enamel.

According to Pukui,[3] the Hawaiians rubbed wood ash or charcoal on and between the teeth and then rinsed the mouth with fresh or salt water. Teeth were extracted by pulling them out with a strong olona cord.

Comparing the results of the present study with

3. Personal correspondence, 1958.

Table C1. TEETH DECAYED AND MISSING

Pre-European Hawaiians

| Age range (years) | | Males | | | | Females | |
	No.	Decayed or missing	Av. per indiv.		No.	Decayed or missing	Av. per indiv.
1 - 5	6	12	2.0		10	3	0.3
6 - 10	4	1	0.3		7	4	0.6
11 - 15	5	2	0.4		10	13	1.3
16 - 20	1	0	0.0		6	3	0.5
21 - 25	9	48	5.3		41	81	2.0
26 - 30	26	129	5.0		45	224	5.0
31 - 35	23	223	9.8		16	142	8.9
36 - 40	27	220	8.1		15	212	14.1
41 - 50	6	123	21.0		4	63	15.8

Department of Health, California, 1957

| Age range (years) | Males | | Females | |
	No.	Decayed, missing or filled (av. per indiv.)	No.	Decayed, missing or filled (av. per indiv.)
20 - 24	102	13.6	81	16.9
25 - 29	170	15.1	99	17.8
30 - 34	228	16.1	165	16.8
35 - 39	220	16.1	191	18.8
40 - 44	261	17.9	180	19.2

those of a study made in 1957 by the Department of Health of California on 1,697 residents of that state between the ages of 20 and 44, we find that the dentition of the pre-European Hawaiians had a lower rate of decay between the ages of 20 to 40. After the age of 40 the decay rate of the Hawaiians exceeded that of modern man. (See Table C1.)

This study of the oral remains of pre-European Hawaiians from Mokapu revealed that, in general, their oral anatomical features were very similar to those of present-day man. There are, however, three characteristics that identify these Hawaiian mandibles: the location of the mental foramen, the presence of enamel extensions on molar teeth, and the rocker contour.

Contrary to the common belief that the natives of Hawaii had teeth free of decay, this examination of their dentition showed that decay was definitely present.

LITERATURE CITED

Chappell, H. G.
1927 Jaws and teeth of ancient Hawaiians. *Bernice P. Bishop Museum Memoirs* 9:249-68. Honolulu.

Jones, Martha R.; Larsen, Nils P.; and Pritchard, George P.
1930 Dental disease in Hawaii. *Dental Cosmos*, May-Aug. 1930.

Marshall, D. S., and Snow, C. E.
1956 An evaluation of Polynesian craniology. *Am. J. Phys. Anthropol.* 14(3):405–27.

Sweet, A. P. S.
1959 Radiodontic study of the mental foramen. *Dental Radiography and Photography* 32 (2):28–33.

APPENDIX D

Hawaiian Folkways of Posture and Body Molding

Mary Kawena Pukui

According to Kamakau, the Hawaiian historian, planting methods varied between wet and dry districts. The people of Hilo on Hawaii were said to have a *ha'aheo* or "proud method," that is, their *'o'o* digging sticks were long like spears and people stood upright to work, keeping their loincloths clean. The ground was constantly wet, hence easy to work. After clearing the ground, a day or so was allowed to elapse before planting. The workers made a game of it, one line moving along with their sticks, raising, thrusting, and turning the sticks in unison as they advanced. Planters came behind them dropping the cuttings into each hole.

My own people, who came from Ka'u, an arid area on southwestern Hawaii, had to squat and work the soil patiently with shorter digging sticks. The dust soiled the flap of the loincloth and so in derision those of the wet districts called the latter *malo 'eka* (dirty loincloth), and *kuawehi* (black backs) because the sun darkened the backs of the squatting workers. This squatting position was called *ki'elelei* in some localities, and *ki'enenei* in others.

The *'oku'u* position was similar to the *ki'elelei*, except that in the former the knees were not close together but were held apart to facilitate working the soil. While sitting to watch the children or tending the fire in cooking, many of my folks took the *'oku'u* position. It was common to hear the answer, when someone asked a person who was doing nothing in particular just what he was doing, *"E 'oku'u wale a'e ana no,"* or "Just *'oku'u.*"

During a cholera epidemic while Kamehameha was on Oahu, the pain caused the people to assume the *'oku'u* position while holding their aching abdomens; for that reason the disease was given the name *'oku'u.*

I was told in my childhood that those trained in the art of *lua* fighting, both male and female, preferred to sit in an *'oku'u* position even when eating. It made springing to the feet much easier and quicker. *Lua* was an art similar to judo but said to be better. The practise of *lua* was discouraged by law long before I was born.

Boys and men were permitted to sit crosslegged because the flap of the loincloth fell gracefully between the thighs in that position. This was called *noho 'aha'aha.* Girls were taught to sit with knees together and feet to one side, in a position called *noho kapae.* The hem of the skirt was tucked under the knees and prevented women from exposing themselves.

When plaiting mats, which were often large, women sat in any position that seemed comfortable. The work required a stooping forward to plait and the *'oku'u* was not very comfortable. Sometimes one leg was tucked under the other and one knee set upright. This was called *noho kukulu* or "set upright" sitting, and in my childhood I was not encouraged to sit this way. It was believed that the pressure of the knee against the breast caused the latter to grow too large. Whether it was so or not, I cannot say.

In the hula, all sitting dances and drumming were done in a kneeling position, sitting on the heels, as the Japanese do. The knees were neither too close together nor too wide apart, but comfortable enough to permit free movement of the body. This position is the *kukuli.* I have seen both men and women twist fibers into a cord in this position—the fibers rolled over the bare thigh with the palm of one hand while the other held the fibers as the twisting was being done.

Sitting flat on the ground with legs extended and feet out was not encouraged when I was a child. Such a position required a support for the back. Someone was bound to say, *"Ua make o Keawe me kona kalele"* (Keawe and the one he leaned on are both dead)—a disapproving rebuke. It was a lazy position, and furthermore exposing the soles of the feet to people was not regarded as polite.

My own people practiced body and head molding, but discontinued the latter before I was born. Body molding went on for a while after that, and then was discontinued as the old folks and their ways passed away.

When my husband and I adopted a Japanese child, my mother noticed that she had no bridge to her nose and began to mold one by pressing finger and thumb together on both sides of the nose. This pressing in one place is called *'opa.* The same child's fingers were tapered by running the finger and thumb up the sides of the small fingers and gently rolling the tips between them. This is called *ʻomi-lomilo*.

Mothers were warned to hold up the breast with the hand while nursing lest the weight resting on the child's nose flatten it. Flat noses and protruding ears were not considered attractive among my people, and attention was paid that the ears did not fold over while lying down. Ears were pressed with the hand back against the head. For boys, the buttocks were guarded against pressure on the lap, lest a flattening result. A flat seat was called *kikala pai*. As a man's body was mostly exposed, except for the part covered by a loincloth, those who reared him watched that his body was perfect by their standards. In order to remove imperfections the body was massaged daily with a rubbing of mashed kukui nuts in a cloth. This had been warmed before being rubbed over the body.

From my mother (who learned the art of *lomilomi* from her father, a medical *kahuna*) I learned some of the names of the hand manipulations. Pressure with the lower part of the palm of the hand or with all the fingers is called *kaomi*, while squeezing with the lower part of the palm and the fingers or with finger and thumb is *ʻopa*. A gentle rubbing of the hand over the pained area is a *hamohamo*. Massaging was done not only with the hands but with the feet. The person being massaged would lie on his stomach while the one working on him walked up and down his back with feet on either side of the spine. Care was taken not to make any jerky movements lest there be an *ʻanuʻu*, that is, a dislocation of the spine. *Kaomi* was done firmly with the heel of the foot as well as the base of the palm.

A corrective, or reshaping, treatment was called *pakolea* by my people. This term was used also by John ʻIʻi in speaking of a kukui tree whose branch was trained to bend in an arch over the Nuʻuanu trail. As a small child I fell off my father's bed, where he had laid me, and injured my spine. My grandmother treated me with the *pakolea*. I was buried daily in sand up to my armpits. Then she slipped her hands under my arms and lifted me slowly and gently out of the sand. Massage with the warmed oil of kukui nuts always followed. Then the treatments were spaced to every other day, to every two days, to every three, and so on until she saw that I needed no more. I have never since had any trouble with my back.

I saw only one head molded with a gourd shell, that of a cousin who was much older than I. I asked older relatives why his head was not like those of the others and was told that as a baby his head was laid in a gourd shell lined with soft *tapa*. A head like his was a mark of distinction. How long it took I do not know, for when my childish curiosity was satisfied, I asked no more questions.

A head with a bulging forehead, *poʻo puʻu*, or one that bulged in the back, *poʻo ololo* (as seen among some *haoles* [whites]) was not considered attractive at all. Grandmothers warned against letting a baby lie in one position too long lest that side flatten, *ʻopaha*, giving the head the appearance of a misshapen melon.

These were the folkways of my own people of Kaʻu. Whether or not they were generally practiced I cannot say.

The Influence of Foods and Food Habits upon the Stature and Teeth of the Ancient Hawaiians

Carey D. Miller

Modern scientific knowledge has firmly established the effect of good and poor food upon growth and teeth. Although heredity may determine the potential stature of an individual, food to furnish the needed nutrients in the right proportions at the proper time is the chief factor in determining whether or not the individual will achieve his potential.

It is easy to gain the notion from some accounts that all the ancient Hawaiians were large and strong, but a careful examination of the records shows that the early explorers and travelers appraised the situation rather well. In the account of Captain Cook's third voyage, written by Captain James King in March 1779 (1784, pp. 125, 126), one may read:

The Natives of these islands [Hawaii] are, in general, above the middle size, and well made; they walk very gracefully, run nimbly, and are capable of bearing great fatigue; though, upon the whole, the men are somewhat inferior, in point of strength and activity, to the Friendly islanders, and the women less delicately limbed than those of Otaheite. . . .

The same superiority that is observable in the persons of the Erees, through all the other islands, is found also here. Those whom we saw were, without exception, perfectly well formed; whereas the lower sort, besides their general inferiority, are subject to all the variety of make and figure that is seen in the populace of other countries. Instances of deformity are more frequent here, than in any of the other islands. Whilst we were cruising off Owhyhee, two dwarfs came on board, one an old man, four feet two inches high, but exactly proportioned, and the other a woman, nearly of the same height. We afterward saw three natives, who were humpbacked, and a young man, born without hands or feet. Squinting is also

This paper was written in 1957 and approved for publication in December 1957 by the Director of the Hawaii Agricultural Experiment Station as Miscellaneous Paper No. 94.

very common amongst them, and a man, who, they said, had been born blind, was brought to us to be cured.

Ellis (1836, p. 23) in 1823 wrote, "The natives are in general rather above the middle stature, well formed, with fine muscular limbs, open countenances, and features frequently resembling those of Europeans. Their gait is graceful, and sometimes stately. The chiefs in particular are tall and stout, and their personal appearance is so much superior to that of the common people, that some have imagined them a distinct race. This, however, is not the fact; the great care taken of them in childhood, and their better living, have probably occasioned the difference." Kamakau Kelou of Kona (Ellis, 1836, p. 64) is described as a chief of considerable rank and influence in old Hawaii. "His person, like that of the chiefs in general, is noble and engaging. He is about six feet high, stout, well proportioned, and more intelligent and enterprising than the people around him."

Stewart, another keen observer, who was in Hawaii from 1823 through 1825, states (1839, p. 104): "The nobles of the land are so strongly marked by their external appearance, as at all times to be easily distinguishable from the common people. They seem indeed in size and stature to be almost a distinct race. They are all large in their frame, and often excessively corpulent, while the common people are scarce of the ordinary height of Europeans, and of a thin rather than full habit."

There seems, therefore, to be rather good evidence that the chiefly class was likely to be taller and better formed than most of the common people, because an assured food supply for the ali'i meant that probably they were never subjected to short or prolonged periods of hunger, as were the lower classes.

After noting the sources of information available today regarding the foods of the ancient Hawaiians, I shall list those believed to have been available. In addition to considering what the foods would contribute to each class of nutrients, I shall attempt to appraise the supply and use of the principal foods. The nutritive value of some of these foods has not been studied.

My sources of information regarding the foods eaten in early Hawaii have been the accounts of early explorers and the Westerners who followed them, the writings of old Hawaiians (Malo, 1903), recollections of modern Hawaiians, and evidence of cultivated areas observed by an ethnologist (Handy, 1940). Studies of the nutritive values of these foods have been made at intervals during the past thirty years by me and my associates at the University of Hawaii.

The principal foods of the Hawaiians are listed below in approximately the order of their importance. A list of foods occasionally eaten, either for variety or during famine or shorter periods of scarcity, and one of the foods forbidden to women are also given.

Principal plant foods

Taro corm (as taro and in the form of poi)
Sweet potato
Breadfruit
Yam
Taro leaves, stems, and flowers
Sweet potato leaves and tender stems
Banana (plantain)
Limu (seaweeds)
Coconut
Sugar cane
Mountain apple (in season)

Principal animal foods

Fish
Shellfish
Crustacea
Pigs
Dogs
Birds and wild fowl
Domesticated fowls

Foods occasionally eaten

(Not claimed to be a complete list)

Cyanea, several species
Ferns: stems, shoots and starchy trunks of several species
Kikaweo (*Aspidium cyatheoides* Kaulfuss), several species
Kukui nuts, roasted and used as a relish
Noni (*Morinda citrifolia* L.)
Pala (*Marattia douglasii* Baker)
Popolo (*Solanum nigrum* L.)
Ti Root (*Cordyline terminalis*)

Foods forbidden women

(Malo, 1903, p. 52)

Banana (plantain)

Coconut
Certain choice fishes
Pork
Turtle

Referring again to King's account of Captain Cook's third voyage (1784, p. 141), we find this statement:

The food of the lower class of people consists principally of fish, and vegetables; such as yams, sweet potatoes, tarrow, plantains, sugar canes, and breadfruit. To these, the people of a higher rank add the flesh of hogs and dogs, dressed in the same manner as at the Society Islands. They also eat fowls of the same domestic kind with ours; but they are neither plentiful, nor much esteemed by them. It is remarked by Captain Cook, that the breadfruit and yams appeared scarce amongst them, and were reckoned great rarities. We found this not to be the case on our second visit; and it is therefore most probable, that as these vegetables were generally planted in the interior parts of the country, the natives had not had time to bring them down to us, during the short stay we made in Wymoa Bay. Their fish they salt, and preserve in gourd-shells; not, as we first imagined, for the purpose of providing against any temporary scarcity, but from the preference they give to salted meats. For we also found, that the Erees used to pickle pieces of pork in the same manner, and esteemed it a great delicacy.

NUTRIENTS NEEDED AND FOODS WHICH SUPPLY THEM

The nutrients needed by humans and other animals are commonly grouped under the following headings: calories, protein, minerals, and vitamins. An adequate diet must furnish sufficient calories to satisfy the energy needs, adequate protein to supply all the amino acids necessary for growth and maintenance, a sufficiency of all the required minerals, and all the vitamins needed for good health.

Calories: The human, like other animals, normally takes care of the need for calories, or energy material, by satisfying his hunger. Simple shortages of foods for several days probably occurred often among the ancient Hawaiian commoners, and they undoubtedly experienced occasional famines of longer duration.

Carbohydrates, proteins, and fats all yield energy when oxidized in the body and practically every food will furnish some calories. Those that satisfied the energy needs of the Hawaiians to the greatest degree would have been taro, sweet potatoes, breadfruit, and yams, all of which have relatively large amounts of starches and sugars, but only 1 to 2 percent of protein.

It should be emphasized that the quantity of each of these energy foods would have been greatly influenced by the locality in which the people lived or from which they drew their foods. Handy (1940), gives a well-documented account of the extent to which and the areas where these foods were grown. If we assume that the people buried at Mokapu resided all or most of their lives in the areas still known as Kailua, Kaneohe, and Heeia, then their principal energy food must have been taro, with sweet potatoes as a secondary source. Both breadfruit and yams (*uhi*) were seasonal and available information indicates that they could never have been major factors in the total food supply. The definitive work on the foods of the ancient Hawaiians is Handy and Handy (1972). The reader is referred to it for much interesting and valuable information.

The body has remarkable ability to adjust to low intakes of protein and other nutrients when the calories are sufficient to cover the energy requirement. Therefore, if any of these three or four principal foods were adequate for energy needs, there should have been no deleterious effects upon health resulting from intermittent low intakes of fish and other protein foods.

The ancient Hawaiians recognized several hundred forms of taro. Handy (1940) lists 346, and Whitney *et al.* (1939) classified 84 varieties in the University Experiment Station collections. A recent list of taro varieties in the Lyon Arboretum, University of Hawaii (1970), indicates only 56 cultivars of Hawaiian taro, and 62 from other Polynesian islands. However, Handy and Handy (1972, p. 83) state, "Unquestionably 300 is a fair figure for the number of varieties grown and known to planters in different localities [in Hawaii] in prediscovery days." While all varieties of cooked taro corms may be used as such, some varieties were considered especially good for *luau* (tender leaves used as greens) and others for "table taros," but the greatest number were used for poi.

No part of the taro plant is edible in the raw state. Thorough cooking is required to break down the calcium oxalate crystals which cause taro to be irritating to the mucous membranes of the mouth and throat (Miller, 1927, p. 5). The Hawaiians were the only Polynesians to consume most of their taro in the form of poi. Poi was made by cooking the taro in an underground or earth oven of hot stones and pounding the cooked corms to a smooth paste with the addition of small amounts of water. Additional water was added to make "one-finger" or "two-finger" poi. Although it may be eaten fresh, most modern Hawaiians prefer poi with about 20 percent solids, when it is at least two to three days old. By this time some fermentation has taken place and the mixture has attained a pH of 4.0 to 3.0, an acidity approximating that of tomatoes and other acid fruits (Miller, 1927, p. 8). Stewart (1839, p. 112) reported in 1823 that the Hawaiians preferred poi when it was four or five days old.

Dietetically it would appear that making taro into poi was an excellent practice. Most baked or boiled taro seems thick, bland, and difficult to masticate thoroughly. Sour poi, on the other hand, stimulates the flow of saliva, mixes readily with it, and is easily swallowed. Being more appetizing, it doubtless stimulates the flow of other digestive juices. The organic acids formed during the fermentation process at room temperature tend to retard the action of yeasts and bacteria that would cause spoilage. The acids, plus possibly other factors, also discourage the growth of certain pathogenic bacteria (Fung and Bushnell, 1948). The most abundant organic acids in poi have been identified by qualitative tests as lactic and acetic acids. The three most common fruit acids, citric, malic, and tartaric, were not found (Bilger and Young, 1935, pp. 48, 49). The Hawaiians had little or no fruit, but poi furnished some of the organic acids which are usually supplied in the diets of other peoples by sour milk or by fruits, including tomatoes.

A number of varieties of sugar cane were growing in the Hawaiian Islands when they were discovered by Captain Cook. Although widely cultivated and used by the ancient Hawaiians, it could not be considered a staple food. It is difficult to extract the juice by chewing or by pounding and squeezing. By weighing and measuring some sugar cane stalks, I have calculated that even if all the sugar could be extracted, one foot of cane would yield only about 35 grams or the equivalent of 3 tablespoons of sugar, which would furnish only 144 calories of the 2,000 to 3,000 needed daily. (The size of the individual and the energy expended govern the caloric requirement.) The amounts of other nutrients furnished would be negligible.

The ancient Hawaiians probably enjoyed sitting

about and gossiping while they chewed sugar cane, and the exercise of chewing would be useful in developing the jaws and teeth. The quantity of carbohydrate that could be obtained in this manner was not sufficiently concentrated to have any ill effects upon the teeth, but if continued, the practice might cause eroded biting edges.

Sugar cane was much used in times of famine and as an emergency ration. Ellis (1832, p. 98) reports that "In a journey, the natives often carry a piece of sugar cane, which furnishes a sweet and nourishing juice, appeasing at once, to a certain degree, both thirst and hunger. . . . A native will sometimes travel, in the course of a day, thirty or forty miles, frequently over mountain and ravine, without taking any refreshment, except the juice from a piece of sugar cane, and apparently experience but little inconvenience from his excursion."

Coconut was a food of minor importance in the diet of the ancient Hawaiians compared to the major role it played in the islands south of the equator (Miller, 1929, pp. 13, 14). The fact that coconut was one of the foods forbidden to women would indicate not only that it was considered a choice food but probably also that it was not very abundant. According to my informants, the ancient Hawaiians made little or no use of expressed coconut "milk" or "cream," as did the more southern Polynesians. They also agree that expressed coconut milk or cream was not used to feed babies nor were they fed the very soft coconut instead of mother's milk, as is sometimes done in the islands to the south.

Protein: Fish was undoubtedly the main source of protein food for all classes of Hawaiians in ancient times, but just as in modern times the phases of the moon and the weather markedly influence the ease or difficulty with which fish may be caught, there must have been times when this important source of protein food failed. The fish from the ancient fish ponds were probably reserved for the chiefs and their families and would have provided them with dependable sources of protein, even when the common people had to go without. Since protein has such a marked effect in promoting growth, this assured supply may well have contributed to the superior stature of the chiefly class.

Stewart (1839, p. 297) tells of visiting a fish pond near Wailuku, Hawaii, in 1825 and states that, since the fish in the pond were tabu to all but the high

chiefs and since no one of rank had lived there lately, the pond was literally full of mullet and hundreds could be taken at any time by a single cast of a small net.

One would judge from early accounts that the pigs and dogs were likely to be reserved for the chiefly class. But since the biological values of fish proteins are just as good as those of land mammals, even the common Hawaiians should not have suffered from poor quality protein if fish were available. The old habit of utilizing the blood and organs of pigs and dogs enhanced the total nutritive value of the flesh. Likewise, the consumption of fish livers and whole small fish meant that, in addition to protein, more vitamins and minerals were obtained than if only the muscle were eaten.

The *opihi*, or Hawaiian limpet, was one of the favored shellfish of the ancient Hawaiians and was available to all classes of people. It is interesting to note that *opihi* shells have been found in the caves on the slopes of Mauna Kea and Mauna Loa, as well as in the crater in Haleakala on Maui. This shellfish has been studied for its nutritive value and found to be a good source of minerals and vitamins, as well as of protein (Miller and Robbins, 1940). The soft parts, which were among the first foods to be fed to young infants, contain a larger proportion of minerals and vitamins than do the tougher foot and mantel (Miller *et al.*, 1956, p. 22). None of the other shellfish or crustacea used by the Hawaiians have been studied.

Although Malo (1903, pp. 62–65) lists a number of birds and wild fowl that the Hawaiians considered "good eating," the methods necessarily used for catching them would probably have prevented them from being consumed in large quantities.

Although some of the early explorers—Cook and King (1784, p. 118), Vancouver (1798), and La Perouse (1807, p. 37)—write of the seemingly inexhaustible supply of hogs, all agree that they were forbidden to women. Later travelers such as Stewart (1839, p. 110) indicate that it was only on rare occasions that the common people had the privilege of eating hog and dog, and that their food consisted of taro, sweet potatoes, and salt, with fish occasionally. Stewart (1839, p. 118) says further, "The poverty of many of the people is such, that they seldom secure a taste of animal food, and live almost exclusively on kalo and salt." But since Ellis (1836, p. 346) about the same time tells of seeing and counting 400 baked dogs with fish, hogs, and vegetables in proportion at a feast for royalty, the common people must have had some share in this animal protein.

Minerals: There are at least thirteen minerals required by the body, but the two most important for growth and for good bones and teeth are calcium and phosphorus. If adequate amounts of these two minerals and iron are obtained from food sources, all the other needed elements are quite certain to be supplied also.

In the diet of the ancient Hawaiians, calcium and phosphorus could be obtained from a number of sources, both plant and animal. Taro has relatively small amounts of these elements, but when taro or poi supplied a large proportion of the calories, they would at the same time furnish a good quota of these two minerals, especially calcium. Experiments with both laboratory animals and humans have shown that these two minerals in poi are well utilized (Potgieter, 1940 a, b). Despite the fact that taro contains a small amount of oxalic acid in the form of oxalate, which is known to interfere with the absorption of calcium, it is not sufficient to reduce the utilization of the calcium in poi, as demonstrated in the studies cited above.

Taro leaves (*luau*) have relatively more calcium oxalate than taro corms (Miller, Ross, and Louis, 1947, p. 21). If eaten in large quantity they would probably prevent the utilization of the calcium in the leaves themselves but would be unlikely to furnish sufficient oxalic acid to interfere with the metabolism of calcium from other sources.

Using biological experiments with rats, the University of Hawaii Nutrition Laboratory proved that the iron in taro and taro leaves was more than 90 percent available and was superior in this respect to thirteen other vegetable foods tested at the same time (Miller and Louis, 1945).

Fish, with bones, may contain ten to fifteen times more calcium and ten times more phosphorus than taro; consequently, the most important sources of these minerals in the diet of the ancient Hawaiians were probably the bones and viscera of the fish that were eaten whole. Most shellfish and crustacea are also good sources of these two minerals. Modern experiments have shown that humans make good use of the calcium and phosphorus in the bones of fish (Basu *et al.*, 1942; Leverton and Payawal, 1951).

For the best utilization of calcium and phosphorus, vitamin D is essential. This vitamin was obtained by the ancient Hawaiians directly from the liver and viscera of fish and shellfish. In addition they had the benefit of ample sunshine which would promote the formation of vitamin D from 7-dehydrocholesterol in the skin.

Limu, or seaweeds, which were available to all classes in old Hawaii, did not take the place of vegetables in the diet, as some have suggested. The Hawaiians with whom I have talked agree that *limu* was used more as a relish than as a salad. Although the composition of dry seaweeds indicates protein contents of from 4 to 28 percent and carbohydrate of from 24 to 55 percent (Chapman, 1950, p. 183) there seems to be considerable doubt about the utilization of these two components by humans (ibid., pp. 186, 187). Analyses of fresh Hawaiian seaweeds made in the University of Hawaii Nutrition Laboratory show large percentages of moisture and relatively small quantities of protein and carbohydrate. *Limu kohu* (unpublished data), *limu ellele*, and *limu lipoa* (Miller, 1927, p. 19), respectively, have the following composition: moisture, 90.8, 90.3, and 84.7 percent; protein, 2.5, 2.8, and 1.6 percent; carbohydrate (by difference) 3.4, 5.2, and 11.1 percent. If the carbohydrate and protein are not digested and the water is held firmly, *limu* would tend to prevent constipation. This might be a desirable factor in a diet with small amounts of crude fiber.

As a source of minerals, *limu* may more logically be compared with common vegetables. Analyses indicate that *limu* are a good source of calcium and a poor source of phosphorus (Miller, 1927, p. 19); but no experiments have been done to give us an idea of how well humans utilize the calcium. Undoubtedly the greatest value of *limu* would have been to give variety to a somewhat monotonous diet.

Since in recent years the role that fluorine plays in decreasing tooth decay has been emphasized, it is interesting to consider the possible sources of fluorine for the ancient Hawaiians. Sea water, which was sometimes used in cooking, could supply fluorine (1.2 to 1.4 ppm) (McClure, 1949, p. 6) and other minor elements. The spring water they used was probably as low in fluorine as the spring water of today (0.06 to 0.44 ppm) (Nekomoto, 1940, p. 24). But if they used brackish water from near the seashore, they would have obtained considerable fluorine, since analyses of one old well near the ocean on Hawaii showed it to have 2.22 ppm as compared with artesian water, which was found to have between 0.10 and 0.35 ppm when analyzed in the same manner (Nekomoto, 1940).

Ellis describes the method used by the old Hawaiians for making salt from sea water (1836, p. 379). Like others, he emphasizes that they used salt very freely. No analyses for the fluorine content of crude salt made in Hawaii are available, and neither are any data available on the fluorine content of *limu*. Both items were generally eaten by everyone, even those living far from the seashore.

Perhaps the most important source of fluorine would have been the animal sea foods, especially fish eaten bones and all. According to McClure (1949, p. 2), whole fresh or canned fish contain from about 4 to 16 ppm of fluorine.

Excess fluorine may have ill effects upon bone calcification, but if there is no evidence of mottled enamel in the teeth of the Mokapu skeletons (see Appendix C, above) it is unlikely that the quantity of fluorine ingested would have been sufficient to have any deleterious effect upon the bones.

Vitamins: There are about twenty unrelated chemical substances classed as vitamins that are needed by the body. Those grouped under the heading of the B-complex, of which thiamine is one of the most important, are vitally concerned in the complex metabolic processes going on in all the cells of the body and are essential for the normal oxidation processes required for the breakdown and utilization of carbohydrate. As they occur in foods, all are water-soluble. The method of cooking in the *imu* would not leach out the vitamins as would boiling in water, though some would be destroyed by the prolonged heating process.

Taro, sweet potatoes, and breadfruit all furnish more than enough thiamine to aid in the metabolism of the carbohydrate in these foods (Miller *et al.*, 1956, p. 32). All three foods furnish more thiamine and niacin than do highly milled rice and white flour. It is highly improbable that the ancient Hawaiians ever suffered from any deficiency of the B vitamins (Miller *et al.*, 1952).

Vitamin A is obtained as vitamin A from animal sources and, as the provitamin, from the yellow pigments which occur in plants. The latter must be changed to vitamin A in the body in order to be utilizable.

Breadfruit and taro are almost devoid of yellow pigment and therefore of provitamin A. So far as can be learned, most of the sweet potatoes favored by the ancient Hawaiians were not deeply pigmented and would consequently not be good sources of the

provitamin. Most of the plantains (cooking bananas) have no more provitamin than the light yellow sweet potatoes, but taro leaves have 8 to 10 times more yellow pigment (masked by the green chlorophyll) than the sweet potatoes and plantains. Any green leaves such as sweet potato tops are better sources of provitamin A than are bananas, but taro leaves have been found superior in this respect to any other Hawaiian food tested (Miller *et al.*, 1956, p. 26).

The most important sources of vitamin A per se for the ancient Hawaiians of all classes may have been the viscera of fish and shellfish, and, for those who were privileged to partake of them, the liver and other viscera of pigs, dogs, and fowls. Animal foods such as eggs, whole milk, liver, and other viscera contain not only preformed vitamin A, but the provitamins in the form of yellow pigments. Both forms together constitute the total vitamin A *value* of these foods. The vitamin A not immediately needed by the body is stored in the liver and other organs, so that even though sources of supply may have been intermittent, body stores could be drawn upon.

Modern research has shown the necessity of vitamin D for the proper utilization of calcium and phosphorus and the building of strong bones and teeth. From the viscera of mammals, fowls, fish, and shellfish, as well as from whole fish (Miller, Louis, Yanazawa, 1947), the Hawaiians obtained fat-soluble vitamin D, which can be stored in the body if an excess is ingested. In addition, the Hawaiians had sufficient sunshine, the ultraviolet rays of which activate the 7-dehydrocholesterol in the skin to form vitamin D.

Since the Hawaiians were keen observers, they probably made the same deduction as did the Tahitians reported by Ellis (1832, p. 83):

At the time of birth, the complexion of Tahitian infants is but little if any darker than that of European children, and the skin only assumes the bronze or brown hue as they grow up under repeated or constant exposure to the sun. Those least exposed are lightest, those most exposed (fishermen) darkest. Darkness of color was generally considered an indication of strength; and fairness of complexion, the contrary. Hence, the men were not solicitous either to cover their persons, or avoid the sun's rays, from any apprehension of the effect it would produce on the skin. When they searched the field of battle for the bones of the slain, to use them in the manufacture of chisels, gimlets, or fish hooks, they always selected those whose skins were dark, as they supposed their bones were strongest. When I have seen the natives looking at a very dark man, I have sometimes heard them say, "The man, how dark, good bones are his."

This would appear to indicate an appreciation of the effects of the sun's rays on bone calcification centuries before modern science proved the relationship.

So far as it is possible to evaluate the ancient Hawaiian diet, on the basis of our present standards, the vitamin most likely to have been in short supply was ascorbic acid, commonly known as vitamin C. This vitamin is considered the most labile of all the vitamins, since it is water-soluble and readily destroyed by heat and oxidation unless the medium is distinctly acid in reaction.

Taro corms are generally a poor source of ascorbic acid, but when taro or poi was used to supply all or a large part of the calories, they would probably furnish enough ascorbic acid to prevent scurvy. The other two important energy foods, sweet potatoes and breadfruit, contain more vitamin C in the raw state than does taro, although a considerable portion of the vitamin may be destroyed in the cooking process, depending upon its length.

The plantains eaten raw and cooked, and mountain apples used only in the raw state, would have been good sources of vitamin C, but it seems safe to speculate that neither were regularly available in any quantity for the common people.

Of the two most common greens generally available, taro leaves are far superior to sweet potato tops as sources of ascorbic acid. Taro leaves (luau), cooked by modern methods sufficiently to destroy the irritating effect of the calcium oxalate crystals, contain, weight for weight, about as much vitamin C as do oranges, providing the water in which the leaves are cooked is also consumed (Miller, Louis, Yanazawa, 1947, p. 19).

The Hawaiians did not collect the sap from the coconut blossom or inflorescence as did the Micronesians and others (Murai, Pen, and Miller, 1958, p. 62), and thus did not avail themselves of this good source of ascorbic acid. Mature, fresh coconut is a very poor source of ascorbic acid and the water from even immature coconuts has only small amounts of the vitamin.

Protein foods such as fish, shellfish, hog, and dog provide little or no vitamin C, especially in the cooked state. Only negligible amounts of ascorbic acid, if any, can be obtained by chewing sugar cane.

A rough calculation of the amount of ascorbic acid that the ancient Hawaiians could have obtained if they consumed enough of the foods assumed to have been available to furnish 2,000 to 3,000 calories daily greatly exceeds the 5 mg. which the English have determined is sufficient to prevent scurvy in adult human volunteers, or 10 mg., which they state will cure clinical scurvy (Stewart and Guthrie, 1953, p. 432). These quantities seem small in comparison with the recommendations of the National Research Council (1953, p. 22) of 70–75 mg. for adults, which, in turn, are probably more than the common pre-Cook Hawaiians obtained. These present standards, or "allowances," are based on a number of considerations in addition to the prevention of scurvy; most especially on the quantity of ascorbic acid necessary to maintain human tissue concentrations comparable "to those observed in animals in which the vitamin is maintained under physiological control by tissue synthesis" (ibid., p. 20).

Vitamin C is essential for the formation and maintenance of the intercellular substance in cartilage, bone, and teeth, as well as all the soft tissues. Scurvy, which plagued the early explorers in northern regions and on long sea voyages, was the result of prolonged periods without fresh foods which would normally supply vitamin C. The literature of such voyages describes some of the characteristic symptoms, which include bleeding gums and the fact that the teeth "commonly become quite loose, and often fall out" (Stewart and Guthrie, 1953, p. 124). The European explorers in the Pacific were familiar with the manifestations of scurvy, but there appear to be no accounts of their recognizing any similar symptoms in the Hawaiians or other tropical island people with whom they came in contact.

Since vitamin C is essential for the formation of normal teeth, as well as for the maintenance of a good condition of the gums and the alveolar processes once the teeth are formed, it is difficult to understand how the ancient Hawaiians could have sufficient ascorbic acid for proper tooth formation and yet not enough to maintain the alveolar processes in adult life.

Loss of the teeth in the living human with scurvy apparently occurred only after the disease had existed for months and had reached a severe stage, with many other serious symptoms such as no early traveler in Hawaii ever described. Mild scurvy, on the other hand, might cause some deterioration of the alveolar processes so that in skulls long buried, the loss of all organic matter and slight loss of minerals might cause the teeth to fall out.

SUMMARY

An appraisal of the nutritive value of the diet of the ancient Hawaiians (pre-Cook), especially those living in the Kailua, Kaneohe, and Heeia districts has been made. Assumptions about the foods which probably made up the diet are based on the accounts of early explorers in the Pacific and later writers, studies by ethnologists, and conversations with modern Hawaiians over the past 35 years.

Taro was the principal energy food, with sweet potatoes rating second. Breadfruit was seasonal and of minor importance, especially for the common people. Fish and shellfish were the most important sources of protein, with occasional fowl or wild birds, and on rare occasions hog and dog.

Taro leaves and sweet potato tips and leaves were the most frequently used greens, with *limu* the principal relish. For the common people plantains (bananas), coconuts, and mountain apples were rare treats. Other foods were probably eaten occasionally, but were of little significance in the total diet.

Women did not have the privilege of eating bananas, coconut, pig, turtle, and some choice fish, but if other fish, shellfish, and crustacea were abundant they doubtless fared very well in having a good supply of protein of high biological value.

Even though the principal energy food, poi, has relatively small amounts of calcium and phosphorus, these minerals were well utilized. The bones of small fish and certain shellfish and crustacea were the best sources of calcium and phosphorus, and in addition furnished other minerals such as fluorine.

Taro and sweet potato supplied adequate amounts of thiamine and some other B vitamins. Taro and sweet potato tops provided provitamin A, and additional foods with high vitamin A values were to be had in the whole fish, shellfish, and viscera of larger fish, and of mammals and fowls when available.

Unless the method used for cooking (the underground *imu*) destroyed more of the ascorbic acid than we can judge from modern cooking methods, the principal energy foods would have furnished sufficient ascorbic acid to prevent scurvy.

Vitamin D would have been obtained from some sea foods and the ample sunshine would have enabled the Hawaiians to make additional quantities of this vitamin needed to promote good calcification of teeth and bones.

The diet of the ancient Hawaiians, like that of most primitive peoples, was simple and monotonous, but, except for food shortages, temporary or prolonged, was of sufficiently high nutritive value to promote and maintain good health.

LITERATURE CITED

Basu, K. P.; Nade, H.; and Basak, M. N.
1942 The bones of small fish as a source of nutritionally available calcium and phosphorus. *Indiana J. Med. Res.* 30:417–22.

Bilger, Leonora Neuffer, and Young, Hong Yip
1935 A chemical investigation of the fermentations occurring in the process of poi manufacture. *J. Agri. Res.* 51:45–50.

Chapman, Valentine J.
1950 *Seaweeds and their uses.* London: Methuen.

Ellis, William
1832, 1836 *Polynesian researches.* 2d ed. Vols. 1, 4. London.

Fung, George, and Bushnell, O. A.
1948 The possible role of poi in the epidemiology of infectious intestinal diseases. *Hawaii Med. J.* 7:296–99.

Handy, E. S. Craighill
1940 *The Hawaiian planter.* Bernice P. Bishop Museum Bulletin 161. Honolulu.

Handy, E. S. Craighill, and Handy, Elizabeth Green
1972 *Native planters in old Hawaii: their life, lore, and environment.* Bernice P. Bishop Museum Bulletin 233. Honolulu.

King, James
1784 *A voyage to the Pacific Ocean . . . 1776–1780.* Vol. 3. London.

La Perouse, Jean François de Galaup de
1807 *A voyage around the world. . . .* 3d ed. Vol. 2. London.

Leverton, Ruth M., and Payawal, Soledad Ramos
1951 The physiological availability of calcium, phosphorus, and nitrogen from the bones and flesh of dilis, a small fish used in the Filipino diet. *Philippine J. Science* 80:23–32.

Lyon Arboretum
1970 *Checklist of taro cultivars (Colocasia*

exculenta [L.] Schott) in the Harold L. Lyon Arboretum, University of Hawaii. Honolulu.

Malo, David
  1903 *Hawaiian antiquities (Moolelo Hawaii).* Trans. by N. B. Emerson. Ed. by W. D. Alexander. Bernice P. Bishop Museum Special Publication 2. Honolulu.

McClure, F. J.
  1949 Fluorine in foods: survey of recent data. *Public Health Reports* 64:1061–74.

Miller, Carey D.
  1927 *Food values of poi, taro, and limu.* Bernice P. Bishop Museum Bulletin 37. Honolulu.
  1929 *Food values of breadfruit, taro leaves, coconut, and sugar cane.* Bernice P. Bishop Museum Bulletin 64. Honolulu.

Miller, Carey D.; Bauer, Adelia; and Denning, Helen
  1952 Taro as a source of thiamine, riboflavin, and niacin. *J. Amer. Dietetic Assoc.* 28:435–38.

Miller, Carey D.; Branthoover, Barbara; Sekiguchi, Nao; Denning, Helen; and Bauer, Adelia
  1956 Vitamin values of foods used in Hawaii. Hawaii Agricultural Experiment Station Technical Bulletin 30. Honolulu.

Miller, Carey D., and Louis, Lucille
  1945 The availability of the iron in Hawaiian-grown vegetables. *J. Nutrition* 30:485–94.

Miller, Carey D.; Louis, Lucille; and Yanazawa, Kisako
  1947 Vitamin values of foods in Hawaii. Hawaii Agricultural Experiment Station Technical Bulletin 6. Honolulu.

Miller, Carey D., and Robbins, Ruth C.
  1940 Chemical analysis and vitamin assays of opihi, the Hawaiian limpet. *Philippine J. Science* 71:141–63.

Miller, Carey D.; Ross, Winifred; and Louis, Lucille
  1947 Hawaiian-grown vegetables. Hawaii Agricultural Experiment Station Technical Bulletin 5. Honolulu.

Murai, Mary; Pen, Florence; and Miller, Carey D.
  1958 *Some tropical South Pacific island foods: description, history, use, composition, and nutritive value.* Honolulu: University of Hawaii Press.

National Research Council
  1953 *Recommended dietary allowances.* Rev. ed. Pub. 302. Washington, D.C.: National Academy of Sciences.

Nekomoto, Robert Seiso
  1940 The determination of fluorine in Hawaiian waters. Master of Science thesis, University of Hawaii.

Potgieter, Martha
  1940a The utilization of the calcium and phosphorus of taro by young rats. *J. Amer. Dietetic Assoc.* 16:670–73.
  1940b The utilization of the calcium and phosphorus of taro by young women. *J. Amer. Dietetic Assoc.* 16:898–904.

Stewart, C. P., and Guthrie, Douglas, eds.
  1953 *Lind's treatise on scurvy.* London and Edinburgh: Edinburgh University Press.

Stewart, C. S.
  1839 *Journal of a residence in the Sandwich Islands.* 5th ed. Boston.

Vancouver, George
  1798 *A voyage of discovery to the North Pacific Ocean. . . .* Vol. 2. London.

Whitney, Leo D.; Bowers, F. A.; and Takahashi, M.
  1939 Taro varieties in Hawaii. *Hawaii Agri. Exper. Sta. Bull.* 84.

Index

Acetabulum: measurements of, 110; in sex assessment, 4
Acquired features, 77. *See also* Functional adaptation
Adults: age determination of, 4; in census, 7; osteoporosis in, 60; sex assessment of, 4; with shaped heads, 31
Age at death: average adult, 7; compared with other populations, 9–10, 81
Age determination, 3–4, 7
Amputation, 75
Animals as food, 168, 170
Ankle joint: functional adaptation of, 51–52
Archaeology: early Polynesian, 129; history of on windward Oahu, 130–33
Arm bones: musculature of, 47. *See also specific bones*
Arthritis: in age determination, 3; eburnation with, 67, 121; in femur, 154; of joints, 121; occupations related to, 68; occurrence in adults, 67, 68; of postcranial bones, 67–68; of skull, 64; of spine, 67–68; mentioned, 11
Artifacts, 136, 143–44
Asymmetry: of face, 64; of head, 61–64; of muscular development, 51; of paired bones, 45, 114; of skull base, 61, 64; of sternum, 49

Bishop Museum, 1, 56, 132, 133, 147
Body molding, 165–66
Body proportions: indices of, 54, 120, 121
Bone: extra deposits of, 67; healing of, 75; modeling of, 46–47
Bones: measurement of fragmentary, 6; preparation of, for storage, 2; state of preservation, 43. *See also by name*
Burial: associated remains in, 140–44; body orientation in, 140; body positions in, 139–40; body preparation for, 136–38; chronology of sites, 134–35; dating of, 1, 10, 136; multiple, 146; practices according to class, 134; in sand dunes, 129, 130, 131, 132; secondary, 146; sites, 129, 132; vandalized, 144–45 (*see also* Skeleton, mutilated). *See also* Disposal of the dead

Calcaneus: asymmetry of, 114; indices of, 111; measurements of, 111; morphology of, 118; pathology of, 155, 156, 157; variations of, 53
Calcium: sources of, 171
Calories, 168–70
Caries, dental: compared to California study, 163; occurrence by age and sex, 66, 160; sites of, 160–62
Census, 7–10; adults, 80; subadults, 81; total, 79
Cheek bone: fracture of zygomatic arch, 160; morphology of, 88
Chronology: of burial sites, 134–35
Class (social), 134
Clavicle: asymmetry of, 114; fracture of, 72; indices of, 106; measurements of, 105–06; morphology of, 45, 47, 115–16; as tool handle, 55; mentioned, 7
Clubfoot, 72, 155, 156, 157
Coconut: as food, 170

Demography, 2, 7, 9
Dental arch: indices of, 24, 25, 91, 92; measurements of, 24, 25, 91, 92

Dentition: in age determination, 3, 4; in sex assessment, 4. *See also* Teeth
Disposal of the dead: methods of, 129–30

Ear: pathology of, 60
Excavations, 1, 132–33

Face: asymmetry of, 61, 63; compared to other Hawaiians, 41–42; features of, 13, 15, 21; features in sex assessment, 4, 5; morphology of, 87–88; osteoporosis of, 60; subnasal pits in, 60–61; mentioned, 10
Femur: asymmetry of, 114; for fish hooks, 56; fracture of, 72; functional adaptation of, 52; head of, in sex assessment, 5, 43; indices of, 43, 107–08; measurements of, 43, 106–07; morphology of, 43, 46, 47, 51, 116–17; pathology of, 153–54; technique of measurement, 6
Fibula: asymmetry of, 114; fracture of, 72; index of, 109; measurements of, 109; morphology of, 47, 117
Figurine, 37, 55
Fish: as source of nutrients, 170, 171
Fluorine: sources of, 171
Food: accounts of, by early explorers, 167–68; for energy, 169; principal, 168; tabus, 168, 170
Fracture: of postcranial bones, 72–75; of skull, 60, 160; treatment of, 75; mentioned, 11
Frontal bone: morphology of, 86; pathology of, 152–53
Functional adaptation: muscularity of arms and legs as, 47; shape of leg bones as, 43; to squatting, 51–52; variations in spine as, 50; mentioned, 11. *See also* Acquired features; Morphology

Genetic characters, 76–77; mentioned, 13, 23, 46
Genotype, 17–18, 76
Grave pits, 138

Hawaii: discovery of, 1
Head shaping: as cultural mark, 32; dimensions and indices affected by, 15–16, 17; early references to, 32; in modern Hawaiians, 42; in other populations, 32; process of, 32, 166; skull characteristics described, 31–32; mentioned, 10
Hip: functional adaptation of joint, 52; pathology of, 72. *See also specific bones*
Homogeneity: of skulls, 13, 17; of teeth, 27; according to statistical measures, 76; mentioned, 10
Humerus: asymmetry of, 114; elbow articulations of, 119; fracture of, 72; indices of, 43, 45, 104–05; measurements of, 6, 43, 104; morphology of, 47, 115; septal aperture of, 49; in sex assessment, 5; technique of measurement of, 6; as tool handle, 55; variations in, at elbow joint, 49

Indices: of body proportions, 54, 120, 121; of calcaneus, 111; of clavicle, 106; definition of, 5; of dental arch, 24, 25, 91, 92; of femur, 43, 107–08; of fibula, 109; of humerus, 43, 45, 104–05; of innominate, 43, 110; intermembral, 112; of pelvis, 44, 46, 111; of postcranial bones, 43–45, 104–12; of radius, 105; of sacrum, 44, 110; of scapula, 106; of talus, 112; of tibia, 43, 109; of tooth crown, 24, 27, 94, 95; of ulna, 105
Innominate: in age determination, 4; asymmetry of, 114; indices of, 43, 110; measurements of, 43, 44, 110; morphology of, 47, 117
Intermembral indices, 112
Instruments: for dental measurements, 24, 25; for postcranial measurements, 6–7, 43, 44; for skull measurements, 6–7
Isolate, breeding, 1, 7

Kamehameha, King, 15
Knee joint: functional adaptations of, 52

Land divisions, 133–34
Leg bones: as tool handles, 55–56. *See also specific bones*
Life span. *See* Age at death
Limb bones: in age determination, 3; intermembral index of, 45, 112; length of, for stature, 53; from mutilated skeletons, 55, 145. *See also specific bones*
Limu: as food, 171
Longevity. *See* Age at death

Mandible: fracture of, 60, 160; identifying characteristics of, 163; morphology of, 89; pathology of, 159; in sex assessment, 5. *See also* Rocker jaw
Massage, 166
Measurements: of calcaneus, 111; of clavicle, 105–06; of dental arch, 24, 25, 91, 92; of femur, 43, 106–07; of fibula, 109; of humerus, 6, 43, 104; of innominate, 43, 44, 110; instruments for, 6–7, 24, 25, 43, 44, 79; as method of study, 5–7; of palate, 91; of pelvis, 111; of radius, 105; of scapula, 106; in sex assessment, 4; of skull, 5–6, 15, 82–84; of talus, 111–12; techniques of, 5, 6, 13–14, 24–25, 44; of tibia, 43, 108–09; of tooth crown, 24, 93; of ulna, 105; of vertebra, 43–44, 109–10
Metacarpals: fracture of, 72
Metatarsals: muscular ridges on, 55
Microcephaly, 64
Minerals: in food, 171–72
Mokapu: described, 130; excavations of, 1, 132–33; land divisions, 133–34; map of, 128
Morphological types: of skull, 17–18, 90
Morphology: of calcaneus, 118; of cheek bone, 88; of clavicle, 45, 47, 155–56; of femur, 43, 46, 47, 51, 116–17; of fibula, 47, 117; of frontal bone, 86; of humerus, 47, 115; of innominate, 47, 117; of nose, 88–89; of occipital bone, 86–87; of palate, 88–89, 159; of parietal bone, 86; of pelvis, 45–46, 118; of radius, 47, 115; of sacrum, 46, 118; of scapula, 43, 47, 116; in sex assessment, 4–5; of skull, 18, 86–90; of sternum, 46, 118; of talus, 53, 118; of teeth, 27, 29, 89, 90, 102, 160; of temporal bone, 87–88; of tibia, 43, 47, 51, 117, 119; of ulna, 47, 49, 115; of vertebra, 47
Muscularity: and postcranial bones, 46–47, 53, 54–55, 117; and Wolf's Law, 46; mentioned, 11

Navicular: pathology of, 156–57
Nose: fracture of, 60; morphology of, 88–89; variations in bones of, 39
Nutrients: needed by humans, 168
Nutrition: factor in growth, 167

Observation. *See* Morphology
Occipital bone: morphology of, 86–87
Occlusion, dental: types of, 159
Occupations: action of spine and, 71; arthritis related to, 68; of men and women, 49; postures in, 165; use of teeth in, 66
Origins: of Mokapuans, 77
Osteoporosis: causes of, 60; in femur, 154; in skull, 60, 121, 151

Palate: compared to other populations, 25; measurements of, 91; morphology of, 88–89, 159; in sex assessment, 5; technique of measurement, 24–25; mentioned, 11
Parietal bone: morphology of, 86
Patella: fracture of, 72
Pathology: amputation, 75; from anthropologist's viewpoint, 60; of skull, 61–64; clubfoot, 72, 155, 156, 157; of

hip, 72; of mandible, 159; microcephaly, 64; of rib cage, 75; spina bifida, 71–72; of spine, 68–72; spondylolisthesis, 11, 71; of teeth, 12, 27–29, 61, 66–67, 159–63; of vertebra, 67, 68, 71. *See also* Arthritis; Fracture; Osteoporosis; Periodontal disease
— detailed: of calcaneus, 155, 156, 157; of femur, 153–54; of frontal bone, 152–53; of navicular, 156–57; of skull, 151–52; of talus, 154–55, 156, 157; of tibia, 149, 156; of ulna, 153; of vertebra, 149–51
Pelvis: in age determination, 3; compared with other populations, 44–45, 113; early study of, 1; fracture of, 72; indices of, 44, 46, 111; measurements of, 111; morphology of, 45–46, 118; in sex assessment, 4, 46; technique of measurement, 44; variations in, 50–51. *See also specific bones*
Periodontal disease: symptoms of, 159–60; treatment for, 160; mentioned, 66
Phalanges: muscular ridges of, 55
Phenotype, 17–18
Phosphorus: sources of, 171
Physical types. *See* Morphological skull types
Planting methods, 165
Plants as food, 168
Poi: factor in dental caries, 162; methods of preparation, 169. *See also* Taro
Porosities. *See* Osteoporosis
Positions. *See* Posture
Postcranial bones: compared with other populations, 43–44; fractures of, 72–75; indices of, 43–45, 104–12; measurements of, 6, 43, 104–12; morphology of, 115–18; pathology of, 67–75; series of (total and paired), 6. *See also specific bones*
Posture: bent-knee, 53; Hawaiian names for, 165; and lumbar vertebrae, 43; and occupation, 165; squatting, 51–52, 165
Protein: fish as source of, 170; in food, 170–71
Pubic symphysis, 3, 7, 46

Radius: asymmetry of, 114; fracture of, 72; indices of, 105; measurements of, 105; morphology of, 47, 115
Restored tissue: skulls with, 103; values used for, 41
Ribs: fracture of, 72; pathology of, 75
Rocker jaw: descriptions of, 35, 159; in living Hawaiians, 37; in other populations, 37; in subadults, 37; technique of measurement, 13–14; theories of cause of, 37–39; mentioned, 10

Sacrum: fracture of, 72; indices of, 44, 110; measurements of, 44; morphology of, 46, 118; variations in, 50, 72
Scalp wounds, 60
Scapula: in age determination, 4; asymmetry of, 114; indices of, 106; measurements of, 106; morphology of, 43, 47, 116
Sex assessment, 4–5
Shaped heads. *See* Head shaping
Shellfish: as food, 170
Shoulder, 3, 45. *See also specific bones*
Skeletal material: identifying numbers and letters of, 1; reassembly into individuals, 2; recovery of, 132, 133; storage of, 1, 147
Skeleton: age determination of, 3–4; and body size and build, 53; incomplete, 3, 5; information for each, 2–3; mutilated, 55 (*see also* Burial, vandalized); sex assessment of, 4–5
Skull: in age determination, 3; capacity of, 14–15; compared with other Hawaiians, 13, 41, 42; compared with other populations, 15; early study of, 2; homogeneity of, 13, 17; indices of, 84–85; measurements of, 5–6, 15, 82–84; morphology of, 18, 86–90; osteoporosis of, 60, 121,

151; pathology of, 61–64, 151–52; as phenotype, 17; with restored tissue, 103; in sex assessment, 4, 5; shapes of, 14; statistical measures of, 15–17; sutures, 3, 7; views of, 18–20; mentioned, 10–11. *See also specific bones*

Spina bifida, 71–72

Spine: in age determination, 3; arthritis of, 67–68; pathology of, 68–72; treatment for injury of, 166. *See also specific bones*

Spondylolisthesis, 11, 71

Statistical measures, 15–17

Stature, 10, 53, 119, 167

Sternum: in age determination, 4; asymmetry of, 49; morphology of, 46, 118; mentioned, 7

Subadults: age determination of, 4; anomalies in, 24; in census, 7; death of, 9; dental traits of, 30; lopsided head in, 64; osteoporosis in, 60; rocker jaw in, 37; sex assessment of, 4; with shaped heads, 31–32; mentioned, 10

Sugar cane: as food, 169–70

Sutures, cranial, 3, 7

Talipes equinovarus. *See* Clubfoot

Talus: asymmetry of, 114; functional adaptation of, 51–52; indices of, 112; measurements of, 111–12; morphology of, 53, 118; pathology of, 154–55, 156, 157

Taro: as food, 169; nutrients in, 69, 171, 172, 173; mentioned, 174. *See also* Poi

Teeth: in age determination, 4; anomalies of, 23–24; calcium and phosphorus for, 171; care of, 162; compared with modern Hawaiians, 102; compared with other populations, 27; effect of sugar cane on, 170; fluorine for, 171–72; homogeneity of, 27; morphology of, 27, 29, 89, 90, 102,

160; as ornament, 56; pathology of, 12, 27–29, 61, 66–67, 159–63 (*see also* Caries, dental; Periodontal disease); in sex assessment, 4, 5; technique of measurement, 25; use of, in occupations, 66; vitamin C and, 173; mentioned, 11. *See also* Tooth crown

Temporal bone: fracture of styloid spines of, 60; morphology of, 87–88

Thiamine: sources of, 172

Tibia: asymmetry of, 114; fracture of, 72; functional adaptation of, 11, 43, 51–52, 53; indices of, 43, 109; measurements of, 43, 108–09; morphology of, 43, 47, 51, 117, 119; pathology of, 149, 156; technique of measurement, 6

Tools: from human bone, 55–56, 145

Tooth crown: compared with other populations, 27, 96–101; indices of, 24, 27, 94, 95; measurements of, 24, 93; sex differences in, 95; technique of measurement, 25

Trade objects: and burials, 1, 136

Ulna: asymmetry of, 114; fracture of, 72; indices of, 105; measurements of, 105; morphology of, 47, 49, 115; pathology of, 153; variations in, at elbow joint, 49

Vertebra: in age determination, 4; arthritis of, 67–68; collapse of, 68–71; fracture of, 72; indices of, 44, 110; measurements of, 43–44, 109–10; morphology of, 47; pathology of, 67, 68, 71, 149–51; spondylolisthesis of, 11, 71; variations in articular patterns of, 49–50

Vitamins, 66, 172–73

Work. *See* Occupations